ATS-21b   ADMISSION TEST SERIES

This is your
PASSBOOK for...

Scholastic Aptitude Test (SAT) - Reading

Test Preparation Study Guide
Questions & Answers

COPYRIGHT NOTICE

This book is SOLELY intended for, is sold ONLY to, and its use is RESTRICTED to individual, bona fide applicants or candidates who qualify by virtue of having seriously filed applications for appropriate license, certificate, professional and/or promotional advancement, higher school matriculation, scholarship, or other legitimate requirements of education and/or governmental authorities.

This book is NOT intended for use, class instruction, tutoring, training, duplication, copying, reprinting, excerption, or adaptation, etc., by:

1) Other publishers
2) Proprietors and/or Instructors of "Coaching" and/or Preparatory Courses
3) Personnel and/or Training Divisions of commercial, industrial, and governmental organizations
4) Schools, colleges, or universities and/or their departments and staffs, including teachers and other personnel
5) Testing Agencies or Bureaus
6) Study groups which seek by the purchase of a single volume to copy and/or duplicate and/or adapt this material for use by the group as a whole without having purchased individual volumes for each of the members of the group
7) Et al.

Such persons would be in violation of appropriate Federal and State statutes.

PROVISION OF LICENSING AGREEMENTS – Recognized educational, commercial, industrial, and governmental institutions and organizations, and others legitimately engaged in educational pursuits, including training, testing, and measurement activities, may address request for a licensing agreement to the copyright owners, who will determine whether, and under what conditions, including fees and charges, the materials in this book may be used them. In other words, a licensing facility exists for the legitimate use of the material in this book on other than an individual basis. However, it is asseverated and affirmed here that the material in this book CANNOT be used without the receipt of the express permission of such a licensing agreement from the Publishers. Inquiries re licensing should be addressed to the company, attention rights and permissions department.

All rights reserved, including the right of reproduction in whole or in part, in any form or by any means, electronic or mechanical, including photocopying, recording, or by any information storage and retrieval system, without permission in writing from the Publisher.

Copyright © 2025 by
National Learning Corporation

212 Michael Drive, Syosset, NY 11791
(516) 921-8888 • www.passbooks.com
E-mail: info@passbooks.com

PASSBOOK® SERIES

THE *PASSBOOK® SERIES* has been created to prepare applicants and candidates for the ultimate academic battlefield – the examination room.

At some time in our lives, each and every one of us may be required to take an examination – for validation, matriculation, admission, qualification, registration, certification, or licensure.

Based on the assumption that every applicant or candidate has met the basic formal educational standards, has taken the required number of courses, and read the necessary texts, the *PASSBOOK® SERIES* furnishes the one special preparation which may assure passing with confidence, instead of failing with insecurity. Examination questions – together with answers – are furnished as the basic vehicle for study so that the mysteries of the examination and its compounding difficulties may be eliminated or diminished by a sure method.

This book is meant to help you pass your examination provided that you qualify and are serious in your objective.

The entire field is reviewed through the huge store of content information which is succinctly presented through a provocative and challenging approach – the question-and-answer method.

A climate of success is established by furnishing the correct answers at the end of each test.

You soon learn to recognize types of questions, forms of questions, and patterns of questioning. You may even begin to anticipate expected outcomes.

You perceive that many questions are repeated or adapted so that you can gain acute insights, which may enable you to score many sure points.

You learn how to confront new questions, or types of questions, and to attack them confidently and work out the correct answers.

You note objectives and emphases, and recognize pitfalls and dangers, so that you may make positive educational adjustments.

Moreover, you are kept fully informed in relation to new concepts, methods, practices, and directions in the field.

You discover that you are actually taking the examination all the time: you are preparing for the examination by "taking" an examination, not by reading extraneous and/or supererogatory textbooks.

In short, this PASSBOOK®, used directedly, should be an important factor in helping you to pass your test.

SCHOLASTIC APTITUDE TEST

Reading Test

In the Reading Test, students will encounter questions like those asked in a lively, thoughtful, evidence-based discussion.

The Reading Test focuses on the skills and knowledge at the heart of education: what you've been learning in high school and what you'll need to succeed in college. It's about how you take in, think about, and use information.

- All Reading Test questions are multiple choices and based on passages.
- Some passages are paired with other passages.
- Informational graphics, such as tables, graphs, and charts, accompany some passages—but no math is required.
- Prior topic-specific knowledge is not tested.
- The Reading Test is part of the Evidence-Based Reading and Writing section.

When you take the Reading Test, you'll read passages and interpret informational graphics. Then you'll use what you've read to answer questions.

Some questions ask you to locate a piece of information or an idea stated directly. But you'll also need to understand what the author's words imply. In other words, you have to read between the lines.

To succeed in college and a career, you'll need to apply reading skills in all sorts of subjects. Not coincidentally, you'll also need those skills to do well on the Reading Test.
The Reading Test always includes

- One passage from a classic or contemporary work of U.S. or world literature.
- One passage or a pair of passages from either a U.S. founding document or a text in the Great Global Conversation they inspired. The U.S. Constitution or a speech.
- A selection about economics, psychology, sociology, or some other social science.
- Two science passages (or one passage and one passage pair) that examine foundational concepts and developments in Earth science, biology, chemistry, or physics.

A lot more goes into reading than you might realize—and the Reading Test measures a range of reading skills.

Some questions ask you to:
- Find evidence in a passage (or pair of passages) that best supports the answer to a previous question or serves as the basis for a reasonable conclusion.
- Identify how authors use evidence to support their claims.
- Find a relationship between an informational graphic and the passage it's paired with.

From the official announcement for educational purposes

Many questions focus on important, widely used words and phrases that you'll find in texts in many different subjects. The words are ones that you'll use in college and the workplace long after test day.

The SAT focuses on your ability to:

- Use contextual clues in a passage to figure out which meaning of a word or phrase is being used.
- Decide how an author's word choice shapes meaning, style, and tone.

The Reading Test includes passages in the fields of history, social studies, and science. You'll be asked questions that require you to draw on the reading skills needed most to succeed in those subjects. For instance, you might read about an experiment then see questions that ask you to:
- Examine hypotheses.
- Interpret data.
- Consider implications.

Answers are based only on the content stated in or implied by the passage.

Writing and Language Test

The SAT Writing and Language Test asks you to be an editor and improve passages that were written especially for the test—and that include deliberate errors.

When you take the Writing and Language Test, you'll do three things that people do all the time when they write and edit:

1. Read.
2. Find mistakes and weaknesses.
3. Fix them.

- All questions are multiple choices and based on passages.
- Some passages are accompanied by informational graphics, such as tables, graphs, and charts—but no math is required.
- Prior topic knowledge is never tested.
- The Writing and Language Test is part of the Evidence-Based Reading and Writing section.

To answer some questions, you'll need to look closely at a single sentence. Others require reading the entire piece and interpreting a graphic. For instance, you might be asked to choose a sentence that corrects a misinterpretation of a scientific chart or that better explains the importance of the data.

The passages you improve will range from arguments to nonfiction narratives and will be about careers, history, social studies, the humanities, and science.

Questions on the Writing and Language Test measure a range of skills.

Questions that test command of evidence ask you to improve the way passages develop information and ideas. For instance, you might choose an answer that sharpens an argumentative claim or adds a relevant supporting detail.

Some questions ask you to improve word choice. You'll need to choose the best words to use based on the text surrounding them. Your goal will be to make a passage more precise or concise, or to improve syntax, style, or tone.

Analysis in History/Social Studies and in Science

You'll be asked to read passages about topics in history, social studies, and science with a critical eye and make editorial decisions that improve them.

Some questions ask about a passage's organization and its impact. For instance, you will be asked which words or structural changes improve how well it makes its point and how well its sentences and paragraphs work together.

This is about the building blocks of writing: sentence structure, usage, and punctuation. You'll be asked to change words, clauses, sentences, and punctuation. Some topics covered include verb tense, parallel construction, subject-verb agreement, and comma use.

Math Test

The SAT Math Test covers a range of math practices, with an emphasis on problem solving, modeling, using tools strategically, and using algebraic structure.

Instead of testing you on every math topic there is, the SAT asks you to use the math that you'll rely on most in all sorts of situations. Questions on the Math Test are designed to mirror the problem solving and modeling you'll do in:

- College math, science, and social science courses
- The jobs that you hold
- Your personal life

For instance, to answer some questions you'll need to use several steps—because in the real world a single calculation is rarely enough to get the job done.

- Most math questions will be multiple choices, but some—called grid-ins—ask you to come up with the answer rather than select the answer.
- The Math Test is divided into two portions: Math Test–Calculator and Math Test–No Calculator.
- Some parts of the test include several questions about a single scenario.

The Math Test will focus in depth on the three areas of math that play the biggest role in a wide range of college majors and careers:

- Heart of Algebra, which focuses on the mastery of linear equations and systems.
- Problem Solving and Data Analysis, which is about being quantitatively literate.
- Passport to Advanced Math, which features questions that require the manipulation of complex equations.

The Math Test also draws on Additional Topics in Math, including the geometry and trigonometry most relevant to college and career readiness.
The Math Test is a chance to show that you:

- Carry out procedures flexibly, accurately, efficiently, and strategically.
- Solve problems quickly by identifying and using the most efficient solution approaches. This might involve solving a problem by inspection, finding a shortcut, or reorganizing the information you've been given.

You'll demonstrate your grasp of math concepts, operations, and relations. For instance, you might be asked to make connections between properties of linear equations, their graphs, and the contexts they represent.

These real-world problems ask you to analyze a situation, determine the essential elements required to solve the problem, represent the problem mathematically, and carry out a solution.

Calculators are important tools, and to succeed after high school, you'll need to know how—and when—to use them. In the Math Test–Calculator portion of the test, you'll be able to focus on complex modeling and reasoning because your calculator can save you time.

However, the calculator is, like any tool, only as smart as the person using it. The Math Test includes some questions where it's better not to use a calculator, even though you're allowed to. In these cases, students who make use of structure or their ability to reason will probably finish before students who use a calculator.

The Math Test–No Calculator portion of the test makes it easier to assess your fluency in math and your understanding of some math concepts. It also tests well-learned technique and number sense.

Although most of the questions on the Math Test are multiple choices, 22 percent are student-produced response questions, also known as grid-ins. Instead of choosing a correct answer from a list of options, you'll need to solve problems and enter your answers in the grids provided on the answer sheet.

SAT Essay

The redesigned SAT Essay asks you to use your reading, analysis, and writing skills.

The SAT Essay is a lot like a typical college writing assignment in which you're asked to analyze a text. Take the SAT with Essay and show colleges that you're ready to come to campus and write.

- Read a passage.
- Explain how the author builds an argument to persuade an audience.
- Support your explanation with evidence from the passage.

The prompt (question) shown below, or a nearly identical one, is used every time the SAT is given.

As you read the passage below, consider how [the author] uses evidence, such as facts or examples, to support claims.

- evidence, such as facts or examples, to support claims.
- reasoning to develop ideas and to connect claims and evidence.
- stylistic or persuasive elements, such as word choice or appeals to emotion, to add power to the ideas expressed.

Write an essay in which you explain how [the author] builds an argument to persuade [his/her] audience that [author's claim]. In your essay, analyze how [the author] uses one or more of the features listed above (or features of your own choice) to strengthen the logic and persuasiveness of [his/her] argument. Be sure that your analysis focuses on the most relevant features of the passage. Your essay should not explain whether you agree with [the author's] claims, but rather explain how the author builds an argument to persuade [his/her] audience.

You can count on seeing the same prompt no matter when you take the SAT with Essay, but the passage will be different every time.

All passages have these things in common:

- Written for a broad audience
- Argue a point
- Express subtle views on complex subjects
- Use logical reasoning and evidence to support claims
- Examine ideas, debates, or trends in the arts and sciences, or civic, cultural, or political life
- Always taken from published works

All the information you need to write your essay will be included in the passage or in notes about it.

The SAT Essay shows how well you understand the passage and use it as the basis for a well-written, thought-out discussion. The two people who score your essay will each award between 1 and 4 points in each of these three categories:

Reading: A successful essay shows that you understood the passage, including the interplay of central ideas and important details. It also shows an effective use of textual evidence.

Analysis: A successful essay shows your understanding of how the author builds an argument by:
- Examining the author's use of evidence, reasoning, and other stylistic and persuasive techniques
- Supporting and developing claims with well-chosen evidence from the passage

Writing: A successful essay is focused, organized, and precise, with an appropriate style and tone that varies sentence structure and follows the conventions of standard written English.

You don't have to take the SAT with Essay, but if you do, you'll be able to apply to schools that require it. Find out which schools require or recommend the SAT Essay.

Key Content Features

Many questions on the SAT focus on important, widely used words and phrases found in texts in many different subjects. Some questions ask you to figure out a word's meaning based on context. The words are ones that you will probably encounter in college or in the workplace long after test day.

The Evidence-Based Reading and Writing section and the SAT Essay ask you to interpret, synthesize, and use evidence found in a wide range of sources. These sources include informational graphics, such as tables, charts, and graphs, as well as multiparagraph passages in the areas of literature and literary nonfiction, the humanities, science, history and social studies, and on topics about work and career.

For every passage or pair of passages you'll see during the Reading Test, at least one question will ask you to identify which part of the text best supports the answer to the previous question. In other instances, you'll be asked to find the best answer to a question by pulling together information conveyed in words and graphics.

The Writing and Language Test also focuses on command of evidence. It asks you to do things like analyze a series of sentences or paragraphs and decide if it makes sense. Other questions ask you to interpret graphics and to edit a part of the accompanying passage so that it clearly and accurately communicates the information in the graphics.

The SAT Essay also tests command of evidence. After reading a passage, you'll be asked to determine how the author builds an argument to persuade an audience through the use of evidence, reasoning, and/or stylistic and persuasive devices. Scorers look for cogent, clear analyses supported by critical reasoning and evidence drawn from the text provided.

The redesigned SAT Essay asks you to read a passage and explain how an author builds an argument to persuade an audience. This task closely mirrors college writing assignments because it is asking you to analyze how the author used evidence, reasoning, and stylistic and persuasive elements.

The new Essay is designed to support high school students and teachers as they cultivate close reading, careful analysis, and clear writing. It will promote the practice of reading a wide variety of arguments and analyzing how authors do their work as writers.

The essay prompt will be the same every time the SAT is offered, but the source material students are asked to write about will be different each time.

Not all students will take the SAT with Essay, but some school districts and colleges require it. The SAT is the only assessment in the SAT Suite that includes the Essay.

The Math Test focuses in-depth on three essential areas of math: Problem Solving and Data Analysis, Heart of Algebra, and Passport to Advanced Math.

Problem Solving and Data Analysis is about being quantitatively literate. It includes using ratios, percentages, and proportional reasoning to solve problems in science, social science, and career contexts.

The Heart of Algebra focuses on the mastery of linear equations and systems, which help students develop key powers of abstraction.

Passport to Advanced Math focuses on more complex equations and the manipulation they require.

Current research shows that these areas are used disproportionately in a wide range of majors and careers. The redesigned SAT also includes questions on other topics in math, including the kinds of geometric and trigonometric skills summary that are most relevant to college and careers.

SUMMARY

Throughout the SAT, you'll be asked questions grounded in the real world, directly related to work performed in college and career.

The Evidence-Based Reading and Writing section includes questions on literature and literary nonfiction, but also features charts, graphs, and passages like the ones students are likely to encounter in science, social science, and other majors and careers.

Questions on the Writing and Language Test ask you to do more than correct errors; they ask you to edit, revise, and improve texts from the humanities, history, social science, science, and career contexts.

The Math section features multistep applications to solve problems in science, social science, career scenarios, and other real-life situations. The test sets up a scenario and asks several questions that give you the opportunity to dig in and model it mathematically.

The redesigned SAT asks you to apply your reading, writing, language, and math knowledge and skills to answer questions in science, history, and social studies contexts. In this way, the assessments call on the same sorts of knowledge and skills that you'll use in college, at work, and throughout your life to make sense of recent discoveries, political developments, global events, and health and environmental issues.

The redesigned SAT includes a range of challenging texts and informational graphics that address these sorts of issues and topics in the Evidence-Based Reading and Writing section and the Math section. Questions will require you to read and understand texts, revise texts to be consistent with data presented in graphics, synthesize information presented through texts and graphics, and solve problems that are grounded in science and social science.

When you take the SAT, you'll be asked to read a passage from U.S. founding documents or the global conversation they inspired.

The U.S. founding documents, including the Declaration of Independence, the Bill of Rights, and the Federalist Papers, have been inspired by and have helped to inspire a conversation that continues to this day about the nature of civic life.

The SAT includes texts from this global conversation. The goal is to inspire a close reading of these rich, meaningful, often profound texts, not only as a way to develop valuable college and career readiness skills but also as an opportunity to reflect on and deeply engage with issues and concerns central to informed citizenship.

HOW TO TAKE A TEST

You have studied long, hard and conscientiously.

With your official admission card in hand, and your heart pounding, you have been admitted to the examination room.

You note that there are several hundred other applicants in the examination room waiting to take the same test.

They all appear to be equally well prepared.

You know that nothing but your best effort will suffice. The "moment of truth" is at hand: you now have to demonstrate objectively, in writing, your knowledge of content and your understanding of subject matter.

You are fighting the most important battle of your life—to pass and/or score high on an examination which will determine your career and provide the economic basis for your livelihood.

What extra, special things should you know and should you do in taking the examination?

I. YOU MUST PASS AN EXAMINATION

A. WHAT EVERY CANDIDATE SHOULD KNOW
Examination applicants often ask us for help in preparing for the written test. What can I study in advance? What kinds of questions will be asked? How will the test be given? How will the papers be graded?

B. HOW ARE EXAMS DEVELOPED?
Examinations are carefully written by trained technicians who are specialists in the field known as "psychological measurement," in consultation with recognized authorities in the field of work that the test will cover. These experts recommend the subject matter areas or skills to be tested; only those knowledges or skills important to your success on the job are included. The most reliable books and source materials available are used as references. Together, the experts and technicians judge the difficulty level of the questions.
Test technicians know how to phrase questions so that the problem is clearly stated. Their ethics do not permit "trick" or "catch" questions. Questions may have been tried out on sample groups, or subjected to statistical analysis, to determine their usefulness.
Written tests are often used in combination with performance tests, ratings of training and experience, and oral interviews. All of these measures combine to form the best-known means of finding the right person for the right job.

II. HOW TO PASS THE WRITTEN TEST

A. BASIC STEPS

1) Study the announcement

How, then, can you know what subjects to study? Our best answer is: "Learn as much as possible about the class of positions for which you've applied." The exam will test the knowledge, skills and abilities needed to do the work.

Your most valuable source of information about the position you want is the official exam announcement. This announcement lists the training and experience qualifications. Check these standards and apply only if you come reasonably close to meeting them. Many jurisdictions preview the written test in the exam announcement by including a section called "Knowledge and Abilities Required," "Scope of the Examination," or some similar heading. Here you will find out specifically what fields will be tested.

2) Choose appropriate study materials

If the position for which you are applying is technical or advanced, you will read more advanced, specialized material. If you are already familiar with the basic principles of your field, elementary textbooks would waste your time. Concentrate on advanced textbooks and technical periodicals. Think through the concepts and review difficult problems in your field.

These are all general sources. You can get more ideas on your own initiative, following these leads. For example, training manuals and publications of the government agency which employs workers in your field can be useful, particularly for technical and professional positions. A letter or visit to the government department involved may result in more specific study suggestions, and certainly will provide you with a more definite idea of the exact nature of the position you are seeking.

3) Study this book!

III. KINDS OF TESTS

Tests are used for purposes other than measuring knowledge and ability to perform specified duties. For some positions, it is equally important to test ability to make adjustments to new situations or to profit from training. In others, basic mental abilities not dependent on information are essential. Questions which test these things may not appear as pertinent to the duties of the position as those which test for knowledge and information. Yet they are often highly important parts of a fair examination. For very general questions, it is almost impossible to help you direct your study efforts. What we can do is to point out some of the more common of these general abilities needed in public service positions and describe some typical questions.

1) General information

Broad, general information has been found useful for predicting job success in some kinds of work. This is tested in a variety of ways, from vocabulary lists to questions about current events. Basic background in some field of work, such as sociology or economics, may be sampled in a group of questions. Often these are principles which have become familiar to most persons through exposure rather than through formal training. It is difficult to advise you how to study for these questions; being alert to the world around you is our best suggestion.

2) Verbal ability

An example of an ability needed in many positions is verbal or language ability. Verbal ability is, in brief, the ability to use and understand words. Vocabulary and grammar tests are typical measures of this ability. Reading comprehension or paragraph interpretation questions are common in many kinds of civil service tests. You are given a paragraph of written material and asked to find its central meaning.

IV. KINDS OF QUESTIONS

1. Multiple-choice Questions

Most popular of the short-answer questions is the "multiple choice" or "best answer" question. It can be used, for example, to test for factual knowledge, ability to solve problems or judgment in meeting situations found at work.

A multiple-choice question is normally one of three types:
- It can begin with an incomplete statement followed by several possible endings. You are to find the one ending which best completes the statement, although some of the others may not be entirely wrong.
- It can also be a complete statement in the form of a question which is answered by choosing one of the statements listed.
- It can be in the form of a problem – again you select the best answer.

Here is an example of a multiple-choice question with a discussion which should give you some clues as to the method for choosing the right answer:

When an employee has a complaint about his assignment, the action which will best help him overcome his difficulty is to
- A. discuss his difficulty with his coworkers
- B. take the problem to the head of the organization
- C. take the problem to the person who gave him the assignment
- D. say nothing to anyone about his complaint

In answering this question, you should study each of the choices to find which is best. Consider choice "A" – Certainly an employee may discuss his complaint with fellow employees, but no change or improvement can result, and the complaint remains unresolved. Choice "B" is a poor choice since the head of the organization probably does not know what assignment you have been given, and taking your problem to him is known as "going over the head" of the supervisor. The supervisor, or person who made the assignment, is the person who can clarify it or correct any injustice. Choice "C" is, therefore, correct. To say nothing, as in choice "D," is unwise. Supervisors have and interest in knowing the problems employees are facing, and the employee is seeking a solution to his problem.

2. True/False

3. Matching Questions

Matching an answer from a column of choices within another column.

V. RECORDING YOUR ANSWERS

Computer terminals are used more and more today for many different kinds of exams.

For an examination with very few applicants, you may be told to record your answers in the test booklet itself. Separate answer sheets are much more common. If this separate answer sheet is to be scored by machine – and this is often the case – it is highly important that you mark your answers correctly in order to get credit.

VI. BEFORE THE TEST

YOUR PHYSICAL CONDITION IS IMPORTANT

If you are not well, you can't do your best work on tests. If you are half asleep, you can't do your best either. Here are some tips:

1) Get about the same amount of sleep you usually get. Don't stay up all night before the test, either partying or worrying—DON'T DO IT!
2) If you wear glasses, be sure to wear them when you go to take the test. This goes for hearing aids, too.
3) If you have any physical problems that may keep you from doing your best, be sure to tell the person giving the test. If you are sick or in poor health, you relay cannot do your best on any test. You can always come back and take the test some other time.

Common sense will help you find procedures to follow to get ready for an examination. Too many of us, however, overlook these sensible measures. Indeed, nervousness and fatigue have been found to be the most serious reasons why applicants fail to do their best on civil service tests. Here is a list of reminders:

- Begin your preparation early – Don't wait until the last minute to go scurrying around for books and materials or to find out what the position is all about.
- Prepare continuously – An hour a night for a week is better than an all-night cram session. This has been definitely established. What is more, a night a week for a month will return better dividends than crowding your study into a shorter period of time.
- Locate the place of the exam – You have been sent a notice telling you when and where to report for the examination. If the location is in a different town or otherwise unfamiliar to you, it would be well to inquire the best route and learn something about the building.
- Relax the night before the test – Allow your mind to rest. Do not study at all that night. Plan some mild recreation or diversion; then go to bed early and get a good night's sleep.
- Get up early enough to make a leisurely trip to the place for the test – This way unforeseen events, traffic snarls, unfamiliar buildings, etc. will not upset you.
- Dress comfortably – A written test is not a fashion show. You will be known by number and not by name, so wear something comfortable.
- Leave excess paraphernalia at home – Shopping bags and odd bundles will get in your way. You need bring only the items mentioned in the official notice you received; usually everything you need is provided. Do not bring reference books to the exam. They will only confuse those last minutes and be taken away from you when in the test room.

- Arrive somewhat ahead of time – If because of transportation schedules you must get there very early, bring a newspaper or magazine to take your mind off yourself while waiting.
- Locate the examination room – When you have found the proper room, you will be directed to the seat or part of the room where you will sit. Sometimes you are given a sheet of instructions to read while you are waiting. Do not fill out any forms until you are told to do so; just read them and be prepared.
- Relax and prepare to listen to the instructions
- If you have any physical problem that may keep you from doing your best, be sure to tell the test administrator. If you are sick or in poor health, you really cannot do your best on the exam. You can come back and take the test some other time.

VII. AT THE TEST

The day of the test is here and you have the test booklet in your hand. The temptation to get going is very strong. Caution! There is more to success than knowing the right answers. You must know how to identify your papers and understand variations in the type of short-answer question used in this particular examination. Follow these suggestions for maximum results from your efforts:

1) Cooperate with the monitor

The test administrator has a duty to create a situation in which you can be as much at ease as possible. He will give instructions, tell you when to begin, check to see that you are marking your answer sheet correctly, and so on. He is not there to guard you, although he will see that your competitors do not take unfair advantage. He wants to help you do your best.

2) Listen to all instructions

Don't jump the gun! Wait until you understand all directions. In most civil service tests you get more time than you need to answer the questions. So don't be in a hurry. Read each word of instructions until you clearly understand the meaning. Study the examples, listen to all announcements and follow directions. Ask questions if you do not understand what to do.

3) Identify your papers

Civil service exams are usually identified by number only. You will be assigned a number; you must not put your name on your test papers. Be sure to copy your number correctly. Since more than one exam may be given, copy your exact examination title.

4) Plan your time

Unless you are told that a test is a "speed" or "rate of work" test, speed itself is usually not important. Time enough to answer all the questions will be provided, but this does not mean that you have all day. An overall time limit has been set. Divide the total time (in minutes) by the number of questions to determine the approximate time you have for each question.

5) Do not linger over difficult questions

If you come across a difficult question, mark it with a paper clip (useful to have along) and come back to it when you have been through the booklet. One caution if you do this – be sure to skip a number on your answer sheet as well. Check often to be sure that you have not lost your place and that you are marking in the row numbered the same as the question you are answering.

6) Read the questions
   Be sure you know what the question asks! Many capable people are unsuccessful because they failed to read the questions correctly.

7) Answer all questions
   Unless you have been instructed that a penalty will be deducted for incorrect answers, it is better to guess than to omit a question.

8) Speed tests
   It is often better NOT to guess on speed tests. It has been found that on timed tests people are tempted to spend the last few seconds before time is called in marking answers at random – without even reading them – in the hope of picking up a few extra points. To discourage this practice, the instructions may warn you that your score will be "corrected" for guessing. That is, a penalty will be applied. The incorrect answers will be deducted from the correct ones, or some other penalty formula will be used.

9) Review your answers
   If you finish before time is called, go back to the questions you guessed or omitted to give them further thought. Review other answers if you have time.

10) Return your test materials
    If you are ready to leave before others have finished or time is called, take ALL your materials to the monitor and leave quietly. Never take any test material with you. The monitor can discover whose papers are not complete, and taking a test booklet may be grounds for disqualification.

VIII. EXAMINATION TECHNIQUES

1) Read the general instructions carefully. These are usually printed on the first page of the exam booklet. As a rule, these instructions refer to the timing of the examination; the fact that you should not start work until the signal and must stop work at a signal, etc. If there are any special instructions, such as a choice of questions to be answered, make sure that you note this instruction carefully.

2) When you are ready to start work on the examination, that is as soon as the signal has been given, read the instructions to each question booklet, underline any key words or phrases, such as least, best, outline, describe and the like. In this way you will tend to answer as requested rather than discover on reviewing your paper that you listed without describing, that you selected the worst choice rather than the best choice, etc.

3) If the examination is of the objective or multiple-choice type – that is, each question will also give a series of possible answers: A, B, C or D, and you are called upon to select the best answer and write the letter next to that answer on your answer paper – it is advisable to start answering each question in turn. There may be anywhere from 50 to 100 such questions in the three or four hours allotted and you can see how much time would be taken if you read through all the questions before beginning to answer any. Furthermore, if you

come across a question or group of questions which you know would be difficult to answer, it would undoubtedly affect your handling of all the other questions.

4) If the examination is of the essay type and contains but a few questions, it is a moot point as to whether you should read all the questions before starting to answer any one. Of course, if you are given a choice – say five out of seven and the like – then it is essential to read all the questions so you can eliminate the two that are most difficult. If, however, you are asked to answer all the questions, there may be danger in trying to answer the easiest one first because you may find that you will spend too much time on it. The best technique is to answer the first question, then proceed to the second, etc.

5) Time your answers. Before the exam begins, write down the time it started, then add the time allowed for the examination and write down the time it must be completed, then divide the time available somewhat as follows:
   - If 3-1/2 hours are allowed, that would be 210 minutes. If you have 80 objective-type questions, that would be an average of 2-1/2 minutes per question. Allow yourself no more than 2 minutes per question, or a total of 160 minutes, which will permit about 50 minutes to review.
   - If for the time allotment of 210 minutes there are 7 essay questions to answer, that would average about 30 minutes a question. Give yourself only 25 minutes per question so that you have about 35 minutes to review.

6) The most important instruction is to read each question and make sure you know what is wanted. The second most important instruction is to time yourself properly so that you answer every question. The third most important instruction is to answer every question. Guess if you have to but include something for each question. Remember that you will receive no credit for a blank and will probably receive some credit if you write something in answer to an essay question. If you guess a letter – say "B" for a multiple-choice question – you may have guessed right. If you leave a blank as an answer to a multiple-choice question, the examiners may respect your feelings but it will not add a point to your score. Some exams may penalize you for wrong answers, so in such cases only, you may not want to guess unless you have some basis for your answer.

7) Suggestions
   a. Objective-type questions
      1. Examine the question booklet for proper sequence of pages and questions
      2. Read all instructions carefully
      3. Skip any question which seems too difficult; return to it after all other questions have been answered
      4. Apportion your time properly; do not spend too much time on any single question or group of questions
      5. Note and underline key words – all, most, fewest, least, best, worst, same, opposite, etc.
      6. Pay particular attention to negatives
      7. Note unusual option, e.g., unduly long, short, complex, different or similar in content to the body of the question
      8. Observe the use of "hedging" words – probably, may, most likely, etc.

9. Make sure that your answer is put next to the same number as the question
10. Do not second-guess unless you have good reason to believe the second answer is definitely more correct
11. Cross out original answer if you decide another answer is more accurate; do not erase until you are ready to hand your paper in
12. Answer all questions; guess unless instructed otherwise
13. Leave time for review

b. Essay questions
  1. Read each question carefully
  2. Determine exactly what is wanted. Underline key words or phrases.
  3. Decide on outline or paragraph answer
  4. Include many different points and elements unless asked to develop any one or two points or elements
  5. Show impartiality by giving pros and cons unless directed to select one side only
  6. Make and write down any assumptions you find necessary to answer the questions
  7. Watch your English, grammar, punctuation and choice of words
  8. Time your answers; don't crowd material

8) Answering the essay question

Most essay questions can be answered by framing the specific response around several key words or ideas. Here are a few such key words or ideas:

M's: manpower, materials, methods, money, management
P's: purpose, program, policy, plan, procedure, practice, problems, pitfalls, personnel, public relations

a. Six basic steps in handling problems:
  1. Preliminary plan and background development
  2. Collect information, data and facts
  3. Analyze and interpret information, data and facts
  4. Analyze and develop solutions as well as make recommendations
  5. Prepare report and sell recommendations
  6. Install recommendations and follow up effectiveness

b. Pitfalls to avoid
1. Taking things for granted – A statement of the situation does not necessarily imply that each of the elements is necessarily true; for example, a complaint may be invalid and biased so that all that can be taken for granted is that a complaint has been registered
2. Considering only one side of a situation – Wherever possible, indicate several alternatives and then point out the reasons you selected the best one
3. Failing to indicate follow up – Whenever your answer indicates action on your part, make certain that you will take proper follow-up action to see how successful your recommendations, procedures or actions turn out to be
4. Taking too long in answering any single question – Remember to time your answers properly

EXAMINATION SECTION

READING COMPREHENSION

PROBLEM SOLVING TECHNIQUES

1. Identify the type of question

   A. Basic information questions (easy)
   B. Inferential questions (hard)
   C. Vocabulary in context (easy)

2. Underline or circle key words in question.

   The author's main purpose is apparently to
   A. <u>criticize</u> present methods of helping the poor
   B. <u>discuss</u> various types of power and how they can be used by the poor
   C. <u>describe</u> the various causes of poverty
   D. <u>propose</u> a way in which the poor can be more effectively helped
   E. <u>describe</u> the psychological and social effects of power

   The primary purpose of the passage is to
   A. <u>expose</u> those who support government anti-poverty programs
   B. <u>distinguish</u> between the pre- and post-Second World War poor
   C. <u>argue</u> for social investment by the federal government to alleviate poverty
   D. <u>reveal</u> the practices of society that perpetuate poverty
   E. <u>distinguish</u> among the first, second, and third New Deal approaches to reducing unemployment

   The information in the passage suggests that the author is most likely
   A. <u>an historian</u> who is concerned about the validity of his sources
   B. <u>a Chicano</u> who is interested in bringing the Chicanos together
   C. <u>a literary critic</u> who questions the conclusions of historians
   D. <u>an educator</u> primarily concerned with the future of Chicano children
   E. <u>a researcher</u> who is interested in discovering new facts about the Mexican Indians

3. With two word answers, focus on the second word Example:

   The author's attitude toward Aristotle's writings is best described as one of
   A. unqualified <u>endorsement</u>
   B. apologetic <u>approval</u>
   C. analytical <u>objectivity</u>
   D. skeptical <u>reserve</u>
   E. scholarly <u>dissatisfaction</u>

   The tone of Josephy's statement about the location of Aztlan can best be described as one of
   a. apologetic <u>regret</u>
   b. disguised <u>irony</u>
   c. cautious <u>speculation</u>
   d. dramatic <u>revelation</u>
   e. philosophical <u>resignation</u>

4. Mark up the passage underlining important sections, words or sentences so that you can look back at the circled markings as you answer the questions. Be careful not to mark up too much or it will not help.

5. You should skim the questions and select the ones you can answer quickly. Then go back to find the ones you still want to answer. Do not jump from passage to passage because you will waste time rereading the passage in order to answer questions.

6. Choose the reading selection you are most comfortable with to do first. Be careful about matching your answers with the number on the answer sheet. Remember this is especially important when you skip questions.

7. Notes on some types of questions
    A. ATTITUDE - Answer will be usually positive or negative
    B. TONE - Ethnic passages are almost always inspirational or positive
    C. GENERAL STYLE - Never choose answers with these words: indifferent, apathetic, ambivalent, dogmatic
    D. MAIN IDEAS FOR FACTUAL PASSAGE - to discuss; to describe
    E. MAIN IDEAS FOR OPINION PASSAGE - to argue; to urge; to present; to propose
    F. MAIN IDEAS FOR FICTION PASSAGE - to portray; to present; to describe

Recognizing Inference Questions

This exercise has a series of inference questions following a reading passage Read the passage and answer the questions that follow. Circle the letter of the BEST response, and then write, in the space provided, the supporting evidence that led you to that answer.

A flash of bright blue in the green depths of the piney woods caught the eye of wildlife biologist Hilbert Siegler of the Texas Game Commission. Then a second spot of blue stirred as another jay sailed on silent wings to the same branch.
(5) The newcomer, holding a morsel of food in its beak, hopped closer to the first bird. Turning eagerly, the first jay lifted its crested head and accepted hungrily the gift its visitor poked down into its throat.
Siegler was astonished. In fledgling season, young birds often continue
(10) coaxing food from their parents even after they have grown up; in courting season bird swains often bestow dainties upon the females they are wooing. But this wasn't the season for fledglings, nor was it courting time. This was the dead of winter.
Hastily the wildlife expert raised his binoculars and got the answer.
The recipient of the bounty was an adult jay, a grizzled veteran. The lower mandible of its beak had been broken off nearly at the base. It had no way to pick up its food.

(20) This impulse to share and cooperate is familiarly awakened in creatures of The wild by members of their immediate families. But here Seemed to be something close to the human ideal of sharing.

Nature's creatures often exhibit impulses of self-assertion and competition.
(25) But all through life's vast range, these instincts are balanced by another kind of drive. Nature does not implant in her children just the single message: *Take care of*
(30) *yourself.* There is a second ancient and universal injunction: *Get together.* It is as vital as the breath of life.

1. What do you think made Hilbert Siegler go into the piney woods with his binoculars?
    A. He liked walking.
    B. It was a nice day.
    C. It was part of his job.
    D. He wanted to get away.

    Supporting evidence: _____

2. It can be inferred from the information in the second paragraph that Siegler
    A. is familiar with the habits of wildlife
    B. thinks jays are interesting to watch
    C. is hopelessly puzzled by the actions of birds
    D. has little curiosity

    Supporting evidence: _____

3. The fourth paragraph suggests that the author of the passage,
    A. disapproves of the birds' behavior described in the first paragraph
    B. thinks blue jays have little regard for each other
    C. regards most interpretations of animal behavior with suspicion
    D. admires what Hilbert Siegler saw the birds doing

    Supporting evidence: _____

4. From the incident described, the author concludes that
    A. nature is based on competition
    B. the laws of nature are not yet fully understood
    C. the laws of nature allow for competition and cooperation
    D. nature favors the strongest

    Supporting evidence: _____

READING COMPREHENSION
UNDERSTANDING AND INTERPRETING WRITTEN MATERIAL

STRATEGIES

SURVEYING PASSAGES, SENTENCES AS CUES

While individual readers develop unique reading styles and skills, there are some known strategies which can assist any reader in improving his or her reading comprehension and performance on the reading subtest. These strategies include understanding how single paragraphs and entire passages are structured, how the ideas in them are ordered, and how the author of the passage has connected these ideas in a logical and sequential way for the reader.

The section that follows highlights the importance of reading a passage through once for meaning, and provides instruction on careful reading for context cues within the sentences before and after the missing word.

SURVEY THE ENTIRE PASSAGE

To get a sense of the topic and the organization of ideas in a passage, it is important to survey each passage initially in its entirety and to identify the main idea. (The first sentence of a paragraph usually states the main idea.) Do not try to fill in the blanks initially. The purpose or surveying a passage is to prepare for the more careful reading which will follow. You need a sense of the big picture before you start to fill in the details; for example, a quick survey of the passage on page 11 indicate that the topic is the early history of universities. The paragraphs are organized to provide information on the origin of the first universities, the associations formed by teachers and students, the early curriculum, and graduation requirements.

READ PRECEDING SENTENCES CAREFULLY

The missing words in a passage cannot be determined by reading and understanding only the sentences in which the deletions occur. Information from the sentences which precede or follow can provide important cues to determine the correct choice. For example, if you read the first sentence from the passage about universities which contains a blank, you will notice that all the alternatives make sense if this one sentence is read in isolation:

Nobody actually _____ them.
   A. started   B. guarded   C. blamed
   D. compared   E. remembered

The only way that you can make the correct word choice is to read the preceding sentences. In the excerpt below, notice that the first sentence tells the reader what the passage will be about: how universities developed. A key word in the first sentence is *emerged*, which is closely related in meaning to one of the five choices for the first blank. The second sentence explains the key word *emerged*, by pointing out that we have no historical record of a decree or a date indicating when the first university was established. Understanding the ideas in the first two sentences makes it possible to select the correct word for the blank. Look at the sentence with the deleted word in the context of the preceding sentences and think about why you are now able to make the correct choice.

> The first universities emerged at the end of the 11th century and beginning of the 12th. These institutions were not founded on any particular date or created by any formal action. Nobody actually _____ them.
> A. started B. guarded C. blamed
> D. compared E. remembered

Started is the best choice because it fits the main idea of the passage and is closely related to the key word *emerged*.

READ THE SENTENCE WHICH FOLLOWS TO VERIFY YOUR CHOICE

The sentences which follow the one from which a word has been deleted may also provide cues to the correct choice. For example, look at an excerpt from the passage about universities again, and consider how the sentence which follows the one with the blank helps to reinforce the choice of the word *started*.

> The first universities emerged at the end of the 11th century and the beginning of the 12th. These institutions were not founded on any particular date or created by any formal action. Nobody actually _____ them. Instead, they developed gradually in places like Paris, Oxford, and Bologna, where scholars had long been teaching students.
> A. started B. guarded C. blamed
> D. compared E. remembered

The words *developed gradually* mean the same as the key word *emerged*. The signal word *instead* helps to distinguish the difference between starting on a specific date as a result of some particular act or event and emerging over a period of time as a result of various factors.

Here is another example of how the sentence which follows the one from which a word is deleted might help you decide which of two good alternatives is the correct choice. This excerpt is from the practice passage about bridges (page 10).

> Bridges are built to allow a continuous flow of highway and railway traffic across water lying in their paths. But engineers cannot forget that river traffic, too, is essential to our economy. The role of _____ is important. To keep these vessels moving freely, bridges are built big enough, when possible, to let them pass underneath.
> A. wind B. boats C. weight
> D. wires E. experience

After the first two sentences, the reader may be uncertain about the direction the writer intended to take in the rest of the paragraph. If the writer intended to continue the paragraph with information concerning how engineers make choices about the relative importance and requirements of land traffic and rive traffic, *experience* might be the appropriate choice for the missing word. However, the sentence following the one in which the deletion occurs makes it clear that *boats* is the correct choice. It provides the synonym *vessels*, which in the noun phrase *these vessels* must refer back to the previous sentence or sentences. The phrase *to let them pass underneath* also helps make it clear that *boats* is the appropriate choice. *Them* refers back to *these vessels* which, in turn, refers back to *boats* when the word *boats* is placed in the previous sentence. Thus, the reader may use these cohesive ties (the pronoun referents) to verify the final choice.

Even when the text following a sentence with a deletion is not necessary to choose the best alternative, it may be helpful in other ways. Specifically, complete sentences provide important transitions into a related topic which is developed in the rest of the paragraph or in the next paragraph of the same passage. For example, the first paragraph in the passage about universities ends with a sentence which introduces the term *guilds*: *But, over time, they joined together to form guilds.* Prior to this sentence, information about the slow emergence of universities and about how independently scholars had acted was introduced. The next paragraph begins with two sentences about guilds in general. Someone who had not read the last sentence in the first paragraph might have missed the link between guilds and scholars and universities and, thus, might have been unnecessarily confused.

COHESIVE TIES AS CUES

Sentences in a paragraph may be linked together by several devices called cohesive ties. Attention to these ties may provide further cues about missing words. This section will describe the different types of cohesive ties and show how attention to them can help you to select the correct word.

PERSONAL PRONOUNS

Personal pronouns (e.g., he, she, they, it, its) are often used in adjoining sentences to refer back to an already mentioned person, place, thing, or idea. The word to which the pronoun refers is called the antecedent.

Tools used in farm work changed very slowly from ancient times to the eighteenth century, and the changes were minor. Since the eighteenth century *they* have changed quickly and dramatically.

The word *they* refers back to *tools* in the example above.

In the examination reading subtest, a deleted word sometimes occurs in a sentence in which the sentence subject is a pronoun that refers back to a previously mentioned noun. You must correctly identify the referent for the particular pronoun in order to interpret the sentence and select the correct answer. Here is an example from the passage about bridges.

An ingenious engineer designed the bridge so that it did not have to be raised above traffic. Instead it was _____.
  A. burned   B. emptied   C. secured
  D. shared   E. lowered

Q. What is the antecedent of *it* in both cases in the example?
A. The antecedent, of course, is *bridge*.

DEMONSTRATIVE PRONOUNS

Demonstrative pronouns (e.g., this, that, these) are also used to refer to a specific, previously mentioned noun. They may occur alone as noun replacements, or they may accompany and modify nouns.

I like jogging, swimming, and tennis. *These* are the only sports I enjoy.

In the sentence above, the word *these* is a replacement noun. However, demonstrative pronouns may also occur as adjectives modifying nouns.

I like jogging, swimming, and tennis. *These* sports are the only ones I enjoy.

The word *these* in the example above is an adjective modifier. The word *these* in each of the two previous examples refers to *jogging, swimming,* and *tennis*.

Here is an example from the passage about universities on page 11.

Undergraduates took classes in Greek philosophy, Latin grammar, arithmetic, music, and astronomy. These were the only _____ available.
  A. rooms   B. subjects   C. clothes
  D. pens   E. company

Q. Which word is a noun replacement?
A. The word *these* is the replacement for *Greek philosophy, Latin grammar, arithmetic, music,* and *astronomy*.

Here is another example from the same passage.

The concept of a fixed program of study leading to a degree first evolved in Medieval Europe. This _____ had not appeared before.
  A. idea   B. desk   C. library   D. capital

Q. What is the antecedent of *this*?
A. The antecedent is *the concept of a fixed program of study leading to a degree*.

COMPARATIVE ADJECTIVES AND ADVERBS

When comparative adjectives and adverbs (e.g., so, such, better, more) occur, they refer to something else in the passage, otherwise a comparison could not be made.

The hotels in the city were all full; so were the motels and boarding houses.

Q. To what in the first sentence does the word *so* refer?
A. So tells us to compare the *motels* and *boarding houses* to the *hotels in the city*.

Q. In what way are the *hotels, motels,* and *boarding houses* similar to each other?
A. The *hotels, motels,* and *boarding houses* are similar in that they were all *full*.

Look at an example from the passage about universities.

Guilds were groups of tradespeople, somewhat akin to modern trade unions. In the Middle Ages, all the crafts had such
  A. taxes   B. secrets   C. products
  D. problems   E. organizations

Q. To what in the first sentence does the word *such* refer?
A. *Such* refers to *groups of tradespeople*.

SUBSTITUTIONS

Substitution is another form of cohesive tie. A substitution occurs when one linguistic item (e.g., a noun) is replaced by another. Sometimes the substitution provides new or contrasting information. The substitution is not identical to the original, or antecedent, idea. A frequently occurring substitution involves the use of *one*. A noun substitution may involve another member of the same class as the original one.

My car is falling apart. I need a new one.

Q. What in the first sentence is replaced in the second sentence with *one*?
A. *One* is a substitute for the specific car mentioned in the first sentence. The contrast comes from the fact that the *new one* isn't the writer's current car.

The substitution may also pinpoint a specific member of a general class.

1. There are many unusual courses available at the university this summer. The *one* I am taking is called *Death and Dying*.
2. There are many unusual courses available at the university this summer. *Some* have never been offered before.

Q. In these examples, what is the general class in the first sentence that is replaced by *one* and by *some*?
A. In both cases the words *one* and *some* replace *many unusual* courses.

SYNONYMS

Synonyms are words that have similar meaning. In the examination reading subtest, a synonym of a deleted word is sometimes found in one of the sentences before and/or after the sentence with the deletion. Examine the following excerpt from the passage about bridges again.

But engineers cannot forget that river traffic, too, is essential to our economy. The role of _____ is important. To keep these vessels moving freely, bridges are built high enough, when possible, to let them pass underneath.
  A. wind   B. boats   C. weight
  D. wires   E. experience

Q. Can you identify synonyms in the sentences, before and after the sentence containing the deletion, which are cues to the correct deleted word?
A. If you identified the correct words, you probably noticed that *river traffic* is not exactly a synonym since it is a slightly more general term than the word *boats* (the correct choice). But the word *vessels* is a direct synonym. Demonstrative pronouns (this, that, these, those) are sometimes used as modifiers for synonymous nouns in sentences which follow those containing deletions. The word *these* in *these vessels* is the demonstrative pronoun (modifier) for the synonymous noun *vessels*.

ANTONYMS

Antonyms are words of opposite meaning. In the examination reading subtest passages, antonyms may be cues for missing words. A contrasting relationship, which calls for the use of an antonym, is often signaled by the connective words *instead, however, but*, etc. Look at an excerpt from the passage about bridges.

An ingenious engineer designed the bridges so that it did not have to be raised above traffic. Instead it was
  A. burned   B. emptied   C. secured
  D. shared   E. lowered

Q: Can you identify an antonym in the first sentence for one of the five alternatives?
A. The word *raised* is an antonym for the word *lowered*.

SUBORDINATE-SUBORDINATE WORDS

In the examination reading subtest, a passage sometimes contains a general term which provides a cue that a more specific term is the appropriate alternative. At other times, the passage may contain a specific term which provides cues that a general term is the appropriate alternative for a particular deletion. The general and more specific words are said to have superordinate-subordinate relationships.

Look at Example 1 below. The more specific word *boy* in the first sentence serves as the antecedent for the more general word *child* in the second sentence. In Example 2, the relationship is reversed. In both examples, the words *child* and *boy* reflect a superordinate-subordinate relationship.

1. The *boy* climbed the tree. Then the *child* fell.
2. The *child* climbed the tree. Then the *boy* fell.

In the practice passage about bridges on Page 11, the phrase *river traffic* is a general term that is superordinate to the alternative *boats* (Item 1). Later in the passage about bridges the following sentences also contain superordinate-subordinate words:

A lift bridge was desired, but there were wartime shortages of steel and machinery needed for the towers. It was hard to find enough _____.
  A. work   B. material   C. time
  D. power   E. space

Q. Can you identify two words in the first sentence that are specific examples for the correct response in the second sentence?
A. Of course, the words *steel* and *machinery* are the specific examples for the more general term *material*.

WORDS ASSOCIATED BY ENTAILMENT

Sometimes the concept described by one word within the context of the passage entails, or implies, the concept described by another word. For example, consider again Item 7 in the practice passage about bridges. Notice how the follow-up sentence to Item 7 provides a cue to the correct response.

An ingenious engineer designed the bridge so that it did not have to be raised above traffic. Instead it was _____. It could be submerged seven meters below the surface of the river.
   A. burned   B. emptied   C. secured
   D. shared   E. lowered

Q. What word in the sentence after the blank implies the concept of an alternative?
A. *Submerged* implies *lowered*. The concept of submerging something implies the idea of lowering the object beneath the surface of the water.

WORDS ASSOCIATED BY PART-WHOLE RELATIONSHIPS

Words may be related because they involve part of a whole and the whole itself; for example, *nose* and *face*. Words may also be related because they involve two parts of the same whole; for example, *radiator* and *muffler* both refer to parts of a car.

The captain of the ship was nervous. The storm was becoming worse and worse. The hardened man paced the _____.
   A. floor   B. hall   C. deck   D. court

Q. Which choice has a part-whole relationship with a word in the sentences above?
A. A *deck* is a part of a *ship*. Therefore, *deck* has a part-whole relationship with *ship*.

CONJUNCTIVE AND CONNECTIVE WORDS AND PHRASES

Conjunctions or connectives are words or phrases that connect parts of sentences or parts of a passage to each other. Their purpose is to help the reader understand the logical and conceptual relationships between ideas and events within a passage. Examples of these words and phrases include coordinate conjunctions (e.g., and, but, yet), subordinate conjunctions (e.g., because, although, since, after), and other connective words and phrases (e.g., too, also, on the other hand, as a result).

Listed below are types of logical relationships expressed by conjunctive, or connective words. Also listed are examples of words used to cue relationships to the reader.

Additive and comparative words and phrases: and, in addition to, too, also, furthermore, similarly.

Adversative and contrastive words and phrases: yet, though, only, but, however, instead, rather, on the other hand, conversely.

Causal words or phrases: so, therefore, because, as a result, if…then, unless, except, in that case, under the circumstances.

Temporal words and phrases: before, after, when, while, initially, lastly, finally, until.

Examples

1. I enjoy fast-paced sports like tennis and volleyball, but my brother prefers _____ sports.
   A. running   B. slower   C. team   D. active

   Q. What is the connective word that tells you to look for a contrast relationship between the two parts of the sentence?
   A. The connective word *but* signals that a contrast relationship exists between the two parts of the sentence.

   Q. Of the four options, what is the best choice for the blank?
   A. The word *slower* is the best response here.

2. The child stepped to close to the edge of the brook. As a result, he _____ in.
   A. fell   B. waded   C. ran   D. jumped

   Q. What is the connective phrase that links the two sentences?
   A. The connective phrase *as a result* links the two sentences.

   Q. Of the four relationships of words and phrases listed previously, what kind of relationship between the two sentences does the connective phrase in the example signal to the reader?
   A. The phrase *as a result* signals that a cause and effect relationship exists between the two sentences.

   Q. Identify the correct response which makes the second sentence reflect and cause and effect relationship.
   A. The correct response is *fell*.

Understanding connectives is very important to success on the examination reading subtest. Sentences with deletions are often very closely related to adjacent sentences in meaning, and the relationships often signaled by connective words or phrases. Here is an example from the practice passage about universities.

At first, these tutors had not been associated with one another. Rather, they had been _____. But, over time, they joined together to form guilds.
   A. curious   B. poor   C. religious
   D. ready   E. independent

Q. Identify the connective and contrastive words and phrases in the example.
A. *At first* and *over time* are connective phrases that set up temporal progression. *Rather* and *but* are contrastive items. The use of *rather* in the sentence with the deletion tells the reader that the missing word has to convey a meaning in contrast to *associated with one another*. (Notice also that *rather* occurs after a negative statement.) The use of *but* in the sentence after the one with the deletion indicates that the deleted word in the previous sentence has to reflect a meaning that contrasts with *joined together*. Thus, the reader is given two substantial cues to the meaning of the missing word. *Independent* is the only choice that meets the requirement for contrastive meaning.

SAMPLE QUESTIOINS

DIRECTIONS: There are two passages on the following pages. In each passage some words are missing. Wherever a word is missing, there is a blank line with a number on it. Below the passage you will find the same number and five words. Choose the word that makes the best sense in the blank. You may not be sure of the answer to a question until you read the sentences that come after the blank, so be sure to read enough to answer the questions. As you work on these passages, you will find that the second passage is harder to read than the first. Answer as many questions as you can.

    Bridges are built to allow a continuous flow of highway and railway traffic across water lying in their paths. But engineers cannot forget that river traffic, too, is essential to our economy. The role of __1__ is important. To keep these vessels moving freely, bridges are built high enough, when possible, to let them pass underneath. Sometimes, however, channels must accommodate very tall ships. It may be uneconomical to build a tall enough bridge. The __2__ would be too high. To save money, engineers build movable bridges.

    In the swing bridge, the middle part pivots or swings open. When the bridge is closed, this section joins the two ends of the bridge, blocking tall vessels. But this section __3__. When swung open, it is perpendicular to the ends of the bridge, creating two free channels for river traffic. With swing bridges channel width is limited by the bridge's piers. The largest swing bridge provides only a 75-meter channel. Such channels are sometimes __4__. In such cases, a bascule bridge may be built.

    Bascule bridges are drawbridges with two arms that swing upward. They provide an opening as wide as the span. They are also versatile. These bridges are not limited to being fully opened or fully closed. They can be __5__ in many ways. They can be fixed at different angles to accommodate different vessels.

    In vertical lift bridges, the center remains horizontal. Towers at both ends allow the center to be lifted like an elevator. One interesting variation of this kind of bridge was built during World War II. A lift bridge was desired, but there were wartime shortages of the steel and machinery needed for the towers. It was hard enough to find enough __6__. An ingenious engineer designed the bridge so that it did not have to be raised above traffic. Instead it was __7__. It could be submerged seven meters below the surface of the river. Ships sailed over it.

1. A. wind   B. boats   C. experience
   D. wires   E. experience

2. A. levels   B. cost   C. standards
   D. waves   E. deck

3. A. stands   B. floods   C. wears
   D. turns   E. supports

4. A. narrow   B. rough   C. long
   D. deep   E. straight

5. A. crossed   B. approached   C. lighted
   D. planned   E. positioned

6. A. work   B. material   C. time   6.____
    D. power   E. space

7. A. burned   B. emptied   C. secured   7.____
    D. shared   E. lowered

The first universities emerged at the end of the 11th century and beginning of the 12th. These institutions were not founded on any particular date or created by any formal action. Nobody actually __8__ them. Instead, they developed gradually in places like Paris, Oxford, and Bologna, where scholars had long been teaching students. At first, these tutors had not been associated with one another. Rather, they had been __9__. But, over time, they joined together to form guilds.

Guilds were groups of tradespeople, somewhat akin to modern unions. In the Middle Ages, all the crafts had such __10__. The scholars' guilds built school buildings and evolved an administration which charged fees and set standards for the curriculum. It set prices for members' services and fixed requirements for entering the profession.

Professors were not the only schoolpeople forming associations. In Italy, students joined guilds to which teachers had to swear obedience. The students set strict rules, fining professors for beginning class a minute late. Teachers had to seek their students' permission to marry, and such permission was not always granted. Sometimes the students __11__. Even if they said yes, the teacher got only one day's honeymoon.

Undergraduates took classes in Greek philosophy, Latin grammar, arithmetic, music, and astronomy. These were the only __12__ available. More advanced study was possible in law, medicine, and theology, but one could not earn such postgraduate degrees quickly. It took a long time to __13__. Completing the requirements in theology, for example, took at least 13 years.

The concept of a fixed program of study leading to a degree first evolved in medieval Europe. This __14__ had not appeared before, in earlier academic settings, notions about *meeting requirements meeting requirements* and *graduating* had been absent. Since the middle ages, though, we have continued to view education as a set curriculum culminating in a degree.

8. A. started   B. guarded   C. blamed   8.____
    D. compared   E. remembered

9. A. curious   B. poor   C. religious   9.____
    D. ready   E. independent

10. A. taxes   B. secrets   C. products   10.____
    D. problems   E. organizations

11. A. left   B. copied   C. refused   11.____
    D. paid   E. prepared

12. A. rooms   B. subjects   C. clothes   12.____
    D. pens   E. markets

13. A. add   B. answer   C. forget   13.____
    D. finish   E. travel

14. A. idea   B. desk   C. library   14._____
    D. capital   E. company

KEY (CORRECT ANSWERS)

1. B	6. B	11. C
2. B	7. E	12. B
3. D	8. A	13. D
4. A	9. E	14. A
5. E	10. E	

EXAMINATION SECTION
TEST 1
READING

DIRECTIONS: Each statement or passage in this test is followed by a question or questions based on its content. After reading a statement or passage, choose the best answer to each question from among the five choices given. Answer all questions following a statement or passage on the basis of what is STATED or IMPLIED in that statement or passage. *PRINT THE LETTER OF THE CORRECT ANSWER IN THE SPACE AT THE RIGHT.*

1. In the future, men's and women's basketball and gymnastics teams will be allotted equal practice time and equal access to the equipment. Though men's basketball and women's gymnastics bring in more revenue for the school, they are no longer entitled to preferential treatment by the Westdale High Athletic Department.
   The new rule requiring equal practice time is probably intended to benefit which two of the following teams?
   I. Men's basketball team
   II. Women's basketball team
   III. Men's gymnastics team
   IV. Women's gymnastics team

   The CORRECT answer is:
   A. I and II
   B. I and III
   C. I and IV
   D. II and III
   E. II and IV

2. Many students who were outstanding in their high school studies find it more difficult to adjust to college than do those who were academically average or those who did poorly in high school; the reason is that many of these formerly outstanding students find in college not only that there are any number of students who are as outstanding academically as they are, but also that there are a large number who are even more gifted.
   Which of the following BEST summarizes the main idea of this statement?
   A. Some students who worked hard and who were academically outstanding in high school do not work as hard in college.
   B. Some students who showed themselves to be of average or low ability in their high school work are happier in college than they were in high school.
   C. Many students who did well in high school do not seem to learn as much once they get to college.
   D. Many students do not do as well in college as they did in high school because they are upset by the large number of students in their classes.
   E. Many outstanding students find that, because of the high level of academic competition, it is more difficult to do well in college than it was in high school.

17

Questions 3-5.

DIRECTIONS: Questions 3 through 5 are to be answered on the basis of the following passage.

Shakespeare wrote four types of plays: histories, comedies, tragedies, and tragicomedies. Some scholars contend that Shakespeare's choice of three of these types of dramatic forms reflects his various psychological states. As a young man making a name for himself in London, he wrote comedies. Then, saddened by the death of his son, he turned to tragedies. Finally, seasoned by life's joys and sorrows, he produced tragicomedies. But a look at the theater scene of his day reveals that Shakespeare was not so much writing out of his heart as into his pocketbook. When comedies were the vogue, he wrote comedies; when tragedies were the rage, he wrote tragedies; and when tragicomedies dominated the stage, he produced tragicomedies.

3. The primary purpose of the passage is to
   A. examine Shakespeare's life in light of his dramatic works
   B. contest a theory that attempts to explain why Shakespeare wrote the kinds of plays he did
   C. explain the terms "comedy," "tragedy," and "tragicomedy" as they are used in discussions of Shakespeare's plays
   D. compare Shakespeare's plays with the works of other dramatists of his day
   E. discuss what is known about Shakespeare's psychological states

4. The passage supplies information for answering which of the following questions?
   A. What types of plays were popular when Shakespeare was writing?
   B. What is the difference between a comedy and a tragicomedy?
   C. In which years did Shakespeare write his major comedies, tragedies, and histories?
   D. What, other than plays, did Shakespeare write?
   E. Were Shakespeare's plays produced only in London?

5. If added to the end of the passage, which of the following would be the BEST summary statement?
   A. Tragicomedies are a hybrid type of drama; they mix both comic and tragic elements.
   B. Shakespeare also wrote histories, but these can be forced into one of the other three categories: comedies, tragedies, and tragicomedies.
   C. Shakespeare's greatest comedy was written when he was happiest; his greatest tragedy when he was most saddened by the death of his son; and his greatest tragicomedy when he accepted fully that life contains both joy and sorrow.
   D. Those playwrights who write of their emotions usually write better plays than do those who are primarily concerned with making money.
   E. The image of Shakespeare as an artist who wrote particular plays because of what was happening in his personal life is almost surely false; rather he was a shrewd businessman who happened to be an artistic genius.

6. Although Sara Burstall was willing to concede that women in the United States had greater educational opportunities than did women in Britain because of the prevalence in the United States of coeducation, she insisted that women teachers, administrators, and school board members in the United States had much less influence on pedagogy at the time of her writing (1908) than did their counterparts in Britain.
According to the statement above, Sara Burstall believed that which of the following elements in the educational system in the United States accounted for the greater educational opportunities that women in the United States enjoyed over women in Britain?
   A. Teachers' influence
   B. Administrators' influence
   C. School boards' influence
   D. Coeducational schooling
   E. Pedagogical philosophy

6.____

7. Keats must be the finest poet to have written in the English language; after all, he wrote the finest poem.
The author of the statement assumes which of the following?
   A. A poet should be judged by his or her best poem.
   B. Most of Keats' poetry is great.
   C. Poets are concerned about how their poems are judged.
   D. Keats' poetry is widely read.
   E. There are better poets than Keats, but they did not write in English.

7.____

Questions 8-12.

DIRECTIONS: Questions 8 through 12 are to be answered on the basis of the following passage.

Recently, increasing attention has been called to the fact that the four freedoms of universities – the freedom to determine who may teach, what will be taught, how it will be taught, and who may study what is taught – are being threatened by the many regulations imposed on universities by the federal government.

Surprisingly, much of this criticism of governmental regulation has come from the universities themselves. After all, universities eagerly accepted the money that was made available for research and scholarships by the National Defense Education Act, which was a governmental response to the launching of Sputnik I in 1957 by the Soviet Union. As its name implies, the National Defense Education Act was concerned with a governmental goal, the national defense. Moreover, the federal government made it clear from the very beginning that it intended to control how such money was spent. Similarly, universities actively supported the Higher Education Act of 1965, which was part of a governmental attempt to end discrimination – a goal that can accurately be described as political.

Clearly, any attempt by the federal government to limit the four freedoms of universities is undesirable. But it is also important to remember that the federal government became involved in university education because it was seeking admirable goals, goals that were also sought by universities.

8. The author mentions the Higher Education Act of 1965 as an example of a(n)
   A. regulation that did not affect any of the four freedoms
   B. regulation that should be made more comprehensive
   C. attempt to lessen the effect of regulation on universities
   D. attempt to attain a desirable political goal
   E. attempt to improve communication between the government and universities

8.____

9. The author asserts which of the following?
   A. Universities should withdraw their support of the National Defense Education Act.
   B. Universities should not criticize the regulations proposed by the federal government.
   C. Universities are partly responsible for the governmental regulations that they now criticize.
   D. The federal government has an obligation to regulate the behavior of some universities.
   E. The federal government should reconsider some of its most recent regulations.

9.____

10. The author would be LEAST likely to agree with which of the following statements about governmental regulation and universities?
    A. Universities are better able to define their four freedoms than is the federal government.
    B. Universities are going to continue to criticize governmental regulation in the near future.
    C. The federal government should consult with university personnel before imposing new regulations.
    D. The federal government passed the National Defense Education Act in order to attain a desirable goal.
    E. The federal government should limit the four freedoms of universities if the goal it seeks is a desirable one.

10.____

11. Why is the author surprised that much of the criticism of governmental regulation is coming from universities?
    A. Universities have willingly accepted government-regulated funds at times in the past.
    B. Universities are less affected by governmental regulation than is private business.
    C. Universities have been reluctant to criticize the federal government in the past.
    D. The federal government has not imposed a new regulation on universities since 1965.
    E. The federal government has sought goals that can be described as political.

11.____

12. The passage would be MOST likely to appear in which of the following? 12.____
    A. A civics textbook
    B. An educational psychology textbook
    C. An essay for university teachers and administrators
    D. A pamphlet for new government employees
    E. A book on the history of primary education

13. The new regulations require that in rainy weather student crossing-guards 13.____
    wear raincoats, hats, and boots. Ponchos may be substituted for raincoats and
    hats. In the event of snow, these students must wear gloves in addition to the
    outerwear required above.
    On a snowy day, which of the following combinations of outerwear would meet
    the new regulations?
    I.   Raincoats, hats, boots, and gloves
    II. Ponchos, gloves, and boots
    III. Ponchos, hats, and gloves

    The CORRECT answer is:
    A. I only   B. II only   C. III only
    D. I and II only   E. I, II, and III

Questions 14-15.

DIRECTIONS: Questions 14 and 15 are to be answered on the basis of the following passage.

    Under our traditional grading system, in which 90-100 is an A, 80-89 a B, and so on, students who take an examination with four essay questions and answer only three, however brilliantly, cannot get a grade higher than a C. This is because, even if a student scores 100 percent on each of the three answered questions, a zero on the fourth lowers the student's average score to 75 percent. This grading practice teaches students to pace themselves and prevents them from skipping questions for which they are unprepared. On the other hand, it penalizes students who prefer to discuss less material in greater depth.

14. The author's primary purpose is to 14.____
    A. suggest a new method of grading examinations
    B. argue that the traditional method of grading examinations needs
       improvement
    C. describe the traditional method of grading essay examinations and its
       drawbacks
    D. point out an inconsistency in the mathematical procedure used in the
       traditional method of grading examinations
    E. question the traditional practice of scoring essay examinations on a
       percentage basis instead of with letter grades

15. Which of the following is the MOST accurate description of the students mentioned in the passage's final sentence?
They usually
   A. finish an examination earlier than do other students
   B. work on an examination at a more even pace than do other students
   C. have failed to study all the material covered in an examination
   D. receive higher grades on examinations than on term papers
   E. answer all the questions they attempt on an examination thoroughly and in detail

15.____

16. Predominantly Black land-grant colleges in the United States have a long tradition of supporting cooperative education programs. These programs combine work experience that carries academic credit with academic courses. This tradition has made these colleges the leaders in the recent movement in American education toward career-oriented curriculums.
According to the statement above, predominantly Black land-grant colleges in the United States are leaders in carrier-oriented education because they
   A. have had cooperative education programs as part of their curriculum for many years
   B. were among the first colleges in the United States to shift away from career-oriented curriculums
   C. offer their students academic credit for their work experience prior to entering college
   D. have a long tradition of cooperation with local business and community leaders
   E. provide opportunities for students to work on campus to earn money for tuition

16.____

Questions 17-22.

DIRECTIONS: Questions 17 through 22 are to be answered on the basis of the following passage.

The new hand-held "talking" spelling computer asks the user to spell a word, which it clearly pronounces. To the user's typed response, it then either gives praise or suggests another try. For spelling practice, there may be nothing better. For teaching spelling there may be nothing worse, since few, if any, of the programs for this device provide instruction in an order that exposes the patterns in English spelling.
Left to learn spelling by rote, children will be unable to detect or predict the regularities that characterize their written language. They will be ill-prepared to reason about and choose correctly among the many options available for translating speech sounds into written representation.
Admittedly, spelling instruction isolated from the logic of the language still takes place in some classrooms. And something can be said for electronic evaluations that urge a second trial before they correct and fade, unlike single, written trials graded in the permanence of red ink. But for all their mechanized patience, feedback, and reinforcement, spelling computers cannot replace the teacher. For mastery in spelling comes not only from learning which spellings are right and which are wrong; it also comes from learning why they are so.

17. The main idea of the passage is that   17._____
    A. a child can perfect spelling skills only through practice
    B. the new spelling computers are limited in their ability to teach children to spell correctly
    C. classroom methods for spelling instruction need to be improved
    D. patience, feedback, and reinforcement are the keys to effective teaching
    E. the new spelling computers provide one of the best possible forms of spelling practice

18. According to the passage, what negative effect might the spelling computer   18._____
    have on children who use it?
    They will
    A. not learn to formulate general rules for correct spelling
    B. not gain practice in handwriting
    C. become too reliant on mechanical devices
    D. become more concerned with the theory than with the practice of spelling
    E. not learn when to seek aid from the teacher

19. Which of the following words in the first sentence of the passage could be   19._____
    enclosed in quotation marks for the same reason that "talking" (line 1) is?
    A. "new"   B. "asks"   C. "user"   D. "spell"   E. "word"

20. According to the passage, which of the following is a MAJOR drawback of   20._____
    the spelling computer?
    A. It does not give the speller more than two tries at a word.
    B. It does not display the correct spelling of a misspelled word.
    C. It does not help the user determine why an incorrect spelling of a word is wrong.
    D. It cannot use a range of words to illustrate different representations of a given speech sound.
    E. It cannot praise the user for correct performance as warmly as a teacher can.

21. The passage supplies information that would answer which of the following   21._____
    questions?
    A. What are some patterns in English spelling?
    B. What determines the correctness of any given spelling?
    C. How widely are the new spelling computers used in public schools?
    D. What are some of the shortcomings of traditional spelling instruction as it sometimes now takes place?
    E. What research has been done recently to determine the effectiveness of the new spelling computers?

22. The author's description of the spelling computer informs us of which of the following?
    I. The computer's approximate size
    II. The method by which the computer gives praise
    III. The sequence of events in one of the computer's learning trials

    The CORRECT answer is:
    A. I only
    B. II only
    C. I and III only
    D. II and III only
    E. I, II, and III

23. Though the changes fostered by desegregation of much of American public education have been profound, we have not yet fully achieved our ultimate goal of comparable educational opportunities for all our citizens.
    The author's attitude toward the effectiveness of "the changes fostered by desegregation" in achieving "our ultimate goal" can BEST be described as
    A. highly critical
    B. deeply disappointed
    C. strongly pessimistic
    D. cautiously positive
    E. enthusiastically optimistic

Questions 24-25.

DIRECTIONS: Questions 24 and 25 are to be answered on the basis of the following passage.

MEMORANDUM FOR GUIDANCE COUNSELORS
AT CITY HIGH SCHOOL

Juniors must select courses according to the following new regulations:

1. Juniors must take six courses; either four or five of these must be academic courses.
2. Juniors taking four academic courses must take physical education and, in addition, must select one of the following music courses: band, chorus, music appreciation, or orchestra.
3. Juniors taking five academic courses must take physical education unless they play an instrument that is needed by the band or orchestra (this year, violin and clarinet only), in which case they will be excused from physical education if they select band or orchestra.

24. A City High School junior who is taking five academic courses and who plays the cello has asked permission to take orchestra instead of physical education. Which of the following responses to the request is MOST consistent with the new regulations?
    Permission is
    A. granted, since orchestra is a music course
    B. granted, since the student is taking five academic courses
    C. denied, since the orchestra has enough cello players this year
    D. denied, since all juniors must take music appreciation
    E. denied, since the student did not take orchestra in previous years

25. Which of the following sets of courses, chosen by a City High School junior who plays the clarinet, would comply with the new regulations?
    I.   Four academic courses, band, and orchestra
    II. Four academic courses, orchestra, and physical education
    III. Five academic courses and band

25.____

26. One of the findings of a recent study of students who are employed in part-time jobs is that those students who derived the greatest learning from their jobs were those who had the most difficulty learning in school.
    Which of the following can be inferred from the findings of the study mentioned in the statement above?
    A. Students who are employed make greater improvement in their school performance than do students who are not employed.
    B. Students who do well in school generally do not learn much from their jobs.
    C. Being employed seems to help students who have difficulty in school improve their academic performance.
    D. Students who have difficulty in school are more likely to be employed than are students who perform adequately in school.
    E. Students who learn easily in school do not learn as much from their jobs as do students who have difficulty in school.

26.____

Questions 27-28.

DIRECTIONS: Questions 27 and 28 are to be answered on the basis of the following passage.

With the influx of Cuban citizens into Miami in 1959, thousands of Spanish-speaking children enrolled in Florida's public schools. Since teachers had been among the professional groups who left Cuba, Florida schools had access to teachers who shared the language and culture of the new students. The school boards had to decide whether the children should learn English before entering school or whether education in both languages should be tried. Fortunately, the latter method was chosen. This event had a significant influence in the acceptance and growth of bilingual education in the United States

27. The author implies that, if Spanish-speaking children had been obliged to learn English before entering Florida's public schools, which of the following MOST probably would have resulted?
    A. Spanish-speaking children would not have entered Florida's public schools.
    B. English-speaking students would not have had the opportunity to learn Spanish.
    C. Bilingual education in the United States would not have grown as rapidly as it did.
    D. Spanish-speaking children would have forgotten their language and culture.
    E. Spanish-speaking children would have needed to work harder to excel in school.

27.____

28. Which of the following statements BEST expresses the author's main point in the passage?
    A. Florida's public schools were among the first in the country to offer bilingual education to Spanish-speaking children.
    B. School systems considering bilingual education programs would do well to model their programs after those used in the Miami public schools.
    C. Bilingual education programs in Florida schools have been very successful and deserve more national recognition.
    D. Florida school boards made the right choice when they decided in 1959 to offer bilingual education to Spanish-speaking children.
    E. Bilingual education was revived in Florida in the 1960's because of an influx of Spanish-speaking students into the public schools.

29. Sentence I: I recently took my daughter to the Virgin Islands on vacation.
    Sentence II: That part of the world is surely one of the most beautiful.
    Sentence III: The day we arrived was sunny; the temperature was 82 degrees.
    Sentence IV: I don't think that my daughter, who is only 5 years old, has ever been more excited.
    Sentence V: She said that she wanted to go straight to the ocean for a swim.

    If the writer is not intending to deceive his or her audience, which of the following descriptions of these sentence is ACCURATE?
    A. Only Sentences I and III state facts.
    B. Sentences I, III, IV, and V state facts only.
    C. Sentences II and IV state opinions and not facts.
    D. Sentence IV states both fact and opinion.
    E. Sentence V states both fact and opinion.

30. Students who receive little or no praise at home for success in school can hardly be expected to be motivated in the classroom.
    Which of the following is the MOST accurate inference from the above statement?
    A. Students who are motivated will do well in school even if they are not openly praised by their teachers.
    B. Children whose families reward good school performance with praise are more likely than other children to try to do well in school.
    C. When children have almost no experience of success in school, they are likely to give up hope and stop trying to do well in the classroom.
    D. Students are unlikely to accept criticism willingly if those students are continually praised at home.
    E. Motivation in students results from the double reward of success in the classroom and praise in the home.

KEY (CORRECT ANSWERS)

1.	D	11.	A	21.	D
2.	E	12.	C	22.	C
3.	B	13.	D	23.	D
4.	A	14.	C	24.	C
5.	E	15.	E	25.	E
6.	D	16.	A	26.	E
7.	A	17.	B	27.	C
8.	D	18.	A	28.	D
9.	C	19.	B	29.	D
10.	E	20.	C	30.	B

READING COMPREHENSION
UNDERSTANDING AND INTERPRETING WRITTEN MATERIAL

EXAMINATION SECTION

TEST 1

DIRECTIONS: Each question or incomplete statement is followed by several suggested answers or completions. Select the one that BEST answers the question or completes the statement. *PRINT THE LETTER OF THE CORRECT ANSWER IN THE SPACE AT THE RIGHT.*

Questions 1-3.

DIRECTIONS: Questions 1 through 3 are to be answered SOLELY on the basis of the following passage.

    Every organization needs a systematic method of checking its operations as a means to increase efficiency and promote economy. Many successful private firms have instituted a system of audit or internal inspections to accomplish these ends. Law enforcement organizations, which have an extremely important service to *sell*, should be no less zealous in developing efficiency and economy in their operations. Periodic, organized, and systematic inspections are one means of promoting the achievement of these objectives. The necessity of an organized inspection system is perhaps greatest in those law enforcement groups which have grown to such a size that the principal officer can no longer personally supervise or be cognizant of every action taken. Smooth and effective operation demands that the head of the organization have at hand some tool with which he can study and enforce general policies and procedure and also direct compliance with day-to-day orders, most of which are put into execution outside his sight and hearing. A good inspection system can serve as that tool.

1. The central thought of the above passage is that a system of inspections within a police department
    A. is unnecessary for a department in which the principal officer can personally supervise all official actions taken
    B. should be instituted at the first indication that there is any deterioration in job performance by the force
    C. should be decentralized and administered by first-line supervisory officers
    D. is an important aid to the police administrator in the accomplishment of law enforcement objectives

1.____

2. The MOST accurate of the following statements concerning the need for an organized inspection system in a law enforcement organization is: It is
    A. never needed in an organization of small size where the principal officer can give personal supervision
    B. most needed where the size of the organization prevents direct supervision by the principal officer
    C. more needed in law enforcement organizations than in private firms
    D. especially needed in an organization about to embark upon a needed expansion of services

2.____

3. According to the above passage, the head of the police organization utilizes the internal inspection system
   A. as a tool which must be constantly re-examined in the light of changing demands for police service
   B. as an administrative technique to increase efficiency and promote economy
   C. by personally visiting those areas of police operation which are outside his sight and hearing
   D. to augment the control of local commanders over detailed field operations

Questions 4-10.

DIRECTIONS: Questions 4 through 10 are to be answered SOLELY on the basis of the following passage.

Job evaluation and job rating systems are intended to introduce scientific procedures. Any type of approach, when properly used, will give satisfactory results. The Point System, when properly validated by actual use, is more likely to be suitable for general use than the ranking system. In many aspects, the Factor Comparison Plan is a point system tied to money values. Of course, there may be another system that combines the ranking system with the point system, especially during the initial stages of the development of the program. After the program has been in use for some time, the tendency is to drop off the ranking phase and continue the use of the point system.

In the ranking system of rating of jobs, every job within the plant is arranged in some order, either from the one with the simplest qualifications to the one with maximum requirements, or in the reverse order. This system should be preceded by careful job analysis and the writing of accurate job descriptions before the rating process is undertaken. It is possible, of course, to take the jobs as they are found in the business enterprise and use the names as they are without any attempt at standardization, and merely rank them according to the general overall impression of the raters. Such a procedure is certain to fall short of what may reasonably be expected of job rating. Another procedure that is in reality merely a modification of the simple rating described above is to establish a series of grades or zones and arrange all he jobs in the plant into groups within these grades and zones. The practice in most common use is to arrange all the jobs in the plant according to their requirements by rating them and then to establish the classification or groups.

The actual ranking of jobs may be done by one individual, several individuals, or a committee. If several individuals are working independently on the task, it will usually be found that, in general, they agree but that their rankings vary in certain details. A conference between the individuals, with each person giving his reasons why he rated one way or another, usually produces agreement. The detailed job descriptions are particularly helpful when there is disagreement among raters as to the rating of certain jobs. It is not only possible but desirable to have workers participate in the construction of the job description and in rating the job.

4. The MAIN theme of this passage is
   A. the elimination of bias in job rating
   B. the rating of jobs by the ranking system
   C. the need or accuracy in allocating points in the point system
   D. pitfalls to avoid in selecting key jobs in the Factor Comparison Plan

5. The ranking system of rating jobs consists MAINLY of
   A. attaching a point value to each ratable factor of each job prior to establishing an equitable pay scale
   B. arranging every job in the organization in descending order and then following this up with a job analysis of the key jobs
   C. preparing accurate job descriptions after a job analysis and then arranging all jobs either in ascending or descending order based on job requirements
   D. arbitrarily establishing a hierarchy of job classes and grades and then fitting each job into a specific class and grade based on the opinions of unit supervisors

6. The above passage states that the system of classifying jobs MOST used in an organization is to
   A. organize all jobs in the organization in accordance with their requirements and then create categories or clusters of jobs
   B. classify all jobs in the organization according to the titles and rank by which they are currently known in the organization
   C. establish a pre-arranged series of grades or zones and then fit all jobs into one of the grades or zones
   D. determine the salary currently being paid for each job and then rank the jobs in order according to salary

7. According to the above passage, experience has shown that when a group of raters is assigned to the job evaluation task and each individual rates independently of the others, the raters GENERALLY
   A. *agree* with respect to all aspects of their rankings
   B. *disagree* with respect to all or nearly all aspects of the rankings
   C. *disagree* on overall ratings, but agree on specific rating factors
   D. *agree* on overall rankings, but have some variance in some details

8. The above passage states that the use of a detailed job description is of special value when
   A. employees of an organization have participated in the preliminary step involved in actual preparation of the job description
   B. labor representatives are not participating in ranking of the jobs
   C. an individual rater who is unsure of himself is ranking the jobs
   D. a group of raters is having difficulty reaching unanimity with respect to ranking a certain job

9. A comparison of the various rating systems as described in the above passage shows that
   A. the ranking system is not as appropriate for general use as a properly validated point system
   B. the point system is the same as the Factor Comparison Plan except that it places greater emphasis on money

C. no system is capable of combining the point system and the Factor Comparison Plan
D. the point system will be discontinued last when used in combination with the Factor comparison System

10. The above passage implies that the PRINCIPAL reason for creating job evaluation and rating systems was to help
    A. overcome union opposition to existing salary plans
    B. base wage determination on a more objective and orderly foundation
    C. eliminate personal bias on the part of the trained scientific job evaluators
    D. management determine if it was overpricing the various jobs in the organizational hierarchy

10.____

Questions 11-13.

DIRECTIONS: Questions 11 through 13 are to be answered SOLELY on the basis of the following passage.

The common sense character of the merit system seems so natural to most Americans that many people wonder why it should ever have been inoperative. After all, the American economic system, the most phenomenal the world has ever known, is also founded on a rugged selective process which emphasizes the personal qualities of capacity, industriousness, and productivity. The criteria may not have always been appropriate and competition has not always been fair, but competition there was, and the responsibilities and the rewards—with exceptions, of course—have gone to those who could measure up in terms of intelligence, knowledge, or perseverance. This has been true not only in the economic area, in the money-making process, but also in achievement in the professions and other walks of life.

11. According to the above passage, economic rewards in the United State have
    A. always been based on appropriate, fair criteria
    B. only recently been based on a competitive system
    C. not going to people who compete too ruggedly
    D. usually gone to those people with intelligence, knowledge, and perseverance

11.____

12. According to the above passage, a merit system is
    A. an unfair criterion on which to base rewards
    B. unnatural to anyone who is not American
    C. based only on common sense
    D. based on the same principles as the American economic system

12.____

13. According to the above passage, it is MOST accurate to say that
    A. the United States has always had a civil service merit system
    B. civil service employees are very rugged
    C. the American economic system has always been based on a merit objective
    D. competition is unique to the American way of life

13.____

Questions 14-15.

DIRECTIONS: Questions 14 and 15 are to be answered SOLELY on the basis of the following passage.

In-basket tests are often used to assess managerial potential. The exercise consists of a set of papers that would be likely to be found in the in-basket of an administrator or manager at any given time, and requires the individuals participating in the examination to indicate how they would dispose of each item found in the in-basket. In order to handle the in-basket effectively, they must successfully manage their time, refer and assign some work to subordinates, juggle potentially conflicting appointments and meetings, and arrange for follow-up of problems generated by the items in the in-basket. In other words, the in-basket test is attempting to evaluate the participants' abilities to organize their work, set priorities, delegate, control, and make decisions.

14. According to the above passage, to succeed in an in-basket test, an administrator must
    A. be able to read very quickly
    B. have a great deal of technical knowledge
    C. know when to delegate work
    D. arrange a lot of appointments and meetings

14.____

15. According to the above passage, all of the following abilities are indications of managerial potential EXCEPT the ability to
    A. organize and control
    B. manage time
    C. write effective reports
    D. make appropriate decisions

15.____

Questions 16-19.

DIRECTIONS: Questions 16 through 19 are to be answered SOLELY on the basis of the following passage.

A personnel researcher has at his disposal various approaches for obtaining information, analyzing it, and arriving at conclusions that have value in predicting and affecting the behavior of people at work. The type of method to be used depends on such factors as the nature of the research problem, the available data, and the attitudes of those people being studied to the various kinds of approaches. While the experimental approach, with its use of control groups, is the most refined type of study, there are others that are often found useful in personnel research. Surveys, in which the researcher obtains facts on a problem from a variety of sources, are employed in research on wages, fringe benefits, and labor relations. Historical studies are used to trace the development of problems in order to understand them better and to isolate possible causative factors. Case studies are generally developed to explore all the details of a particular problem that is representative of other similar problems. A researcher chooses the most appropriate form of study for the problem he is investigating. He should recognize, however, that the experimental method, commonly referred to as the scientific method, if used validly and reliably, gives the most conclusive results.

16. The above passage discusses several approaches used to obtain information on particular problems.
Which of the following may be MOST reasonably concluded from the passage? A(n)
    A. historical study cannot determine causative factors
    B. survey is often used in research on fringe benefits
    C. case study is usually used to explore a problem that is unique and unrelated to other problems
    D. experimental study is used when the scientific approach to a problem fails

17. According to the above passage, all of the following are factors that may determine the type of approach a researcher uses EXCEPT
    A. the attitudes of people toward being used in control groups
    B. the number of available sources
    C. his desire to isolate possible causative factors
    D. the degree of accuracy he requires

18. The words *scientific method*, as used in the last sentence of the above passage, refer to a type of study which, according to the above passage
    A. uses a variety of sources
    B. traces the development of problems
    C. uses control groups
    D. analyzes the details of a representative problem

19. Which of the following can be MOST reasonably concluded from the above passage?
    In obtaining and analyzing information on a particular problem, a researcher employs the method which is the
    A. most accurate
    B. most suitable
    C. least expensive
    D. least time-consuming

Questions 20-25.

DIRECTIONS: Questions 20 through 25 are to be answered SOLELY on the basis of the following passage.

The quality of the voice of a worker is an important factor in conveying to clients and co-workers his attitude and, to some degree, his character. The human voice, when not consciously disguised, may reflect a person's mood, temper, and personality. It has been shown in several experiments that certain character traits can be assessed with better than chance accuracy through listening to the voice of an unknown person who cannot be seen.
Since one of the objectives of the worker is to put clients at ease and to present an encouraging and comfortable atmosphere, a harsh, shrill, or loud voice could have a negative effect. A client who displays emotions of anger or resentment would probably be provoked even further by a caustic tone. In a face-to-face situation, an unpleasant voice may be compensated for, to some degree, by a concerned and kind facial expression. However, when one speaks on the telephone, the expression on one's face cannot be seen by the listener. A supervising clerk who wishes to represent himself effectively to clients should try to eliminate as many faults as possible in striving to develop desirable voice qualities.

20. If a worker uses a sarcastic tone while interviewing a resentful client, the client, according to the above passage, would MOST likely
    A. avoid the face-to-face problem
    B. be ashamed of his behavior
    C. become more resentful
    D. be provoked to violence

21. According to the passage, experiments comparing voice and character traits have demonstrated that
    A. prospects for improving an unpleasant voice through training are better than chance
    B. the voice can be altered to project many different psychological characteristics
    C. the quality of the human voice reveals more about the speaker than his words do
    D. the speaker's voice tells the hearer something about the speaker's personality

22. Which of the following, according to the above passage, is a person's voice MOST likely to reveal?
    His
    A. prejudices
    B. intelligence
    C. social awareness
    D. temperament

23. It may be MOST reasonably concluded from the above passage that an interested and sympathetic expression on the face of a worker
    A. may induce a client to feel certain he will receive welfare benefits
    B. will eliminate the need for pleasant vocal qualities in the interviewer
    C. may help to make up for an unpleasant voice in the interviewer
    D. is desirable as the interviewer speaks on the telephone to a client

24. Of the following, the MOST reasonable implication of the above paragraph is that a worker should, when speaking to a client, control and use his voice to
    A. simulate a feeling of interest in the problems of the client
    B. express his emotions directly and adequately
    C. help produce in the client a sense of comfort and security
    D. reflect his own true personality

25. It may be concluded from the above passage that the PARTICULAR reason for a worker to pay special attention to modulating her voice when talking on the phone to a client is that, during a telephone conversation
    A. there is a necessity to compensate for the way in which a telephone distorts the voice
    B. the voice of the worker is a reflection of her mood and character
    C. the client can react only on the basis of the voice and words she hears
    D. the client may have difficulty getting a clear understanding over the telephone

KEY (CORRECT ANSWERS)

1.	D	11.	D
2.	B	12.	D
3.	B	13.	C
4.	B	14.	C
5.	C	15.	C
6.	A	16.	B
7.	D	17.	D
8.	D	18.	C
9.	A	19.	B
10.	B	20.	C

21. D
22. D
23. C
24. C
25. C

TEST 2

DIRECTIONS: Each question or incomplete statement is followed by several suggested answers or completions. Select the one that BEST answers the question or completes the statement. *PRINT THE LETTER OF THE CORRECT ANSWER IN THE SPACE AT THE RIGHT.*

Questions 1-3.

DIRECTIONS: Questions 1 through 3 are to be answered SOLELY on the basis of the following paragraph.

    Suppose you are given the job of printing, collating, and stapling 8,000 copies of a ten-page booklet as soon as possible. You have available one photo-offset machine, a collator with an automatic stapler, and the personnel to operate these machines. All will be available for however long the job takes to complete. The photo-offset machine prints 5,000 impressions an hour, and it takes about 15 minutes to set up a plate. The collator, including time for insertion of pages and stapling, can process about 2,000 booklets an hour. (Answers should be based on the assumption that there are no breakdowns or delays.)

1. Assuming that all the printing is finished before the collating is started, if the job is given to you late Monday and your section can begin work the next day and is able to devote seven hours a day, Monday through Friday, to the job until it is finished, what is the BEST estimate of when the job will be finished?
   A. Wednesday afternoon of the same week
   B. Thursday morning of the same week
   C. Friday morning of the same week
   D. Monday morning of the next week

2. An operator suggests to you that instead of completing all the printing and then beginning collating and stapling, you first print all the pages for 4,000 booklets, so that they can be collated and stapled while the last 4,000 pages are being printed.
   If you accepted this suggestion, the job would be completed
   A. sooner but would require more man-hours
   B. at the same time using either method
   C. later and would require more man-hours
   D. sooner but there would be more wear and tear on the plates

3. Assume that you have the same assignment and equipment as described above, but 16,000 copies of the booklet are needed instead of 8,000.
   If you decided to print 8,000 complete booklets, then collate and staple them while you started printing the next 8,000 booklets, which of the following statements would MOST accurately describe the relationship between this new method and your original method of printing all the booklets at one time, and then collating and stapling them? The
   A. job would be completed at the same time regardless of the method used
   B. new method would result in the job's being completed 3½ hours earlier
   C. original method would result in the job's being completed an hour later
   D. new method would result in the job's being completed 1½ hours earlier

Questions 4-6.

DIRECTIONS: Questions 4 through 6 are to be answered SOLELY on the basis of the following passage.

When using words like company, association, council, committee, and board in place of the full official name, the writer should not capitalize these short forms unless he intends them to invoke the full force of the institution's authority. In legal contracts, in minutes, or in formal correspondence where one is speaking formally and officially on behalf of the company, the term Company is usually capitalized, but in ordinary usage, where it is not essential to load the short form with this significance, capitalization would be excessive. (Example: The company will have many good openings for graduates this June.)
The treatment recommended for short forms of place names is essentially the same as that recommended for short forms of organizational names. In general, we capitalize the full form but not the short form. If Park Avenue is referred to in one sentence, then the *avenue* is sufficient in subsequent references. The same is true with words like building, hotel, station, and airport, which are capitalized when part of a proper name changed (Pan Am Building, Hotel Plaza, Union Station, O'Hare Airport), but are simply lower-cased when replacing these specific names.

4. The above passage states that USUALLY the short forms of names of organizations
   A. and places should not be capitalized
   B. and places should be capitalized
   C. should not be capitalized, but the short forms of names of places should be capitalized
   D. should be capitalized, but the short forms of names of places should not be capitalized

5. The above passage states that in legal contracts, in minutes, and in formal correspondence, the short forms of names of organizations should
   A. usually not be capitalized   B. usually be capitalized
   C. usually not be used   D. never be used

6. It can be inferred from the above passage that decisions regarding when to capitalize certain words
   A. should be left to the discretion of the writer
   B. should be based on generally accepted rules
   C. depend on the total number of words capitalized
   D. are of minor importance

Questions 7-10.

DIRECTIONS: Questions 7 through 10 are to be answered SOLELY on the basis of the following passage.

Use of the systems and procedures approach to office management is revolutionizing the supervision of office work. This approach views an enterprise as an entity which seeks to fulfill definite objectives. Systems and procedures help to organize repetitive work into a routine, thus reducing the amount of decision making required for its accomplishment. As a result, employees are guided in their efforts and perform only necessary work. Supervisors are relieved of any details of execution and are free to attend to more important work. Establishing work guides which require that identical tasks be performed the same way each time permits standardization of forms, machine operations, work methods, and controls. This approach also reduces the probability of errors. Any error committed is usually discovered quickly because the incorrect work does not meet the requirement of the work guides. Errors are also reduced through work specialization, which allows each employee to become thoroughly proficient in a particular type of work. Such proficiency also tends to improve the morale of the employees.

7. The above passage states that the accuracy of an employee's work is INCREASED by
   A. using the work specialization approach
   B. employing a probability sample
   C. requiring him to shift at one time into different types of tasks
   D. having his supervisor check each detail of work execution

8. Of the following, which one BEST expresses the main theme of the above passage? The
   A. advantages and disadvantages of the systems and procedures approach to office management
   B. effectiveness of the systems and procedures approach to office management in developing skills
   C. systems and procedures approach to office management as it relates to office costs
   D. advantages of the systems and procedures approach to office management for supervisors and office workers

9. Work guides are LEAST likely to be used when
   A. standardized forms are used
   B. a particular office task is distinct and different from all others
   C. identical tasks are to be performed in identical ways
   D. similar work methods are expected from each employee

10. According to the above passage, when an employee makes a work error, it USUALLY
    A. is quickly corrected by the supervisor
    B. necessitates a change in the work guides
    C. can be detected quickly if work guides are in use
    D. increases the probability of further errors by that employee

Questions 11-12.

DIRECTIONS: Questions 11 and 12 are to be answered SOLELY on the basis of the following passage.

The coordination of the many activities of a large public agency is absolutely essential. Coordination, as an administrative principle, must be distinguished from and is independent of cooperation. Coordination can be of either the horizontal or the vertical type. In large organizations, the objectives of vertical coordination are achieved by the transmission of orders and statements of policy down through the various levels of authority. It is an accepted generalization that the more authoritarian the organization, the more easily may vertical coordination be accomplished. Horizontal coordination is arrived through staff work, administrative management, and conferences of administrators of equal rank. It is obvious that of the two types of coordination, the vertical kind is more important, for at best horizontal coordination only supplements the coordination effected up and down the line,

11. According to the above passage, the ease with which vertical coordination is achieved in a large agency depends upon
    A. the extent to which control is firmly exercised from above
    B. the objectives that have been established for the agency
    C. the importance attached by employees to the orders and statements of policy transmitted through the agency
    D. the cooperation obtained at the various levels of authority

12. According to the above passage,
    A. vertical coordination is dependent for its success upon horizontal coordination
    B. one type of coordination may work in opposition to the other
    C. similar methods may be used to achieve both types of coordination
    D. horizontal coordination is at most an addition to vertical coordination

Questions 13-17.

DIRECTIONS: Questions 13 through 17 are to be answered SOLELY on the basis of the following situation.

Assume that you are a newly appointed supervisor in the same unit in which you have been acting as a provisional for some time. You have in your unit the following workers:

WORKER I: He has always been an efficient worker. In a number of his cases, the clients have recently begun to complain that they cannot manage on the departmental budget.

WORKER II: He has been under selective supervision for some time as an experienced, competent worker. He now begins to be late for his supervisory conferences and to stress how much work he has to do.

WORKER III: He has been making considerable improvement in his ability to handle the details of his job. He now tells you, during an individual conference, that he does not need such close supervision and that he wants to operate more independently. He says that Worker II is always available when he needs a little information or help but, in general, he can manage very well by himself.

5 (#2)

WORKER IV: He brings you a complex case for decision as to eligibility. Discussion of the case brings out the fact that he has failed to consider all the available resources adequately but has stressed the family's needs to include every extra item in the budget. This is the third case of a similar nature that his worker has brought to you recently. This worker and Worker I work in adjacent territory and are rather friendly.

In the following questions, select the option that describes the method of dealing with these workers that illustrate BEST supervisory practice.

13. With respect to supervision of Worker I, the assistant supervisor should 13.____
    A. discuss with the worker, in an individual conference, any problems that he may be having due to the increase in the cost of living
    B. plan a group conference for the unit around budgeting, as both Workers I and IV seem to be having budgetary difficulties
    C. discuss with Workers I and IV together the meaning of money as acceptance or rejection to the clients
    D. discuss with Worker I the budgetary data in each case in relation to each client's situation

14. With respect to supervision of Worker II, the supervisory should 14.____
    A. move slowly with this worker and give him time to learn that the supervisor's official appointment has not changed his attitudes or methods of supervision
    B. discuss the worker's change of attitude and asks him to analyze the reasons for his change in behavior
    C. take time to show the worker how he is avoiding his responsibility in the supervisor-worker relationship and that he is resisting supervision
    D. hold an evaluatory conference with the worker and show him how he is taking over responsibilities that are not his by providing supervision for Worker III

15. With respect to supervision of Worker III, the supervisor should discuss with this worker 15.____
    A. why he would rather have supervision from Worker II than from the supervisor
    B. the necessity for further improvement before he can go on selective supervision
    C. an analysis of the improvement that has been made and the extent to which the worker is able to handle the total job for which he is responsible
    D. the responsibility of the supervisor to see that clients receive adequate service

16. With respect to supervision of Worker IV, the supervisor should 16.____
    A. show the worker that resources figures are incomplete but that even if they were complete, the family would probably be eligible for assistance
    B. ask the worker why he is so protective of these families since there are three cases so similar

C. discuss with the worker all three cases at the same time so that the worker may see his own role in the three situations
D. discuss with the worker the reasons for departmental policies and procedures around budgeting

17. With respect to supervision of Workers I and IV, since these two workers are friends and would seem to be influencing each other, the supervisor should
    A. hold a joint conference with them both, pointing out how they should clear with the supervisor and not make their own rules together
    B. handle the problems of each separately in individual conferences
    C. separate them by transferring one to another territory or another unit
    D. take up the problem of workers asking help of each other rather than from the supervisor in a group meeting

17._____

Questions 18-20.

DIRECTIONS: Questions 18 through 20 are to be answered SOLELY on the basis of the following passage.

One of the key supervisory problems in a large municipal recreation department is that many leaders are assigned to isolated playgrounds or small centers, where it is difficult to observe their work regularly. Often their facilities are extremely limited. In such settings, as well as in larger recreation centers, where many recreation leaders tend to have other jobs as well, there tends to be a low level of morale and incentive. Still, it is the supervisor's task to help recreation personnel to develop pride in their work and to maintain a high level of performance. With isolated leaders, the supervisor may give advice or assistance. Leaders may be assigned to different tasks or settings during the year to maximize their productivity and provide new challenges. When it is clear that leaders are no willing to make a real effort to contribute to the department, the possibility of penalties must be considered, within the scope of departmental policy and the union contract. However, the supervisor should be constructive, encourage and assist workers to take a greater interest in their work, be innovative, and try to raise morale and to improve performance in positive ways.

18. The one of the following that would the MOST appropriate title for the above passage is
    A. Small Community Centers – Pro and Con
    B. Planning Better Recreation Programs
    C. The Supervisor's Task in Upgrading Personnel Performance
    D. The Supervisor and the Municipal Union – Rights and Obligations

18._____

19. The above passage makes clear that recreation leadership performance in all recreation playgrounds and centers throughout a large city is
    A. generally above average, with good morale on the part of most recreation leaders
    B. beyond description since no one has ever observed or evaluated recreation leaders

19._____

C. a key test of the personnel department's effort to develop more effective hiring standards
D. of mixed quality, with many recreation leaders having poor morale and a low level of achievement

20. According to the above passage, the supervisor's role is to 20.____
    A. use disciplinary action as his major tool in upgrading performance
    B. tolerate the lack of effort of individual employees since they are assigned to isolated playgrounds or small centers
    C. employ encouragement, advice, and, when appropriate, disciplinary action to improve performance
    D. inform the county supervisor whenever malfeasance or idleness is detected

Questions 21-25.

DIRECTIONS: Questions 21 through 25 are to be answered SOLELY on the basis of the following passage.

EMPLOYEE LEAVE REGULATIONS

Peter Smith, as a full-time permanent city employee under the Career and Salary Plan, earns an *annual leave allowance*. This consists of a certain number of days off a year with pay and may be used for vacation, personal business, and for observing religious holidays. As a newly appointed employee, during his first 8 years of city service, he will earn an annual leave allowance of 20 days off a year (an average of $1^2/_3$ days off a month). After he has finished 8 full years of working for the city, he will begin earning an additional 5 days off a year. His annual leave allowance, therefore, will then be 25 days a year and will remain at this amount for seven full years. He will begin earning an additional two days off a year at this amount for seven full years. He will begin earning an additional two days off a year after he has completed a total of 15 years of city employment. Therefore, in his sixteenth year of working for the city, Mr. Smith will be earning 27 days off a year as his annual leave allowance (an average of $2\frac{1}{4}$ days off a month).

A *sick leave allowance* of one day a month is also given to Mr. Smith, but it can be used only in cases of actual illness. When Mr. Smith returns to work after using sick leave allowance, he must have a doctor's note if the absence is for a total of more than 3 days, but he may also be required to show a doctor's note for absences of 1, 2, or 3 days.

21. According to the above passage, Mr. Smith's annual leave allowance consists 21.____
    of a certain number of days off a year which he
    A. does not get paid for
    B. gets paid for at time and a half
    C. may use for personal business
    D. may not use for observing religious holidays

22. According to the above passage, after Mr. Smith has been working for the city 22.____
    for 9 years, his annual leave allowance will be _____ days a year.
    A. 20   B. 25   C. 27   D. 37

23. According to the above passage, Mr. Smith will begin earning an average of 2 days off a month as his annual leave allowance after he has worked for the city for _____ full years.
    A. 7   B. 8   C. 15   D. 17

24. According to the above passage, Mr. Smith is given a sick leave allowance of
    A. 1 day every 2 months
    B. 1 day per month
    C. $1^{2}/_{3}$ days per month
    D. 2¼ days a month

25. According to the above passage, when he uses sick leave allowance, Mr. Smith may be required to show a doctor's note
    A. even if his absence is for only 1 day
    B. only if his absence is for more than 2 days
    C. only if his absence is for more than 3 days
    D. only if his absence is for 3 days or more

KEY (CORRECT ANSWERS)

1.	C	11.	A
2.	C	12.	D
3.	D	13.	D
4.	A	14.	A
5.	B	15.	C
6.	B	16.	C
7.	A	17.	B
8.	D	18.	C
9.	B	19.	D
10.	C	20.	C

21. C
22. B
23. C
24. B
25. A

TEST 3

DIRECTIONS: Each question or incomplete statement is followed by several suggested answers or completions. Select the one that BEST answers the question or completes the statement. *PRINT THE LETTER OF THE CORRECT ANSWER IN THE SPACE AT THE RIGHT.*

Questions 1-6.

DIRECTIONS: Questions 1 through 6 are to be answered SOLELY on the basis of the following passage.

    A folder is made of a sheet of heavy paper (manila, kraft, pressboard, or red rope stock) that has been folded once so that the back is about one-half inch higher than the front. Folders are larger than the papers they contain in order to protect them. Two standard folder sizes are *letter size* for papers that are 8½" x 11" and *legal cap* for papers that are 8½" x 13".
    Folders are cut across the top in two ways: so that the back is straight (straight-cut) or so that the back has a tab that projects above the top of the folder. Such tabs bear captions that identify the contents of each folder. Tabs vary in width and position. The tabs of a set of folders that are *one-half cut* are half the width of the folder and have only two positions.
    One-third cut folders have three positions, each tab occupying a third of the width of the folder. Another standard tabbing is *one-fifth cut*, which has five positions. There are also folders with *two-fifths cut*, with the tabs in the third and fourth or fourth and fifth positions.

1. Of the following, the BEST title for the above passage is
   A. Filing Folders
   B. Standard Folder Sizes
   C. The Uses of the Folder
   D. The Use of Tabs

2. According to the above passage, one of the standard folder sizes is called
   A. Kraft cut
   B. legal cap
   C. one-half cut
   D. straight-cut

3. According to the above passage, tabs are GENERALLY placed along the _____ of the folder.
   A. back   B. front   C. left side   D. right side

4. According to the above passage, a tab is GENERALLY used to
   A. distinguish between standard folder sizes
   B. identify the contents of a folder
   C. increase the size of the folder
   D. protect the papers within the folder

5. According to the above passage, a folder that is two-fifths cut has _____ tabs.
   A. no   B. two   C. three   D. five

45

6. According to the above passage, one reason for making folders larger than the papers they contain is that
   A. only a certain size folder can be made from heavy paper
   B. they will protect the papers
   C. they will aid in setting up a tab system
   D. the back of the folder must be higher than the front

Questions 7-15.

DIRECTIONS: Questions 7 through 15 are to be answered SOLELY on the basis of the following passage.

The City University of New York traces its origins to 1847, when the Free Academy, which later became City College, was founded as the first tuition-free municipal college. City and Hunter Colleges were placed under the direction of the Board of Higher Education in 1926, and Brooklyn and Queens Colleges were subsequently added to the system of municipal colleges. In 1955, Staten Island Community College, the first of the two-year colleges sponsored by the Board of Higher Education under the program of the State University of New York, joined the system.

In 1961, the four senior colleges and three community colleges then under the jurisdiction of the Board of Higher Education became the City University of New York, and a University Graduate Division was organized to offer programs leading to the Ph.D. Since then, the university has undergone even more rapid growth. Today, it consists of nine senior colleges, an upper division college which admits students at the junior level, eight community colleges, a graduate division, and an affiliated medical center.

In the summer of 1969, the Board of Higher Education resolved that the time had come to commit the resources of the university to meeting an urgent social need—unrestricted access to higher education for all youths of the City. Determined to prevent the waste of human potential represented by the thousands of high school graduates whose limited educational opportunities left them unable to meet existing admission standards, the Board moved to adopt a policy of Open Admissions. It was their judgment that the best way of determining whether a potential student can benefit from college work is to admit him to college, provide him with the learning assistance he needs, and then evaluate his performance.

Beginning with the class of June 1970, every New York City resident who received a high school diploma from a public or private high school was guaranteed a place in one of the colleges of City University.

7. Of the following, the BEST title for the above passage is
   A. A Brief History of the City University
   B. High Schools and the City University
   C. The Components of the University
   D. Tuition-free Colleges

8. According to the above passage, which one of the following colleges of the City University was ORIGINALLY called the Free Academy?
   A. Brooklyn College   B. City College
   C. Hunter College   D. Queens College

9. According to the above passage, the system of municipal colleges became the City University of New York in
   A. 1926 B. 1955 C. 1961 D. 1969

10. According to the above passage, Staten Island Community College came under the jurisdiction of the Board of Higher Education
    A. 6 years after a Graduate Division was organized
    B. 8 years before the adoption of the Open Admissions Policy
    C. 29 years after Brooklyn and Queens Colleges
    D. 29 years after City and Hunter Colleges

11. According to the above passage, the Staten Island Community College is
    A. a graduate division center   B. a senior college
    C. a two-year college   D. an upper division college

12. According to the above passage, the TOTAL number of colleges, divisions, and affiliated branches of the City University is
    A. 18 B. 19 C. 20 D. 21

13. According to the above passage, the Open Admissions Policy is designed to determine whether a potential student will benefit from college by PRIMARILY
    A. discouraging competition for placement in the City University among high school students
    B. evaluating his performance after entry into college
    C. lowering admission standards
    D. providing learning assistance before entry into college

14. According to the above passage, the FIRST class to be affected by the Open Admissions Policy was the
    A. high school class which graduated in January 1970
    B. City University class which graduated in June 1970
    C. high school class when graduated in June 1970
    D. City University class when graduated in June 1970

15. According to the above passage, one of the reasons that the Board of Higher Education initiated the policy of Open Admission was to
    A. enable high school graduates with a background of limited educational opportunities to enter college
    B. expand the growth of the City University so as to increase the number and variety of degrees offered
    C. provide a social resource to the qualified youth of the City
    D. revise admission standards to meet the needs of the City

Questions 16-18.

DIRECTIONS: Questions 16 through 18 are to be answered SOLELY on the basis of the following passage.

Hereafter, all probationary students interested in transferring to community college career programs (associate degrees) from liberal arts programs in senior colleges (bachelor degrees) will be eligible for such transfers if they have completed no more than three semesters.
For students with averages 1.5 or above, transfer will be automatic. Those with 1.0 to 1.5 averages can transfer provisionally and will be required to make substantial progress during the first semester in the career program. Once transfer has taken place, only those courses in which passing grades were received will be computed in the community college grade-point average.
No request for transfer will be accepted from probationary students wishing to enter the liberal arts programs at the community college.

16. According to the above passage, the one of the following which is the BEST statement concerning the transfer of probationary students is that a probationary student
    A. may transfer to a career program at the end of one semester
    B. must complete three semester hours before he is eligible for transfer
    C. is not eligible to transfer to a career program
    D. is eligible to transfer to a liberal arts program

17. Which of the following is the BEST statement of academic evaluation for transfer purposes in the case of probationary students?
    A. No probationary student with an average under 1.5 may transfer.
    B. A probationary student with an average of 1.3 may not transfer.
    C. A probationary student with an average of 1.6 may transfer.
    D. A probationary student with an average of .8 may transfer on a provisional basis.

18. It is MOST likely that, of the following, the next degree sought by one who already holds the Associate in Science degree would be a(n) _____ degree.
    A. Assistantship in Science   B. Associate in Applied Science
    C. Bachelor of Science   D. Doctor of Philosophy

Questions 19-20.

DIRECTIONS: Questions 19 and 20 are to be answered SOLELY on the basis of the following passage.

Auto: Auto travel requires prior approval by the President and/or appropriate Dean and must be indicated in the *Request for Travel Authorization* form. Employees authorized to use personal autos on official College business will be reimbursed at the rate of 28¢ per mile for the first 500 miles driven and 18¢ per mile for mileage driven in excess of 500 mile. The Comptroller's Office may limit the amount of reimbursement to the expenditure that would have been made if a less expensive mode of transportation (railroad, airplane, bus, etc.) had been utilized. If this occurs, the traveler will have to pick up the excess expenditure as a personal expense.

Tolls, Parking Fees, and Parking Meter Fees are not reimbursable and many not be claimed.

19. Suppose that Professor T gives the office assistant the following memorandum: Used car for official trip to Albany, New York, and return. Distance from New York to Albany is 148 miles. Tolls were $3.50 each way. Parking garage cost $3.00. When preparing the Travel Expense Voucher for Professor T, the figure which should be claimed for transportation is 19.____
    A. $120.88   B. $113.88   C. $82.88   D. $51.44

20. Suppose that Professor V gives the office assistant the following memorandum: Used car for official trip to Pittsburgh, Pennsylvania, and return. Distance from New York to Pittsburgh is 350 miles. Tolls were $3.30, $11.40 going, and $3.30, $2.00 returning.
    When preparing the Travel Expense Voucher for Professor V, the figure which should be claimed for transportation is 20.____
    A. $225.40   B. $176.00   C. $127.40   D. $98.00

Questions 21-25.

DIRECTIONS: Questions 21 through 25 are to be answered SOLELY on the basis of the following passage.

For a period of nearly fifteen years, beginning in the mid-1950's, higher education sustained a phenomenal rate of growth. The factor principally responsible were continuing improvement in the rate of college entrance by high school graduates, a 50 percent increase in the size of the college-age (eighteen to twenty-one) group and—until about 1967—a rapid expansion of university research activity supported by the Federal government.

Today, as one looks ahead to the year 2010, it is apparent that each of these favorable stimuli will either be abated or turn into a negative factor. The rate of growth of the college-age group has already diminished; and from 2000 to 2005, the size of the college-age group has shrunk annually almost as fast as it grew from 1965 to 1970. From 2005 to 2010, this annual decrease will slow down so that by 2010 the age group will be about the same size as it was in 2009. This substantial net decrease in the size of the college-age group (from 1995 to 2010) will dramatically affect college enrollments since, currently, 83 percent of undergraduates are twenty-one and under, and another 11 percent are twenty-to to twenty-four.

21. Which one of the following factors is NOT mentioned in the above passage as contributing to the high rate of growth of higher education? 21.____
    A. A large increase in the size of the eighteen to twenty-one age group
    B. The equalization of educational opportunities among socio-economic groups
    C. The Federal budget impact on research and development spending in the higher education sector
    D. The increasing rate at which high school graduates enter college

22. Based on the information in the above passage, the size of the college-age group in 2010 will be
    A. larger than it was in 2009
    B. larger than it was in 1995
    C. smaller than it was in 2005
    D. about the same as it was in 2000

    22._____

23. According to the above passage, the tremendous rate of growth of higher education started around
    A. 1950   B. 1955   C. 1960   D. 1965

    23._____

24. The percentage of undergraduates who are over age 24 is MOST NEARLY
    A. 6%   B. 8%   C. 11%   D. 17%

    24._____

25. Which one of the following conclusions can be substantiated by the information given in the above passage?
    A. The college-age group was about the same size in 2000 as it was in 1965.
    B. The annual decrease in the size of the college-age group from 2000 to 2005 is about the same as the annual increase from 1965 to 1970.
    C. The overall decrease in the size of the college-age group from 2000 to 2005 will be followed by an overall increase in its size from 2005 to 2010.
    D. The size of the college-age group is decreasing at a fairly constant rate from 1995 to 2010.

    25._____

KEY (CORRECT ANSWERS)

1.	A		11.	C
2.	B		12.	C
3.	A		13.	B
4.	B		14.	C
5.	B		15.	A
6.	B		16.	A
7.	A		17.	C
8.	B		18.	C
9.	C		19.	C
10.	D		20.	B

21.	B
22.	C
23.	B
24.	A
25.	B

READING COMPREHENSION
UNDERSTANDING AND INTERPRETING WRITTEN MATERIAL
EXAMINATION SECTION
TEST 1

DIRECTIONS: Each question or incomplete statement is followed by several suggested answers or completions. Select the one that BEST answers the question or completes the statement. *PRINT THE LETTER OF THE CORRECT ANSWER IN THE SPACE AT THE RIGHT.*

1. The National Assessment of Educational Progress recently released the results of the first statistically valid national sampling of young adult reading skills in the United States. According to the survey, ninety-five percent of United States young adults (aged 21-25) can read at a fourth-grade level or better. This means they can read well enough to apply for a job, understand a movie guide or join the Army. This is a higher literacy rate than the eighty to eighty-five percent usually estimated for all adults. The study also found that ninety-nine percent can write their names, eighty percent can read a map or write a check for a bill, seventy percent can understand an appliance warranty or write a letter about a billing error, twenty-five percent can calculate the amount of a tip correctly, and fewer than ten percent can correctly figure the cost of a catalog or understand a complex bus schedule.
   Which statement about the study is BEST supported by the above passage?
   A. United States literacy rates among young adults are at an all-time high.
   B. Forty percent of young people in the United States cannot write a letter about a billing error.
   C. Twenty percent of United States teenagers cannot read a map,
   D. More than ninety percent of United States young adults cannot correctly calculate the cost of a catalog order.

   1.____

2. It is now widely recognized that salaries, benefits, and working conditions have more of an impact on job satisfaction than on motivation. If they aren't satisfactory, work performance and morale will suffer. But even when they are high, employees will not necessarily be motivated to work well. For example, THE WALL STREET JOURNAL recently reported that as many as forty or fifty percent of newly hired Wall Street lawyers (whose salaries start at upwards of $50,000) quit within the first three years, citing long hours, pressures, and monotony as the prime offenders. It seems there's just not enough of an intellectual challenge in their jobs. An up and coming money-market executive concluded: *Whether it was $1 million or $100 million, the procedure was the same. Except for the tension, a baboon could do my job.* When money and benefits are adequate, the most important additional determinants of job satisfaction are: more responsibility, a sense of achievement, recognition, and a chance to advance. All of these factors have a more significant influence on employee motivation and performance. As a footnote, several studies have found that the absence of these non-monetary factors can lead to serious stress-related illnesses.

   2.____

Which statement is BEST supported by the above passage?
  A. A worker's motivation to perform well is most affected by salaries, benefits, and working conditions.
  B. Low pay can lead to high levels of job stress.
  C. Work performance will suffer if workers feel they are not paid well.
  D. After satisfaction with pay and benefits, the next most important factor is more responsibility.

3. The establishment of joint labor-management production committees occurred in the United States during World War I and again during World War II. Their use was greatly encouraged by the National War Labor Board in World War I and the War Production Board in 1942. Because of the war, labor-management cooperation was especially desired to produce enough goods for the war effort, to reduce conflict, and to control inflation. The committees focused on how to achieve greater efficiency, and consulted on health and safety, training, absenteeism, and people issues in general. During the second world war, there were approximately five thousand labor-management committees in factories, affecting over six million workers. While research has found that only a few hundred committees made significant contributions to productivity, there were additional benefits in many cases. It became obvious to many that workers had ideas to contribute to the running of the organization, and that efficient enterprises could become even more so. Labor-management cooperation was also extended to industries that had never experienced it before. Directly after each war, however, few United States labor-management committees were in operation.
Which statement is BEST supported by the above passage?
  A. The majority of United States labor-management committees during the second world war accomplished little.
  B. A major goal of United States labor-management committees during the first and second world wars was to increase productivity.
  C. There were more United States labor-management committees during the second world war than during the first world war.
  D. There are few United States labor-management committees in operation today.

4. Studies have found that stress levels among employees who have a great deal of customer contact or a great deal of contact with the public can be very high. There are many reasons for this. Sometimes stress results when the employee is caught in the middle—an organization wants things done one way, but the customer wants them done another way. The situation becomes even worse for the employee's stress levels when he or she knows was to more effectively provide the service, but isn't allowed to, by the organization. An example is the bank teller who is required to ask a customer for two forms of identification before he or she can cash a check, even though the teller knows the customer well. If organizational mishaps occur or if there are problems with job design, the employee may be powerless to satisfy the customer, and also powerless to protect himself or herself from the customer's wrath. An example of this is the waitress who is forced to serve poorly prepared food. Studies have also found,

however, that if the organization and the employee design the positions and the service encounter well, and encourage the use of effective stress management techniques, stress can be reduced to levels that are well below average.
Which statement is BEST supported by the above passage?
- A. It is likely that knowledgeable employees will experience greater levels of job-related stress.
- B. The highest levels of occupational stress are found among those employees who have a great deal of customer contact.
- C. Organizations can contribute to the stress levels of their employees by poorly designing customer contact situations.
- D. Stress levels are generally higher in banks and restaurants.

5. It is estimated that approximately half of the United States population suffers from varying degrees of adrenal malfunction. When under stress for long periods of time, the adrenals produce extra cortisol and norepinephrine. By producing more hormones than they were designed to comfortably manufacture and secrete, the adrenals can *burn out* over time and then decrease their secretion. When this happens, the body loses its capacity to cope with stress, and the individual becomes sicker more easily and for longer periods of time. A result of adrenal malfunction may be a diminished output of cortisol. Symptoms of diminished cortisol output include any of the following: craving substances that will temporarily raise serum glucose levels such as caffeine, sweets, soda, juice, or tobacco; becoming dizzy when standing up too quickly; irritability; headaches; and erratic energy levels. Since cortisol is an anti-inflammatory hormone, a decreased output over extended periods of time can make one prone to inflammatory disease such ass arthritis, bursitis, colitis, and allergies. (Many food and pollen allergies disappear when adrenal function is restored to normal.) The patient will have no reserve energy, and infections can spread quickly. Excessive cortisol production, on the other hand, can decrease immunity, leading to frequent and prolonged illnesses.
Which statement is BEST supported by the above passage?
- A. Those who suffer from adrenal malfunction are most likely to be prone to inflammatory diseases such as arthritis and allergies.
- B. The majority of Americans suffer from varying degrees of adrenal malfunction.
- C. It is better for the health of the adrenals to drink juice instead of soda.
- D. Too much cortisol can inhibit the body's ability to resist disease.

6. Psychologist B.F. Skinner pointed out long ago that gambling is reinforced either by design or accidentally, by what he called a variable ratio schedule. A slot machine, for example, is cleverly designed to provide a payoff after it has been played a variable number of times. Although the person who plays it and wins while playing receives a great deal of monetary reinforcement, over the long run the machine will take in much more money than it pays out. Research on both animals and humans has consistently found that such variable reward schedules maintain a very high rate of repeat behavior, and that this behavior is particularly resistant to extinction.

Which statement is BEST supported by the above passage?
  A. Gambling, because it is reinforced by the variable ratio schedule, is more difficult to eliminate than most addictions.
  B. If someone is rewarded or wins consistently, even if it is not that often, he or she is likely to continue that behavior.
  C. Playing slot machines is the safest form of gambling because they are designed so that eventually the player will indeed win.
  D. A cat is likely to come when called if its owner has trained it correctly,

7. Paper entrepreneurialism is an offshoot of scientific management that has become so extreme that it has lost all connection to the actual workplace. It generates profits by cleverly manipulating rules and numbers that only in theory represent real products and real assets. At its worst, paper entrepreneurialism involves very little more than imposing losses on others for the sake of short-term profits. The others may be taxpayers, shareholders who end up indirectly subsidizing other shar holders, consumers, or investors. Paper entrepreneurialism has replaced product entrepreneurialism, is seriously threatening the United States economy, and is hurting our necessary attempts to transform the nation's industrial and productive economic base. An example is the United States company that complained loudly in 1979 that it did not have the $200 million needed to develop a video-cassette recorder, though demand for them had been very high. The company, however, did not hesitate to spend $1.2 billion that same year to buy a mediocre finance company. The video recorder market was handed over to other countries, who did not hesitate to manufacture them.
Which statement is BEST supported by the above passage?
  A. Paper entrepreneurialism involves very little more than imposing losses on others for the sake of short-term profits.
  B. Shareholders are likely to benefit most from paper entrepreneurialism.
  C. Paper entrepreneurialism is hurting the United States economy.
  D. The United States could have made better video-cassette recorders than the Japanese but we ceded the market to them in 1979.

7.____

8. The *prisoner's dilemma* is an almost 40-year-old game-theory model psychologists, biologists, economists, and political scientists use to try to understand the dynamics of competition and cooperation. Participants in the basic version of the experiment are told that they and their *accomplice* have been caught red-handed. Together, their best strategy is to cooperate by remaining silent. If they do this, each will get off with a 30-day sentence. But either person can do better for himself or herself. If you double-cross your partner, you will go scot free while he or she serves ten years. The problem is, if you each betray the other, you will both go to prison for eight years, not thirty days. No matter what your partner chooses, you are logically better off choosing betrayal. Unfortunately, your partner realizes this too, and so the odds are good that you will both get eight years. That's the dilemma. (The length of the prison sentences is always the same for each variation.) Participants at a recent symposium on behavioral economics at Harvard University discussed the many variations on the game that have been used

8.____

over the years. In one standard version, subjects are paired with a supervisor who pays them a dollar for each point they score. Over the long run, both subjects will do best if they cooperate every time. Yet in each round, there is a great temptation to betray the other because no one knows what the other will do. The best overall strategy for this variation was found to be *tit for tat*, doing unto your opponent as he or she has just done unto you. It is a simple strategy, but very effective. The partner can easily recognize it and respond. It is retaliatory enough not to be easily exploited, but forgiving enough to allow a pattern of mutual cooperation to develop.

Which statement is BEST supported by the above passage?
   A. The best strategy for playing *prisoner's dilemma* is to cooperate and remain silent.
   B. If you double-cross your partner, and he or she does not double-cross you, your partner will receive a sentence of eight years.
   C. When playing *prisoner's dilemma*, it is best to double-cross your partner.
   D. If you double-cross your partner, and he or she double-crosses you, you will receive an eight-year sentence.

9. After many years of experience as the vice president and general manager of a large company, I feel that I know what I'm looking for in a good manager. First, the manager has to be comfortable with himself or herself, and not be arrogant or defensive. Secondly, he or she has to have a genuine interest in people. There are some managers who love ideas—and that's fine—but to be a manager, you must love people, and you must make a hobby of understanding them, believing in them and trusting them. Third, I look for a willingness and a facility to manage conflict. Gandhi defined conflict as a way of getting at the truth. Each person brings his or her own grain of truth and the conflict washes away the illusion and fantasy. Finally, a manager has to have a vision, and the ability and charisma to articulate it. A manager should be seen as a little bit crazy. Some eccentricity is an asset. People don't want to follow vanilla leaders. They want to follow chocolate-fudge-ripple leaders.

Which statement is BEST supported by the above passage?
   A. It is very important that a good manager spend time studying people.
   B. It is critical for good managers to love ideas.
   C. Managers should try to minimize or avoid conflict.
   D. Managers should be familiar with people's reactions to different flavors of ice cream.

10. Most societies maintain a certain set of values and assumptions that make their members feel either good or bad about themselves, and either better or worse than other people. In most developed countries, these values are based on the assumption that we are all free to be what we want to be, and that differences in income, work, and education are a result of our own efforts. This may make us believe that people with more income work that is more skilled, more education, and more power are somehow *better* people. We may view their achievements as proof that they have more intelligence, more motivation, and more initiative than those with lower status. The myth tells us that power, income, and education are freely and equally available to all, and that our

failure to achieve them is due to our own personal inadequacy. This simply is not the case.

The possessions we own may also seem to point to our real worth as individuals. The more we own, the more worthy of respect we may feel we are. Or, the acquisition of possessions may be a way of trying to fulfill ourselves, to make up for the loss of community and/or purpose. It is a futile pursuit because lost community and purpose can never be compensated for by better cars or fancier houses. And too often, when these things fail to satisfy, we believe it is only because we don't have enough money to buy better quality items, or more items. We feel bad that we haven't been successful enough to get all that we think we need. No matter how much we do have, goods never really satisfy for long. There is always something else to acquire, and true satisfaction eludes many, many of us.
Which statement is BEST supported by the above passage?
  A. The author would agree with the theory of *survival of the fittest*.
  B. The possessions an individual owns are not a proper measure of his or her real worth.
  C. Many countries make a sincere attempt to ensure equal access to quality education for their citizens.
  D. The effect a society's value system has on the lives of its members is greatly exaggerated.

11. *De nihilo nihil* is Latin for *nothing comes from nothing*. In the first century, the Roman poet Persius advised that if anything is to be produced of value, effort must be expended. He also said, *In nihilum nil posse revorti*—anything once produced cannot become nothing again. It is thought that Persius was parodying Lucretius, who expounded the 500-year-old physical theories of Epicurus. *De nihilo nihil* can also be used as a cynical comment, to negatively comment on something that is of poor quality produced by a person of little talent. The implication here is: *What can you expect from such a source?*
Which statement is BEST supported by the above passage?
  A. *In nihilum nil posse revorti* can be interpreted as meaning, *If anything is to be produced of value, then effort must be expended.*
  B. *De nihilo nihil* can be understood in two different ways,
  C. Lucretius was a great physicist.
  D. Persius felt that Epicurus put in little effort while developing his theories.

11.____

12. A Cornell University study has found that less than one percent of the billion pounds of pesticides used in this country annually strike their intended targets. The study found that the pesticides, which are somewhat haphazardly applied to 370 million acres, or about sixteen percent of the nation's total land area, end up polluting the environment and contaminating almost all 200,000 species of plants and animals, including humans. While the effect of indirect contamination on human cancer rates was not estimated, the study found that approximately 45,000 human pesticide poisonings occur annually, including about 3,000 cases admitted to hospitals and approximately 200 fatalities.

12.____

Which statement is BEST supported by the above passage?
A. It is likely that indirect pesticide contamination affects human health.
B. Pesticides are applied to over one-quarter of the total United States land area.
C. If pesticides were applied more carefully, fewer pesticide-resistant strains of pests would develop.
D. Human cancer rates in this country would drop considerably if pesticide use was cut in half.

13. The new conservative philosophy presents a unified, coherent approach to the world. It offers to explain much of our experience since the turbulent 1960s, and it shows what we've learned since about the dangers of indulgence and permissiveness. But it also warns that the world has become more ruthless, and that as individuals and as a nation, we must struggle for survival. It is necessary to impose responsibility and discipline in order to defeat those forces that threaten us. This lesson is dramatically clear, and can be applied to a wide range of issues.
Which statement is BEST supported by the above passage?
A. The 1970s were a time of permissiveness and indulgence.
B. The new conservative philosophy may help in imposing discipline and a sense of responsibility in order to meet the difficult challenges facing this country.
C. The world faced greater challenges during the second world war than it faces at the present time.
D. More people identify themselves today as conservative in their political philosophy.

14. One of the most puzzling questions in management in recent years has been how usually honest, compassionate, intelligent managers can sometimes act in ways that are dishonest, uncaring, and unethical. How could top-level managers at the Manville Corporation, for example, suppress evidence for decades that proved beyond all doubt that asbestos inhalation was killing their own employees? What drove the managers of a Midwest bank to continue to act in a way that threatened to bankrupt the institution, ruin its reputation, and cost thousands of employees and investors their jobs and their savings? It's been estimated that about two out of three of America's five hundred largest corporations have been involved in some form of illegal behavior. There are, of course, some common rationalizations used to justify unethical conduct: believing that the activity is in the organization's or the individual's best interest, believing that the activity is not *really* immoral or illegal, believing that no one will ever know, or believing that the organization will sanction the behavior because it helps the organization. Ambition can distort one's sense of *duty*.
Which statement is BEST supported by the above passage?
A. Top-level managers of corporations are currently involved in a plan to increase ethical behavior among their employees.
B. There are many good reasons why a manager may act unethically.
C. Some managers allow their ambitions to override their sense of ethics,
D. In order to successfully compete, some organizations may have to indulge in unethical or illegal behavior from time to time.

15. Some managers and supervisors believe that they are leaders because they occupy positions of responsibility and authority. But leadership is more than holding a position. It is often defined in management literature as *the ability to influence the opinions, attitudes and behaviors of others.* Obviously, there are some managers that would not qualify as leaders, and some leaders that are not *technically* managers. Research has found that many people overrate their own leadership abilities. In one recent study, seventy percent of those surveyed rated themselves in the top quartile in leadership abilities, and only two percent felt they were below average as leaders.
Which statement is BEST supported by the above passage?
   A. In a recent study, the majority of people surveyed rated themselves in the top twenty-five percent in leadership abilities.
   B. Ninety-eight percent of the people surveyed in a recent study had average or above-average leadership skills.
   C. In order to be a leader, one should hold a management position.
   D. Leadership is best defined as the ability to be liked by those one must lead.

15.____

KEY (CORRECT ANSWERS)

1.	D	6.	B	11.	B
2.	C	7.	C	12.	A
3.	B	8.	D	13.	B
4.	C	9.	A	14.	C
5.	D	10.	B	15.	A

READING COMPREHENSION
UNDERSTANDING AND INTERPRETING WRITTEN MATERIAL
EXAMINATION SECTION
TEST 1

DIRECTIONS: Each question or incomplete statement is followed by several suggested answers or completions. Select the one that *BEST* answers the question or completes the statement. *PRINT THE LETTER OF THE CORRECT ANSWER IN THE SPACE AT THE RIGHT.*

PASSAGE

It is a common belief that a thing is desirable because it is scarce and thereby has ostentation value. The notion that such a standard of value is an inescapable condition of settled social existence rests on one of two implicit assumptions. The first is that the attempt to educate the human race so that the desire to display one's possessions is not a significant feature of man's social behavior, is an infringement against personal freedom. The greatest obstacle to lucid discourse in these matters is the psychological anti-vaccinationist who uses the word freedom to signify the natural right of men and women to be unhappy and unhealthy through scientific ignorance instead of being healthy and happy through the knowledge which science confers. Haunted by a perpetual fear of the dark, the last lesson which man learns in the difficult process of growing up is "ye shall know the truth, and the truth shall make you free." The professional economist who is too sophisticated to retreat Into the obscurities of this curious conception of liberty may prefer to adopt the second assumption, that the truth does not and cannot make us free because the need for ostentation is a universal species characteristic, and all attempts to eradicate the unconscionable nuisance and discord which arise from overdeveloped craving for personal distinction artificially fostered by advertisement propaganda and so-called good breeding are therefore destined to failure. It may be earnestly, hoped that those who entertain this view have divine guidance. No rational basis for it will be found in textbooks of economics. Whatever can be said with any plausibility in the existing state of knowledge rests on the laboratory materials supplied by anthropology and social history.

1. According to the writer, the second assumption

    A. Is fostered by propaganda and so-called good breeding
    B. is basically opposite to the view of the psychological anti-vaccinationist
    C. is not so curious a conception of liberty as Is the first assumption
    D. is unsubstantiated
    E. is a religious explanation of an economic phenomenon

2. The author's purpose in writing this paragraph is MOST probably to

    A. denounce the psychological anti-vaccinationists
    B. demonstrate that the question under discussion is an economic rather than a psychological problem
    C. prove the maxim "ye shall know the truth, and the truth shall make you free"
    D. prove that ostentation is not an inescapable pheonomenon of settled social existence
    E. prove the inability of economics to account for ostentation

1.____

2.____

3. The writer implies that

   A. neither the psychological anti-vaccinationist nor the professional economist recognizes the undesirability of ostentation
   B. our cultural standards are at fault in enhancing ostentation value
   C. scarcity as a criterion of value Is an inexplicable concept
   D. his main objection Is to the inescapable standard of values
   E. the results of studies of ostentation in anthropology and social history are Irrational

4. The writer believes that both assumptions

   A. are invalid because they ignore the lesson "ye shall know the truth, and the truth shall make you free"
   B. are fallacious because they agree that a thing is desirable because it is scarce
   C. arise from overdeveloped craving for personal distinction
   D. are implicit in the conception of ostentation value
   E. dispute the efficacy of education in eliminating ostentation

5. In his reference to divine guidance, the writer is

   A. being ironic
   B. implying that only divine guidance can solve the problem
   C. showing how the professional economist is opposing divine laws
   D. referring to opposition which exists between religion and science
   E. indicating that the problem is not a matter for divine guidance

6. The writer believes that personal freedom is

   A. less important than is scientific knowledge
   B. a requisite for the attainment of truth
   C. attained by eradicating false beliefs
   D. no concern of the professional economist
   E. an unsophisticated concept

7. We may infer that this writer does NOT believe that

   A. education can solve the problem
   B. people have any "natural rights"
   C. science can solve the problem
   D. the psychological anti-vaccinationist is more than a lipservant of the cause of freedom
   E. people can be happy under the present value system

8. The writer would consider as MOST comparable to the effect of a vaccination on the body, the effect of

   A. fear upon personality
   B. science upon the supposed need for ostentation
   C. truth upon the mind
   D. knowledge upon ignorance
   E. knowledge upon happiness

KEY (CORRECT ANSWERS)

1. D 5. A
2. D 6. C
3. B 7. E
4. D 8. C

TEST 2

DIRECTIONS: Each question or incomplete statement is followed by several suggested answers or completions. Select the one that *BEST* answers the question or completes the statement. *PRINT THE LETTER OF THE CORRECT ANSWER IN THE SPACE AT THE RIGHT.*

PASSAGE

In any country the wages commanded by laborers who have comparable skills but who work in various industries are determined by the productivity of the least productive unit of labor, i.e., that unit of labor which works in the industry which has the greatest economic disadvantage. We will represent the various opportunities of employment in a country like the United States by symbols: A, standing for a group of industries in which we have exceptional economic advantages over foreign countries; B, for a group in which our advantages are less; C, one in which they are still less; D, the group of industries in which they are least of all.

When our population is so small that all our labor can be engaged in the group represented by A, productivity of labor (and therefore wages) will be at their maximum. When our population increases so that some of the labor will have to be set to work in group B, the wages of all labor must decline to the level of the productivity in that group. But no employer, without government aid, will yet be able to afford to hire labor to exploit the opportunities represented by C and D, unless there is a further increase in population.

But suppose that the political party in power holds the belief that we should produce everything that we consume, that the opportunities represented by C and D should be exploited. The commodities that the industries composing C and D will produce have been hitherto obtained from abroad in exchange for commodities produced by A and B. The government now renders this difficult by placing high duties upon the former class of commodities. This means that workers in A and B must pay higher prices for what they buy, but do not receive higher prices for what they sell.

After the duty has gone into effect and the prices of commodities that can be produced by C and D have risen sufficiently, enterprisers will be able to hire labor at the wages prevailing in A and B, and establish industries in C and D. So far as the remaining laborers in A and B buy the products of C and D, the difference between the price which they pay for those products and the price that they would pay if they were permitted to import those products duty-free is a tax paid not to the government, but to the producers in C and D, to enable the latter to remain in business. It is an uncompensated deduction from the natural earnings of the laborers in A and B. Nor are the workers in C and D paid as much, estimated in purchasing power, as they would have received if they had been allowed to remain in A and B under the earlier conditions.

1. When C and D are established, workers in these industries 1.___
    A. receive higher wages than do the workers in A and B
    B. receive lower wages than do the workers in A and B
    C. must be paid by government funds collected from the duties on imports
    D. are not affected so adversely by the levying of duties as are workers in A and B
    E. receive wages equal to those workers in A and B

2. We cannot exploit C and D unless

   A. the productivity of labor in all industries is increased
   B. the prices of commodities produced by A and B are raised
   C. we export large quantities of commodities produced by A and B
   D. the producers in C and D are compensated for the disadvantages under which they operate
   E. we allow duties to be paid to the producers in C and D rather than to the government

3. "No employer; without government aid, will yet be able to afford to hire labor to exploit the opportunities represented by C and D" because

   A. productivity of labor is not at the maximum
   B. we cannot produce everything we consume
   C. the population has increased
   D. enterprisers would have to pay wages equivalent to those obtained by workers in A and B, while producing under greater economic disadvantages
   E. productivity would drop correspondingly with the wages of labor

4. The government, when it places high duties on imported commodities of classes C and D,

   A. raises the price of commodities produced by A and B
   B. is, in effect, taxing the workers in A and B
   C. raises the wages of workers in C and D at the expense of the workers in A and B
   D. does not affect the productivity of the workers in A and B, although the wages of these workers are reduced
   E. is adopting a policy made necessary by the stability of the population

5. The author's MAIN point is that

   A. it is impossible to attain national self-sufficiency
   B. the varying productivity of the various industries leads to the inequalities in wages of workers in these industries
   C. a policy that draws labor from the fields of greater natural productiveness to fields of lower natural productiveness tends to reduce purchasing power
   D. wages ought to be independent of international trade
   E. the government ought to subsidize C and D.

6. The author's arguments in this passage could BEST be used to

   A. refute the belief that it is theoretically possible for us to produce everything that we consume
   B. disprove the theory that national self-sufficiency can be obtained by means of protective tariffs
   C. advocate the levying of duties on imported goods
   D. advocate equal wages for workers who have comparable skills but who work in various industries
   E. advocate free trade

3 (#2)

7. When could C and D, as here defined, be exploited without the assistance of an artificially boosted price and without resultant lowering of wage levels?   7.___

    A. When a duty is placed on competing products from other countries
    B. When the products of C and D are exchanged in trade for other commodities
    C. When the country becomes economically self-sufficient
    D. When there is a favorable balance of trade
    E. At no time

8. In the last sentence in the selection, the statement is made: "Nor are the workers in C and D paid as much, estimated in purchasing power, as they would have received if they had been allowed to remain in A and B under the earlier conditions." This is because   8.___

    A. they must pay higher prices for commodities produced by C and D
    B. C and D cannot pay so high wages as can A and B
    C. products of C and D do not command sufficiently high prices
    D. there has not been an increase in population
    E. wages in all groups have declined

KEY (CORRECT ANSWERS)

1.	E	5.	C
2.	D	6.	E
3.	D	7.	B
4.	B	8.	E

TEST 3

DIRECTIONS: Each question or incomplete statement is followed by several suggested answers or completions. Select the one that *BEST* answers the question or completes the statement. *PRINT THE LETTER OF THE CORRECT ANSWER IN THE SPACE AT THE RIGHT.*

PASSAGE

In the Federal Convention of 1787, the members were fairly well agreed as to the desirability of some check on state laws; but there was sharp difference of opinion whether this check should be political in character as in the form of a congressional veto, or whether the principle of judicial review should be adopted.

Madison was one of the most persistent advocates of the congressional veto and in his discussion of the subject he referred several times to the former imperial prerogative of disallowing provincial statutes. In March, 1787, he wrote to Jefferson, urging the necessity of a federal negative upon state laws. He referred to previous colonial experience in the suggestion that there should be "some emanation" of the federal prerogative "within the several states, so far as to enable them to give a temporary sanction to laws of immediate necessity." This had been provided for in the imperial system through the action of the royal governor in giving immediate effect to statutes, which nevertheless remained subject to royal disallowance. In a letter to Randolph a few weeks later, Madison referred more explicitly to the British practice, urging that the national government be given "a negative, in all cases whatsoever, on the Legislative acts of the States, as the King of Great Britain heretofore had." Jefferson did not agree with Madison; on practical grounds rather than as a matter of principle, he expressed his preference for some form of judicial control.

On July 17, Madison came forward with a speech in support of the congressional veto, again supporting his contention by reference to the royal disallowance of colonial laws: "Its utility is sufficiently displayed in the British System. Nothing could maintain the harmony and subordination of the various parts of the empire, but the prerogative by which the Crown stifles in the birth every Act of every part tending to discord or encroachment. It is true the prerogative is sometimes misapplied thro' ignorance or a partiality to one particular part of the empire: but we have not the same reason to fear such misapplications in our System." This is almost precisely Jefferson's theory of the legitimate function of an imperial veto.

This whole issue shows that the leaders who wrestled with confederation problems during and after the war understood, in some measure at least, the attitude of British administrators when confronted with the stubborn localism of a provincial assembly.

1. Madison was advocating

   A. royal disallowance of state legislation
   B. a political check on state laws
   C. the supremacy of the states over the federal government
   D. the maintenance of a royal governor to give immediate effect to statutes
   E. discord and encroachment among the states

1.____

2. From this passage there is no indication
   A. of what the British System entailed
   B. of Jefferson's stand on the question of a check on state laws
   C. that the royal negative had been misapplied in the past
   D. that Jefferson understood the attitude of British administrators
   E. of what judicial review would entail

3. According to this passage, Madison believed that the federal government
   A. ought to legislate for the states
   B. should recognize the sovereignty of the several states
   C. ought to exercise judicial control over state legislation
   D. should assume the king's veto power
   E. was equivalent to a provincial assembly

4. Madison's conception of a congressional veto
   A. was opposed to Jefferson's conception of a congressional veto
   B. developed from fear that the imperial negative might be misused
   C. was that the federal prerogative should be exercised in disallowing state laws
   D. was that its primary function was to give temporary sanction to laws of immediate necessity
   E. was that its primary function was to prevent such injustices as "taxation without representation"

5. Madison believed that
   A. the congressional veto would not be abused
   B. the royal prerogative ought to have some form of check to correct misapplications
   C. the review of state legislation by the federal government ought to remain subject to a higher veto
   D. the imperial veto had not been misused
   E. utility rather than freedom is the criterion for governmental institutions

6. Jefferson believed that
   A. the congressional veto would interfere with states' rights
   B. Madison's proposal smacked of imperialism
   C. the veto of state legislation was outside the limits of the federal prerogative
   D. the British System would be harmful if applied in the United States
   E. an imperial veto should include the disallowance of all legislation leading to discord

7. Madison's MAIN principle was that
   A. the national interest is more important than the interests of any one state
   B. the national government should have compulsive power over the states
   C. the king can do no wrong
   D. the United States should follow the English pattern of government
   E. the veto power of the royal governor should be included in the federal prerogative

8. Madison thought of the states as 8._____

   A. emanations of the federal government
   B. comparable to provinces of a colonial empire
   C. incapable of creating sound legislation
   D. having no rights specifically delegated to them
   E. incapable of applying judicial review of their legislation

9. Which of the following is the BEST argument which could be made against Madison's proposition? 9._____

   A. The United States has no king.
   B. The federal government is an entity outside the jurisdiction of the states.
   C. Each state has local problems concerning which representatives from other states are not equipped to pass judgment.
   D. The federal prerogative had been misused in the past.
   E. It provides no means of dealing with stubborn localism.

KEY (CORRECT ANSWERS)

1.	B	5.	A
2.	E	6.	D
3.	D	7.	B
4.	C	8.	B
		9.	C

TEST 4

DIRECTIONS: Each question or incomplete statement is followed by several suggested answers or completions. Select the one that *BEST* answers the question or completes the statement. *PRINT THE LETTER OF THE CORRECT ANSWER IN THE SPACE AT THE RIGHT.*

PASSAGE

The nucleus of its population is the local businessmen, whose interests constitute the municipal policy and control its municipal administration. These local businessmen are such as the local bankers, merchants of many kinds and degrees, real estate promoters, local lawyers, local clergymen...The businessmen, who take up the local traffic in merchandising, litigation, church enterprise and the like, commonly begin with some share in the real estate speculation. This affords a common bond and a common ground of pecuniary interest, which commonly masquerades under the name of local patriotism, public spirit, civic pride, and the like. This pretense of public spirit is so consistently maintained that most of these men come presently to believe in their own professions on that head. Pecuniary interest in local land values involves an interest in the continued growth of the town. Hence any creditable misrepresentation of the town's volume of business traffic, population, tributary farming community, or natural resources, is rated as serviceable to the common good. And any member of this business-like community will be rated as a meritorious citizen in proportion as he is serviceable to this joint pecuniary interest of these "influential citizens."

1. The tone of the paragraph is

   A. bitter
   C. complaining
   E. informative
   B. didactic
   D. satirical

2. The foundation for the "influential citizens" interest in their community is

   A. their control of the municipal administration
   B. their interests in trade and merchandising
   C. their natural feeling of civic pride
   D. a pretense of public spirit
   E. ownership of land for speculation

3. The "influential citizens" type of civic pride may be compared with the patriotism of believers in

   A. a balance of power in international diplomacy
   B. racial superiority
   C. laissez faire
   D. a high tariff
   E. dollar diplomacy

4. The IMPORTANT men in the town

   A. are consciously insincere in their local patriotism
   B. are drawn together for political reasons
   C. do not scruple to give their community a false boost
   D. regard strict economy as a necessary virtue
   E. are extremely jealous of their prestige

5. The writer considers that the influential men of the town

    A. are entirely hypocritical in their conception of their motives
    B. are blinded to facts by their patriotic spirit
    C. have deceived themselves into thinking they are altruistic
    D. look upon the welfare of their community as of paramount importance
    E. form a closed corporation devoted to the interests of the town

6. PROBABLY the author's own view of patriotism is that it

    A. should be a disinterested passion untinged by commercial motives
    B. is found only among the poorer classes
    C. is usually found in urban society
    D. grows out of a combination of the motives of selfinterest and altruism
    E. consists in the main of a feeling of local pride

KEY (CORRECT ANSWERS)

1. B   4. C
2. E   5. C
3. E   6. A

TEST 5

DIRECTIONS: Each question or incomplete statement is followed by several suggested answers or completions. Select the one that *BEST* answers the question or completes the statement. *PRINT THE LETTER OF THE CORRECT ANSWER IN THE SPACE AT THE RIGHT.*

PASSAGE

Negative thinking and lack of confidence in oneself or in the pupils are probably the greatest hindrances to inspirational teaching. Confronted with a new idea, one teacher will exclaim: "Oh, my children couldn't do that! They're too young." Another will mutter, "If I tried that stunt, the whole class would be in an uproar." Such are the self-justifications for mediocrity.

Here and there it is good to see a teacher take a bold step away from the humdrum approach. For example, Natalie Robinson Cole was given a class of fourth-year pupils who could hardly speak English. Yet in her book, THE ARTS IN THE CLASSROOM, she describes how she tried clay work, creative writing, interpretive dancing and many other exciting activities with them. Did her control of the class suffer? Were the results poor? Was morale adversely affected? The answer is *NO* on all three counts.

But someone may point out that what Mrs. Cole could do on the fourth-grade could not be done in the primary grades. Wrong again! The young child is more malleable than his older brother. Furthermore, his radiant heritage of originality has not been enveloped in clouds of self-consciousness. Given the proper encouragement, he will paint an interesting design on the easel, contribute a sparkling expression to the "class poem" as it takes shape on the blackboard, make a puppet speak his innermost thoughts, and react with sensitivity in scores of other ways.

All teachers on all grade levels need to think positively and act confidently. Of course, any departure from the commonplace must be buttressed by careful preparation, firm handling of the situation, and consistent attention to routines. Since these assets are within the reach of all teachers there should be no excuse for not putting some imagination into their work.

1. The central idea of the above passage is BEST conveyed by the

   A. first sentence in the first paragraph
   B. last sentence in the first paragraph
   C. first sentence in the second paragraph
   D. last sentence in the passage
   E. third sentence in the third paragraph

2. If the concepts of this passage were to be expanded into a book, the one of the following titles which would be MOST suitable is

   A. THE ARTS IN THE CLASSROOM
   B. THE POWER OF POSITIVE THINKING
   C. THE HIDDEN PERSUADERS
   D. KIDS SAY THE DARNDEST THINGS
   E. ARMS AND THE MAN

3. Of the following reasons for uninspired teaching, the one which is NOT given explicitly in the passage is 3.____

   A. negative thinking
   B. teachers' underestimation of pupils' ability or stability
   C. teachers' failure to broaden themselves culturally
   D. teachers' lack of self-assurance
   E. teachers' rationalizations

4. From reading the passage one can gather that Natalie R. Cole 4.____

   A. teaches in New York City
   B. has been married
   C. is an expert in art
   D. teaches in the primary grades
   E. is a specialist in child psychology

5. An activity for children in the primary grades which is NOT mentioned in the passage is 5.____

   A. creative expression
   B. art work
   C. puppetry
   D. constructing with blocks
   E. work on the blackboard

6. A basic asset of the inspirational teacher NOT mentioned in the passage is 6.____

   A. a pleasant, outgoing personality
   B. a firm hand
   C. a thorough, careful plan
   D. consistent attention to routines
   E. acting confidently

KEY (CORRECT ANSWERS)

1.	A	4.	B
2.	B	5.	D
3.	C	6.	A

TEST 6

DIRECTIONS: Each question or incomplete statement is followed by several suggested answers or completions. Select the one that BEST answers the question or completes the statement. PRINT THE LETTER OF THE CORRECT ANSWER IN THE SPACE AT THE RIGHT.

PASSAGE

Of all the areas of learning the most important is the development of attitudes. Emotional reactions as well as logical thought processes affect the behavior of most people. "The burnt child fears the fire" is one instance; another is the rise of despots like Hitler. Both these examples also point up the fact that attitudes stem from experience. In the one case the experience was direct and impressive; in the other it was indirect and cumulative. The Nazis were indoctrinated largely by the speeches they heard and the books they read.

The classroom teacher in the elementary school is in a strategic position to influence attitudes. This is true partly because children acquire attitudes from these adults whose word they respect. Another reason it is true is that pupils often delve somewhat deeply into a subject in school that has only been touched upon at home or has possibly never occurred to them before. To a child who had previously acquired little knowledge of Mexico, his teacher's method of handling such a unit would greatly affect his attitude toward Mexicans.

The media through which the teacher can develop wholesome attitudes are innumerable. Social studies (with special reference to races, creeds and nationalities), science, matters of health and safety, the very atmosphere of the classroom... these are a few of the fertile fields for the inculcation of proper emotional reactions.

However, when children come to school with undesirable attitudes, it is unwise for the teacher to attempt to change their feelings by cajoling or scolding them. She can achieve the proper effect by helping them obtain constructive experiences. To illustrate, firstgrade pupils afraid of policemen will probably alter their attitudes after a classroom chat with the neighborhood officer in which he explains how he protects them. In the same way, a class of older children can develop attitudes through discussion, research, outside reading and all-day trips.

Finally, a teacher must constantly evaluate her own attitude because her influence can be deleterious if she has personal prejudices. This is especially true in respect to controversial issues and questions on which children should be encouraged to reach their own decisions as a result of objective analysis of all the facts.

1. The central idea conveyed in the above passage is that

   A. attitudes affect our actions
   B. teachers play a significant role in developing or changing pupils' attitudes
   C. by their attitudes, teachers inadvertently affect pupils' attitudes
   D. attitudes can be changed by some classroom experiences
   E. attitudes are affected by experience

1.___

2. The author implies that

   A. children's attitudes often come from those of other children
   B. in some aspects of social studies a greater variety of methods can be used in the upper grades than in the lower grades
   C. the teacher should guide all discussions by revealing her own attitude
   D. people usually act on the basis of reasoning rather than on emotion
   E. parents' and teachers' attitudes are more often in harmony than in conflict

3. A statement NOT made or implied in the passage is that

   A. attitudes cannot easily be changed by rewards and lectures
   B. a child can develop in the classroom an attitude about the importance of brushing his teeth
   C. attitudes can be based on the learning of falsehoods
   D. the attitudes of children are influenced by all the adults in their environment
   E. the children should accept the teacher's judgment in controversial matters

4. The passage SPECIFICALLY states that

   A. teachers should always conceal their own attitudes
   B. whatever attitudes a child learns in school have already been introduced at home
   C. direct experiences are more valuable than indirect ones
   D. teachers can sometimes have an unwholesome influence on children
   E. it is unwise for the teacher to attempt to change children's attitudes

5. The first and fourth paragraphs have all the following points in common EXCEPT

   A. how reading affects attitudes
   B. the importance of experience in building attitudes
   C. how attitudes can be changed in the classroom
   D. how fear sometimes governs attitudes
   E. how differences in approach change attitudes

KEY (CORRECT ANSWERS)

1. B
2. B
3. D
4. D
5. C

TEST 7

DIRECTIONS: Each question or incomplete statement is followed by several suggested answers or completions. Select the one that BEST answers the question or completes the statement. PRINT THE LETTER OF THE CORRECT ANSWER IN THE SPACE AT THE RIGHT.

PASSAGE

The word geology refers to the study of the composition, structure, and history of the earth. The term is derived from the Latin, geologia. coined by Bishop Richard de Bury in 1473 to distinguish lawyers who study "earthy things" from theologians. It was first consistently used in its present sense in the latter part of the 17th century. The great mass of detail that constitutes geology is classified under a number of subdivisions which, in turn, depend upon the fundamental sciences, physics, chemistry and biology.

The principal subdivisions of geology are: mineralogy, petrology, structural geology, physiography (geomorphology), usually grouped under physical or dynamical geology; and paleontology, stratigraphy and paleogeography, grouped under historical geology. The term economic geology usually refers to the study of valuable mineral "ore" deposits, including coal and oil. The economic aspects of geology are, however, much more embracive, including many subjects associated with civil engineering, economic geography, and conservation. Some of the more important of these subjects are: meteorology, hydrology, agriculture, and seismology. Subjects which are also distinctly allied to geology are geophysics, geochemistry, and cosmogony.

1. The statement that geology treats of the history of the earth and its life, especially as recorded in the rocks, is

    A. contrary to the paragraph
    B. made in the paragraph
    C. neither made nor implied in the paragraph
    D. not made, but implied in the paragraph
    E. unclear from the passage

1.___

2. The statement that the principal branches or phases of geology are dynamical geology and historical geology are

    A. contrary to the paragraph
    B. made in the paragraph
    C. neither made nor implied in the paragraph
    D. not made, but implied in the paragraph
    E. unclear from the passage

2.___

3. The statement that mining geology is a subdivision of geophysics is

    A. contrary to the paragraph
    B. made in the paragraph
    C. neither made nor implied in the paragraph
    D. not made, but implied in the paragraph
    E. unclear from the passage

3.___

4. The statement that the study of both the exterior of the earth and its inner constitution constitutes the fundamental subject matter of geology is   4.____

    A. contrary to the paragraph
    B. made in the paragraph
    C. neither made nor implied in the paragraph
    D. not made, but implied in the paragraph
    E. unclear from the passage

5. The statement that geology utilizes the principles of astronomy, zoology, and botany is   5.____

    A. contrary to the paragraph
    B. made in the paragraph
    C. neither made nor implied in the paragraph
    D. not made, but implied in the paragraph
    E. unclear from the passage

6. The statement that geology is synonymous with the study of the attributes of rocks, rock formation, or rock attributes is   6.____

    A. contrary to the paragraph
    B. made in the paragraph
    C. neither made nor implied in the paragraph
    D. not made, but implied in the paragraph
    E. unclear from the passage

KEY (CORRECT ANSWERS)

1.	D	4.	D
2.	B	5.	D
3.	C	6.	A

TEST 8

DIRECTIONS: Each question or incomplete statement is followed by several suggested answers or completions. Select the one that *BEST* answers the question or completes the statement. *PRINT THE LETTER OF THE CORRECT ANSWER IN THE SPACE AT THE RIGHT.*

PASSAGE

1 Schiller was the first to ring a change on this state of things
2 by addressing himself courageously to the entire population of his
3 country in all its social strata at one time. He was the great popularizer of our
4 theatre, and remained for almost a century the guiding
5 spirit of the German drama of which Schiller's matchless tragedies
6 are still by many people regarded as the surpassing manifestoes.
7 Schiller's position, while it demonstrates a whole people's gratitude
8 to those who respond to its desires, does not however furnish a
9 weapon of self-defense to the "popularizers" of drama, or rather its
10 diluters. Schiller's case rather proves that the power of popular
11 influence wrought upon a poet may be vastly inferior to the strength
12 that radiates from his own personality. Indeed, whereas the secret
13 of ephemeral power is only too often found in paltriness or mediocrity,
14 an influence of enduring force such as Schiller exerts on the Germans
15 can only emanate from a strong and self-assertive character. No poet
16 lives beyond his day who does not exceed the average in mental stature
17 or who, through a selfish sense of fear of the general, allows
18 himself to be ground down to the conventional size and shape.
19 Schiller, no less than Ibsen, forced his moral demands tyrannically
20 upon his contemporaries. And in the long run your moral despot, pro-
21 vided he be high-minded, vigorous, and able, has a better chance of
22 fame than the pliant time-server. However, there is a great difference
23 between the two cases. For quite apart from the striking dissimilarities
24 between the poets themselves, the public, through the
25 gradual growth of social organization, has become greatly altered.

1. Schiller's lasting popularity may be attributed to

    A. his meeting the desires of a whole people, not just a segment of the people
    B. his abiding by his inmost convictions
    C. his mediocrity and paltriness
    D. his courageous facing up to the problems of his day
    E. his ability to popularize the unknown

2. In the first line, "on this state of things" refers to

    A. romantic drama
    B. the French play of contrived construction
    C. drama directed to the rich and well-born
    D. the popularizers of the theatre of today
    E. the ruling class

3. In the second sentence from the last, "the two cases" refer to

    A. pliant time-server and moral despot
    B. the one who exceeds the average In mental stature and the one who allows himself to be ground down to conventional size
    C. the popularizer and the poet of enduring fame
    D. Ibsen and Schiller
    E. the man of character and the man of wealth

3.____

4. We may assume that the author

    A. is no believer in the democratic processes
    B. has no high opinions of the "compact majority"
    C. regards popularity with the people as a measure of enduring success
    D. is opposed to the aristocracy
    E. has no fixed opinions

4.____

5. A word used in an ambiguous sense (having two or more possible meanings) in this passage is

    A. "poet" (lines 11, 15, 24)
    B. "power" (lines 10, 13)
    C. "people" (lines 6, 7)
    D. "popularizer" (lines 3, 9)
    E. "moral" (lines 19, 20)

5.____

KEY (CORRECT ANSWERS)

1. B
2. C
3. D
4. B
5. D

TEST 9

DIRECTIONS: Each question or incomplete statement is followed by several suggested answers or completions. Select the one that BEST answers the question or completes the statement. PRINT THE LETTER OF THE CORRECT ANSWER IN THE SPACE AT THE RIGHT.

PASSAGE

In one sense, of course, this is not a new insight: all our great social and philosophical thinkers have been keenly aware of the fact of individual differences. It has remained, however, for psychologists to give the insight scientific precision.

What all this adds up to is more than just a working body of information about this and that skill. It adds up to a basic recognition of one important factor in the maturing of the individual. If each individual has a certain uniqueness of power, his maturing will best be accomplished along the line of that power. To try to develop him along lines that go in directions contrary to that of his major strength is to condition him to defeat. Thus, the non-mechanical person who is arbitrarily thrust into a mechanical occupation cannot help but do his work poorly and reluctantly, with some deep part of himself in conscious or unconscious rebellion.

He may blame himself for the low level of his accomplishment or for his persistent discontent; but not all his self-berating, nor even all his efforts to become more competent by further training, can make up for the original aptitude-lack. Unless he discovers his aptitude-lack, he may be doomed to a lifetime of self-blame, with a consequent loss of self-confidence and a halting of his psychological growth.

Or he may take refuge in self-pity – finding reason to believe that his failure is due to one or another bad break, to the jealousy of a superior, to lack of sympathy and help at home, to an initial bad start, to a lack of appreciation of what he does. If he thus goes the way of self-pity, he is doomed to a lifetime of self-commiseration that makes sound growth impossible.

The characteristic of the mature person is that he affirms life. To affirm life he must be involved, heart and soul, in the process of living. Neither the person who feels himself a failure nor the person who consciously or unconsciously resents what life has done to him can feel his heart and soul engaged in the process of living. That experience is reserved for the person whose full powers are enlisted. This, then, is what this fourth insight signifies: to mature, the individual must know what his powers are and must make them competent for life.

1. It is the author's view that

   A. "all men are created equal"
   B. "each man in his life plays many parts"
   C. "all comes to him who waits"
   D. "no kernel of nourishing corn can come to one but through his toil bestowed on that plot of ground given to him to till...."
   E. "that is what it is not to be alive. To move about in a cloud of ignorance... to live with envy... in quiet despair... to feel oneself sunk into a common grey mass..."

2. Ignorance of this fourth insight

   A. may very likely cause one to take refuge in self pity or conscious or unconscious rebellion
   B. constitutes a failure to understand that each individual is different and must cultivate his special powers in socially rewarding ways
   C. is a major deterrent to a growth to maturity
   D. means unawareness of the fact that each must use all his energy and powers to the best of his ability to make him competent for life
   E. may becloud the use of scientific precision

3. Two possible maladjustments of a man thrust into a position he is unfitted for may be summed up in the phrase,

   A. conscious and unconscious rebellion
   B. guilt-feelings and scapegoating
   C. halting of psychological growth and blaming the "breaks"
   D. "Peccavi—I have sinned" and "all the world is made except thee and me and I am not so sure of thee"
   E. light and darkness

4. We will expect a person placed in a job he is unequal to, to

   A. strike out for himself as an extrepreneur
   B. display quick angers and fixed prejudices
   C. show a great love of life outside of his work
   D. engage in labor union activities
   E. join political and social movements

KEY (CORRECT ANSWERS)

1. D 3. B
2. B 4. B

TEST 10

DIRECTIONS: Each question or incomplete statement is followed by several suggested answers or completions. Select the one that *BEST* answers the question or completes the statement. *PRINT THE LETTER OF THE CORRECT ANSWER IN THE SPACE AT THE RIGHT.*

PASSAGE

1 "For the ease and pleasure of treading the old road, accepting
2 the fashions, the education, the religion of society, he takes the
3 cross of making his own, and, of course, the self-accusation, the
4 faint heart, the frequent uncertainty and loss of time, which are the
5 nettles and tangling vines in the way of the self-relying and self-
6 directed; and the state of virtual hositility in which he seems to
7 stand to society, and especially to educated society. For all this
8 loss and scorn, what offset? He is to find consolation in exercising
9 the highest functions of human nature. He is one who raises himself
10 from private consideration and breathes and lives on public and
11 illustrious thoughts. He is the world's eye. He is the world's
12 heart. He is to resist the vulgar prosperity that retrogrades ever
13 to barbarism, by preserving and communicating heroic sentiments,
14 noble biographies, melodious verse, and the conclusions of history.
15 Whatsoever oracles the human heart, in all emergencies, in all solemn
16 hours, has uttered as its commentary on the world of actions – these
17 he shall receive and impart. And whatsoever new verdict Reason from
18 her inviolable seat pronounces on the passing men and events of
19 today – this he shall hear and promulgate.
20   "These being his functions, it becomes him to feel all confidence
21 in himself, and to defer never to the popular cry. He and he only
22 knows the world. The world of any moment is the merest appearance.
23 Some great decorum, some fetish of a government, some ephemeral
24 trade, or war, or man, is cried up by half mankind and cried down by
25 the other half, as if all depended on this particular up or down.
26 The odds are that the whole question is not worth the poorest thought
27 which the scholar has lost in listening to the controversy. Let him
28 not quit his belief that a popgun is a popgun, though the ancient and
29 honorable of the earth affirm it to be the crack of doom. In silence,
30 in steadiness, in severe abstraction, let him hold by himself; add
31 observation to observation, patient of neglect, patient of reproach,
32 and bide his own time – happy enough if he can satisfy himself alone
33 that this day he has seen something truly. Success treads on every
34 right step. For the instinct is sure, that prompts him to tell his
35 brother what he thinks. He then learns that in going down into the
36 secrets of his own mind he has descended into the secrets of all
37 minds. He learns that he who has mastered any law in his private
38 thoughts, is master to the extent of all translated. The poet, in
39 utter solitude remembering his spontaneous thoughts and recording
40 them, is found to have recorded that which men in crowded cities
41 find true for them also. The orator distrusts at first the fitness

42 of his frank confessions, his want of knowledge of the persons he
43 addresses, until he finds that he is the complement of his hearers—
44 that they drink his words because he fulfills for them their own
45 nature; the deeper he delves into his privatest, secretest presentiment,
46 to his wonder he finds this is the most acceptable, most public, and
47 universally true. The people delight in it; the better part of every
48 man feels. This is my music; this is myself."

1. It is a frequent criticism of the scholar that he lives by himself, in an "ivory tower," remote from the problems and business of the world. Which of these below constitutes the BEST refutation by the writer of the passage to the criticism here noted?

    A. The world's concern being ephemeral, the scholar does well to renounce them and the world.
    B. The scholar lives in the past to interpret the present.
    C. The scholar at his truest is the spokesman of the people.
    D. The scholar is not concerned with the world's doing because he is not selfish and therefore not engrossed in matters of importance to himself and neighbors.
    E. The scholar's academic researches of today are the businessman's practical products of tomorrow.

1.____

2. The scholar's road is rough, according to the passage. Which of these is his GREATEST difficulty?

    A. He must renounce religion.
    B. He must pioneer new approaches.
    C. He must express scorn for, and hostility to, society.
    D. He is uncertain of his course.
    E. There is a pleasure in the main-traveled roads in education, religion, and all social fashions.

2.____

3. When the writer speaks of the "world's eye" and the "world's heart" he means

    A. the same thing
    B. culture and conscience
    C. culture and wisdom
    D. a scanning of all the world's geography and a deep sympathy for every living thing
    E. mind and love

3.____

4. By the phrase, "nettles and tangling vines," the author PROBABLY refers to

    A. "self-accusation" and "loss of time"
    B. "faint heart" and "self accusation"
    C. "the slings and arrows of outrageous fortune"
    D. a general term for the difficulties of a scholar's life
    E. "self-accusation" and "uncertainty"

4.____

5. The various ideas in the passage are BEST summarized in which of these groups?

   1. (a) truth versus society
      (b) the scholar and books
      (c) the world and the scholar
   2. (a) the ease of living traditionally
      (b) the glory of a scholar's life
      (c) true knowledge versus trivia
   3. (a) the hardships of the scholar
      (b) the scholar's function
      (c) the scholar's justifications for disregarding the world's business

   A. 1 and 3 together
   B. 3 only
   C. 1 and 2 together
   D. 1 only
   E. 1, 2, and 3 together

6. "seems to stand" (lines 6 and 7) means

   A. is
   B. gives the false impression of being
   C. ends probably in becoming
   D. is seen to be
   E. the quicksands of time

7. "public and illustrious thoughts" (lines 10 and 11) means

   A. what the people think
   B. thoughts for the good of mankind
   C. thoughts in the open
   D. thoughts transmitted by the people
   E. the conclusions of history

KEY (CORRECT ANSWERS)

1. C   5. B
2. B   6. B
3. C   7. B
4. E

READING COMPREHENSION
UNDERSTANDING AND INTERPRETING
WRITTEN MATERIAL

EXAMINATION SECTION

TEST 1

DIRECTIONS: Each question or incomplete statement is followed by several suggested answers or completions. Select the one that BEST answers the question or completes the statement. *PRINT THE LETTER OF THE CORRECT ANSWER IN THE SPACE AT THE RIGHT.*

In its current application to art, the term *"primitive"* is as vague and unspecific as the term "heathen" is in its application to religion. A heathen sect is simply one which is not affiliated with one or another of three or four organized systems of theology. Similarly, a primitive art is one which flourishes outside the small number of cultures which we have chosen to designate as civilizations. Such arts differ vastly and it is correspondingly difficult to generalize about them. Any statements which will hold true for such diverse aesthetic experiences as the pictographs of the Australians, the woven designs of the Peruvians, and the abstract sculptures of the African tribes must be of the broadest and simplest sort. Moreover, the problem is complicated by the meaning attached to the term "primitive" in its other uses. It stands for something simple, undeveloped, and, by implication, ancestral to more evolved forms. Its application to arts and cultures other than our own is an unfortunate heritage from the nineteenth-century scientists who laid the foundations of anthropology. Elated by the newly enunciated doctrines of evolution, these students saw all cultures as stages in a single line of development and assigned them to places in this series on the simple basis of the degree to which they differed from European culture, which was blandly assumed to be the final and perfect flower of the evolutionary process. This idea has long since been abandoned by anthropologists, but before its demise it diffused to other social sciences and became a part of the general body of popular misinformation. It still tinges a great deal of the thought and writing about the arts of non-European peoples and has been responsible for many misunderstandings.

1. The MAIN purpose of the passage is to 1.____
   A. explain the various definitions of the term "primitive"
   B. show that the term "primitive" can be applied validly to art
   C. compare the use of the term "primitive" to the use of the term "heathen"
   D. deprecate the use of the term "primitive" as applied to art
   E. show that "primitive" arts vary greatly among themselves

2. The nineteenth-century scientists believed that the theory of evolution 2.____
   A. could be applied to the development of culture
   B. was demonstrated in all social sciences
   C. was substantiated by the diversity of "primitive" art
   D. could be applied only to European culture
   E. disproved the idea that some arts are more "primitive" than others

3. With which of the following would the author agree?
   A. The term "primitive" is used only by the misinformed.
   B. "Primitive" arts may be as highly developed as "civilized" arts.
   C. The arts of a culture often indicated how advanced that culture was.
   D. Australian, Peruvian, and African tribal arts are much like the ancestral forms from which European art evolved.
   E. A simple culture is likely to have a simple art.

4. According to the author, many misunderstandings have been caused by the belief that
   A. most cultures are fundamentally different
   B. inferior works of art in any culture are "primitive" art
   C. "primitive" arts are diverse
   D. non-European arts are diverse
   E. European civilization is the final product of the evolutionary process

KEY (CORRECT ANSWERS)

1. D
2. A
3. B
4. E

TEST 2

DIRECTIONS: Each question or incomplete statement is followed by several suggested answers or completions. Select the one that BEST answers the question or completes the statement. *PRINT THE LETTER OF THE CORRECT ANSWER IN THE SPACE AT THE RIGHT.*

One of the ways the intellectual *avant-garde* affects the technical intelligentsia is through the medium of art, and art is, if only implicitly, a critique of experience. The turning upon itself of modern culture in the forms of the new visual art, the utilization of the detritus of daily experience to mock that experience, constitutes a mode of social criticism. Pop art, it is true, does not go beyond the surface of the visual and tactile experience of an industrial (and a commercialized) culture. Dwelling on the surface, it allows its consumers to mock the elements of their daily life, without abandoning it. Indeed, the consumption of art in the organized market for leisure serves at times to encapsulate the social criticism of the *avant-garde*. However, the recent engagement of writers, artists, and theater people in contemporary issues suggests that this sort of containment may have begun to reach its limits.

In an atmosphere in which the intellectually dominant group insists on the contradictions inherent in daily experience, the technical intelligentsia will find it difficult to remain unconscious of those contradictions. The technical intelligentsia have until now avoided contradictions by accepting large rewards for their expertise. As expertise becomes increasingly difficult to distinguish from ordinary service on the one hand, and merges on the other with the change of the social environment, the technical intelligentsia's psychic security may be jeopardized. Rendering of labor services casts it back into spiritual proletarianization; a challenge to the social control exercised by elites, who use the technical intelligentsia's labor power, pushes it forward to social criticism and revolutionary politics. That these are matters, for the moment, of primarily spiritual import does not diminish their ultimate political significance. A psychological precondition for radical action is usually far more important than an "objectively" revolutionary situation—whatever that may be.

The chances for a radicalization of the technical intelligentsia, thus extending the student revolt cannot be even approximated. I believe I have shown there is a chance.

1. It may be *inferred* that the technical intelligentsia are
    I. The executives and employers in society
    II. Critics of *avant-garde* art
    III. Highly skilled technical workers
    The CORRECT answer is:
    A. I only
    B. I and III
    C. I, II, and III
    D. III only
    E. I and II

2. The engagement of the intellectual *avant-garde* in contemporary issues
    A. indicates that people tire of questioning the contradictions inherent in day-to-day living
    B. indicates that the technical intelligentsia are close to the point where they will rebel against the *avant-garde*
    C. could cause a challenge to the social control of the elites
    D. could cause the public to become more leisure-oriented
    E. could cause an increase in the consumption of art in the organized market for leisure services

3. The *possible* effect of the intellectual *avant-garde* on the technical intelligentsia is that
   A. the intellectual *avant-garde* makes the technical intelligentsia conscious of society's contradictions
   B. rapid curtailment of large rewards for expertise will result
   C. it may cause a strong likelihood of a radicalization of the technical intelligentsia
   D. the *avant-garde* will replace the employment of the technical intelligentsia in contemporary issues
   E. the rendering of labor services will be eliminated

4. If it is assumed that the technical intelligentsia becomes fully aware of the contradictions of modern life, it is the author's position that
   A. revolution will result
   B. the technical intelligentsia may refuse to perform manual labor
   C. the technical intelligentsia will be pushed forward to social criticism and revolutionary politics
   D. the technical intelligentsia will experience some psychic dislocation
   E. ordinary service will replace technical expertise

5. According to the author,
   A. the state of mind of a particular group may have more influence on its action than the effect of environmental factors
   B. the influence of art will often cause social upheaval
   C. matters of primarily spiritual import necessarily lack political significance
   D. the detritus of day-to-day living should be mocked by the intellectual *avant-garde*
   E. the technical intelligentsia can only protect their psychic security by self-expression through art

6. With which of the following would the author agree?
   I. As contradictions are less contained, the psychic security of all members of the working class would be jeopardized.
   II. The expertise of the technical intelligentsia evolved from the ownership and management of property.
   III. The technical intelligentsia is not accustomed to rendering labor services.
   The CORRECT answer is:
   A. I only   B. III only   C. I and III
   D. II only   E. None of the above

7. The MAIN purpose of the passage is to
   A. discuss the influence of the *avant-garde* art form on the expertise of the technical intelligentsia
   B. discuss the effect of the intellectual *avant-garde* on the working classes
   C. discuss the social significance of the technical intelligentsia
   D. discuss the possible effects of the de-encapsulation of *avant-garde* social criticism
   E. point out that before a change psychological preconditions are first established

KEY (CORRECT ANSWERS)

1. D
2. C
3. A
4. D
5. A
6. B
7. D

———

TEST 3

DIRECTIONS: Each question or incomplete statement is followed by several suggested answers or completions. Select the one that BEST answers the question or completes the statement. *PRINT THE LETTER OF THE CORRECT ANSWER IN THE SPACE AT THE RIGHT.*

Turbulent flow over a boundary is a complex phenomenon for which there is no really complete theory even in simple laboratory cases. Nevertheless, a great deal of experimental data has been collected on flows over solid surfaces, both in the laboratory and in nature, so that, from an engineering point of view at least, the situation is fairly well understood. The force exerted on a surface varies with the roughness of that surface and approximately with the square of the wind speed at some fixed height above it. A wind of 10 meters per second (about 20 knots, or 22 miles per hour) measured at a height of 10 meters will produce a force of some 30 tons per square kilometer on a field of mown grass or of about 70 tons per square kilometer on a ripe wheat field. On a really smooth surface, such as glass, the force is only about 10 tons per square kilometer.

When the wind blows over water, the whole thing is much more complicated. The roughness of the water is not a given characteristic of the surface but depends on the wind itself. Not only that, the elements that constitute the roughness—the waves—themselves move more or less in the direction of the wind. Recent evidence indicates that a large portion of the momentum transferred from the air into the water goes into waves rather than directly into making currents in the water; only as the waves break, or otherwise lose energy, does their momentum become available to generate currents, or produce Ekman layers. Waves carry a substantial amount of both energy and momentum (typically about as much as is carried by the wind in a layer about one wavelength thick), and so the wave-generation process is far from negligible. A violently wavy surface belies its appearance by acting, as far as the wind is concerned, as though it were very smooth. At 10 meters per second, recent measurements seem to agree, the force on the surface is quite a lot less than the force over mown grass and scarcely more than it is over glass; some observations in light winds of two or three meters per second indicate that the force on the wavy surface is less than it is on a surface as smooth as glass. In some way the motion of the waves seems to modify the airflow so that air slips over the surface even more freely than it would without the waves. This seems not to be the case at higher wind speeds, above about five meters per second, but the force remains strikingly low compared with that over other natural surfaces.

One serious deficiency is the fact that there are no direct observations at all in those important cases in which the wind speed is greater than about 12 meters per second and has had time and fetch (the distance over water) enough to raise substantial waves. The few indirect studies indicate that the apparent roughness of the surface increases somewhat under high-wind conditions, so that the force on the surface increases rather more rapidly than as the square of the wind speed.

Assuming that the force increases at least as the square of the wind speed, it is evident that high-wind conditions produce effects far more important than their frequency of occurrence would suggest. Five hours of 60-knot storm winds will put more momentum into the water than a week of 10-knot breezes. If it should be shown that, for high winds, the force on the surface increases appreciably more rapidly than as the square of the wind speed, then the transfer of momentum to the ocean will turn out to be dominated by what happens during the occasional storm rather than by the long-term average winds.

2 (#3)

1. According to the passage, several hours of storm winds (60 miles per hour) over the ocean would
   A. be similar to the force exerted by light winds for several hours over glass
   B. create an ocean roughness which reduces the force exerted by the high winds
   C. have proved to be more significant in creating ocean momentum than light winds
   D. create a force not greater than 6 times the force of a 10-mile-per-hour wind
   E. eventually affect ocean current

2. According to the passage, a rough-like ocean surface
   A. is independent of the force of the wind
   B. has the same force exerted against it by high and light winds
   C. is more likely to have been caused by a storm than by continuous light winds
   D. nearly always allows airflow to be modified so as to cause the force of the wind to be less than on glass
   E. is a condition under which the approximate square of wind speed can never be an accurate figure in measuring the wind force

3. The author indicates that, where a hurricane is followed by light winds of 10 meters per second or less,
   I. ocean current will be unaffected by the light winds
   II. ocean current will be more affected by the hurricane winds than the following light winds
   III. the force of the light winds on the ocean would be less than that exerted on a wheat field.
   The CORRECT combination is:
   A. I only   B. III only   C. II and III   D. I and III   E. II only

4. The MAIN purpose of the passage is to discuss
   A. oceanic momentum and current
   B. turbulent flow of wind over water
   C. wind blowing over water as related to causing tidal flow
   D. the significance of high wind conditions on ocean momentum
   E. experiments in wind force

5. The author would be incorrect in concluding that the transfer of momentum to the ocean is dominated by the occasional storm if
   A. air momentum went directly into making ocean current
   B. high speed winds slipped over waves as easily as low speed winds
   C. waves did not move in the direction of wind
   D. the force exerted on a wheat field was the same as on mown grass
   E. the force of wind under normal conditions increased as the square of wind speed

6. A wind of 10 meters per second measured at a height of 10 meters will produce a force close to 30 tons per square mile on which of the following? 6.____
   A. Unmown grass
   B. Mown grass
   C. Glass
   D. Water
   E. A football field

KEY (CORRECT ANSWERS)

1. E
2. C
3. C
4. B
5. B
6. A

TEST 4

DIRECTIONS: Each question or incomplete statement is followed by several suggested answers or completions. Select the one that BEST answers the question or completes the statement. *PRINT THE LETTER OF THE CORRECT ANSWER IN THE SPACE AT THE RIGHT.*

    Political scientists, as practitioners of a negligibly formalized discipline, tend to be accommodating to formulations and suggested techniques developed in related behavioral sciences. They even tend, on occasion, to speak of psychology, sociology, and anthropology as "hard core sciences." Such a characterization seems hardly justified. The disposition to uncritically adopt into political science non-indigenous sociological and general systems concepts tends, at times, to involve little more than the adoption of a specific, and sometimes barbarous, academic vocabulary which is used to redescribe reasonably well-confirmed or intuitively-grasped low-order empirical generalizations.
    At its worst, what results in such instances is a runic explanation, a redescription in a singular language style, i.e., no explanation at all. At their best, functional accounts as they are found in the contemporary literature provide explanation sketches, the type of elliptical explanation characteristic of historical and psychoanalytic accounts. For each such account there is an indeterminate number of equally plausible ones, the consequence of either the complexity of the subject matter, differing perspectives, conceptual vagueness, the variety of sometimes mutually exclusive empirical or quasi-empirical generalizations employed, or syntactical obscurity, or all of them together.
    Functional explanations have been most reliable in biology and physiology (where they originated) and in the analysis of servo mechanical and cybernetic systems (to which they have been effectively extended). In these areas we possess a well-standardized body of lawlike generalizations. Neither sociology nor political science has as yet the same resource of well-confirmed lawlike statements. Certainly sociology has few more than political science. What passes for functional explanation in sociology is all too frequently parasitic upon suggestive analogy and metaphor, trafficking on our familiarity with goal-directed systems.
    What is advanced as "theory" in sociology is frequently a non-theoretic effort at classification or "codification," the search for an analytic conceptual schema which provides a typology or a classificatory system serviceable for convenient storage and ready retrieval of independently established empirical regularities. That such a schema takes on a hierarchic and deductive character, imparting to the collection of propositions a *prima facie* theoretical appearance, may mean no more than that the terms employed in the high-order propositions are so vague that they can accommodate almost any inference and consequently can be made to any conceivable state of affairs.

1. The author *implies* that, when the political scientist is at his best, his explanations   1._____
    A. are essentially a retelling of events
    B. only then form the basis of an organized discipline
    C. plausibly account for past occurrences
    D. are prophetic of future events
    E. are confirmed principles forming part of the political scientist's theory

2. With which of the following would the author probably agree?
   I. Because of an abundance of reasonable explanations for past conduct, there is the possibility of contending schools within the field of political science developing.
   II. Political science is largely devoid of predictive power.
   III. Political science has very few verified axioms.
   The CORRECT answer is:
   A. III only   B. I and III   C. I and II   D. I, II, III   E. I only

3. The passage *implies* that many sociological theories
   A. are capable of being widely applied to various situations
   B. do not even appear to be superficially theoretical in appearance
   C. contrast with those of political science in that there are many more confirmed lawlike statements
   D. are derived from deep analysis and exhaustive research
   E. appear theoretical but are really very well proved

4. The author's thesis would be UNSUPPORTABLE if
   A. the theories of the political scientist possessed predictive power
   B. political science did not consist of redescription
   C. political scientists were not restricted to "hard core sciences"
   D. political science consisted of a body of theories capable of application to any situation
   E. none of the above

5. The author believe that sociology as a "hard core science," contains reliable and functional explanations
   A. is never more than a compilation of conceptual schema
   B. is in nearly every respect unlike political science
   C. is a discipline which allows for varied inferences to be drawn from its general propositions
   D. is a science indigenous *prima facie* theoretical appearance containing very little codification posing as theory

KEY (CORRECT ANSWERS)

1. C
2. D
3. A
4. A
5. D

TEST 5

DIRECTIONS: Each question or incomplete statement is followed by several suggested answers or completions. Select the one that BEST answers the question or completes the statement. *PRINT THE LETTER OF THE CORRECT ANSWER IN THE SPACE AT THE RIGHT.*

    James' own prefaces to his works were devoted to structural composition and analytics and his approach in those prefaces has only recently begun to be understood. One of his contemporary critics, with the purest intention to blame, wrote what might be recognized today as sophisticated praise when he spoke of the later James as "an impassioned geometer" and remarked that "what interested him was not the figures but their relations, the relations which alone make pawns significant." James's explanations of his works often are so bereft of interpretation as to make some of our own austere defenses against interpretation seem almost embarrassingly rich with psychological meanings. They offer, with a kind of brazen unselfconsciousness, an astonishingly artificial, even mechanical view of novelistic invention. It's not merely that James asserts the importance of technique; more radically, he tends to discuss character and situation almost entirely as functions of technical ingenuities. The very elements in a Jamesian story which may strike us as requiring the most explanation are presented by James either as a *solution* to a problem of compositional harmony or else as the *donnee* about which it would be irrelevant to ask any questions at all.
    James should constantly be referred to as a model of structuralist criticism. He consistently redirects our attention from the referential aspect of a work of art (its extensions into "reality") to its own structural coherence as the principal source of inspiration.
    What is most interesting about James's structurally functional view of character is that a certain devaluation of what we ordinarily think of as psychological interest is perfectly consistent with an attempt to portray reality. It's as if he came to feel that a kind of autonomous geometric pattern, in which the parts appeal for their value to nothing but their contributive place in the essentially abstract pattern, is the artist's most successful representation of life. Thus, he could perhaps even think that verisimilitude—a word he liked—has less to do with the probability of the events the novelist describes than with those processes, deeply characteristic of life, by which he creates sense and coherence from any event. The only faithful picture of life in art is not in the choice of a significant subject (James always argues against the pseudo realistic prejudice), but rather in the illustration of sense- or design-making processes. James proves the novel's connection with life by deprecating its derivation from life; and it's when he is most abstractly articulating the growth of a structure that James is almost most successfully defending the mimetic function of art (and of criticism). His deceptively banal position that only execution matters means most profoundly that verisimilitude, properly considered, is the grace and the truth of a formal unity.

1. The author suggests that James, in explanations of his own art,   1.____
    A. was not bound by formalistic strictures but concentrated on verisimilitude
    B. was deeply psychological and concentrated on personal insight
    C. felt that his art had a one-to-one connection with reality
    D. was basically mechanical and concentrated on geometrical form
    E. was event-and-character-oriented rather than technique-oriented

2. The passage indicates that James's method of approaching reality was
   A. that objective reality did not exist and was patterned only by the mind
   B. that formalism and pattern were excellent means of approaching reality
   C. not to concentrate on specific events but rather on character development
   D. that the only objective reality is the psychological processes of the mind
   E. that in reality events occur which are not structured but rather as random occurrences

3. The MAIN purpose of the paragraph is to
   A. indicate that James's own approach to his work is only now beginning to be understood
   B. deprecate the geometrical approach towards the novel
   C. question whether James's novels were related to reality
   D. indicate that James felt that society itself could be seen as a geometric structure
   E. discuss James's explanation of his works

4. In discussing his own works, James
   I. talks of people and events as a function of technique to the exclusion of all else
   II. is quick to emphasize the referential aspect of the work
   III. felt that verisimilitude could be derived not from character but rather from the ordering of event
   The CORRECT answer is:
   A. I only   B. II only   C. III only   D. I and III   E. I and II

5. The author
   A. *approves* of James's explanations of his work but *disapproves* his lack of discussion into the psychological makings of his characters
   B. *disapproves* of James's explanation of his own work and his lack of discussion into the psychological makings of his characters
   C. *approves* of James's explanations of his works in terms of structure as being well-rated to life
   D. *disapproves* of James's explanation of his works in terms of structure as lacking verisimilitude
   E. *approves* of James's explanation of his works because of the significance of the subjects chosen

6. The following is NOT true of James's explanation of his own works: He
   A. did not explain intriguing elements of a story except as part of a geometric whole
   B. felt the artist could represent life by its patterns rather than its events
   C. defended the imitative function of art by detailing the growth of a structure
   D. attempted to give the reader insight into the psychology of his characters by insuring that his explanation followed a strict geometrical pattern
   E. was able to devalue psychological interest and yet be consistent with an attempt to truly represent life

7. James believed it to be *essential* to
   A. carefully choose a subject which would lend itself to processes by which sense and cohesion is achieved
   B. defend the mimetic function of art by emphasizing verisimilitude
   C. emphasize the manner in which different facets of a story could fit together
   D. explain character in order to achieve literary harmony
   E. be artificial and unconcerned with representing life

KEY (CORRECT ANSWERS)

1.	D	5.	C
2.	B	6.	D
3.	E	7.	C
4.	C		

TEST 6

DIRECTIONS: Each question or incomplete statement is followed by several suggested answers or completions. Select the one that BEST answers the question or completes the statement. *PRINT THE LETTER OF THE CORRECT ANSWER IN THE SPACE AT THE RIGHT.*

The popular image of the city as it is now is a place of decay, crime, of fouled streets, and of people who are poor or foreign or odd. But what is the image of the city of the future? In the plans for the huge redevelopment projects to come, we are being shown a new image of the city. Gone are the dirt and the noise—and the variety and the excitement and the spirit. That it is an ideal makes it all the worse; these bleak new utopias are not bleak because they have to be; they are the concrete manifestation—and how literally—of a deep, and at times arrogant, misunderstanding of the function of the city.

Being made up of human beings, the city is, of course, a wonderfully resilient institution. Already it has reasserted itself as an industrial and business center. Not so many years ago, there was much talk of decentralizing to campus-like offices, and a wholesale exodus of business to the countryside seemed imminent. But a business pastoral is something of a contradiction in terms, and for the simple reason that the city is the center of things because it is a center, the suburban heresy never came off. Many industrial campuses have been built, but the overwhelming proportion of new office building has been taking place in the big cities. But the rebuilding of downtown is not enough; a city deserted at night by its leading citizens is only half a city. If it is to continue as the dominant cultural force in American life, the city must have a core of people to support its theatres and museums, its shops and its restaurants—even a Bohemia of sorts can be of help. For it is the people who like living in the city who make it an attraction to the visitors who don't. It is the city dwellers who support its style; without them there is nothing to come downtown to.

The cities have a magnificent opportunity. There are definite signs of a small but significant move back from suburbia. There is also evidence that many people who will be moving to suburbia would prefer to stay in the city—and it would not take too much more in amenities to make them stay. But the cities seem on the verge of muffing their opportunity and muffing it for generations to come. In a striking failure to apply marketing principles and an even more striking failure of aesthetics, the cities are freezing on a design for living ideally calculated to keep everybody in suburbia. These vast, barracks-like superblocks are not designed for people who like cities, but for people who have no other choice. A few imaginative architects and planners have shown that redeveloped blocks don't have to be repellent to make money, but so far their ideas have had little effect. The institutional approach is dominant, and, unless the assumptions embalmed in it are re-examined, the city is going to be turned into a gigantic bore.

1. The author would NOT be pleased with   1._____
   A. a crowded, varied, stimulating city
   B. the dedication of new funds to the reconstruction of the cities
   C. a more detailed understanding of the poor
   D. the elimination of assumptions which do not reflect the function of the city
   E. the adoption of a laissez-faire attitude by those in charge of redevelopment

2. "The rebuilding of downtown" (1st sentence, 3rd paragraph) refers to
   A. huge redevelopment projects to come
   B. the application of marketing and aesthetic principles to rejuvenating the city
   C. keeping the city as the center of business
   D. attracting a core of people to support the city's functions
   E. the doing away with barracks-like structures

3. According to the author the city, in order to better itself, *must*
   A. increase its downtown population
   B. attract an interested core of people to support its cultural institutions
   C. adhere to an institutional approach rather than be satisfied with the status quo
   D. erect campus-like business complexes
   E. establish an ideal for orderly future growth

4. The MAIN purpose of the passage is to
   A. show that the present people inhabiting the city do not make the city viable
   B. discuss the types of construction which should and should not take place in the city's future
   C. indicate that imaginative architects and planners have shown that redeveloped areas don't have to be ugly to make money
   D. discuss the human element in the city
   E. point out the lack of understanding by many city planners of the city's functions

5. The author's thesis would be LESS supportable if
   I. city planners presently understood that stereotyped reconstruction is doomed to ultimate failure
   II. the institutional approach referred to in the passage was based upon assumptions which took into account the function of the city
   III. there were signs that a shift back to the city from suburbia were occurring
   The CORRECT answer is:
   A. II only   B. II and III   C. I and II   D. I only   E. III only

KEY (CORRECT ANSWERS)

1. D
2. C
3. B
4. E
5. C

TEST 7

DIRECTIONS: Each question or incomplete statement is followed by several suggested answers or completions. Select the one that BEST answers the question or completes the statement. *PRINT THE LETTER OF THE CORRECT ANSWER IN THE SPACE AT THE RIGHT.*

    In estimating the child's conceptions of the world, the first question is to decide whether external reality is as external and objective for the child as it is for adults. In other words, can the child distinguish the self from the external world? So long as the child supposes that everyone necessarily thinks like himself, he will not spontaneously seek to convince others, nor to accept common truths, nor, above all, to prove or test his opinions. If his logic lacks exactitude and objectivity, it is because the social impulses of mature years are counteracted by an innate egocentricity. In studying the child's thought, not in this case in relation to others but to things, one is faced at the outset with the analogous problem of the child's capacity to dissociate thought from self in order to form an objective conception of reality.
    The child, like the uncultured adult, appears exclusively concerned with things. He is indifferent to the life of thought and the originality of individual points of view escape him. His earliest interests, his first games, his drawings are all concerned solely with the imitation of what is. In short, the child's thought has every appearance of being exclusively realistic.
    But realism is of two types, or, rather, objectivity must be distinguished from realism. Objectivity consists in so fully realizing the countless intrusions of the self in everyday thought and the countless illusions which result—illusions of sense, language, point of view, value, etc.—that the preliminary step to every judgment is the effort to exclude the intrusive self. Realism, on the contrary, consists in ignoring the existence of self and thence regarding one's own perspective as immediately objective and absolute. Realism is thus anthropocentric illusion, finality—in short, all those illusions which teem in the history of science. So long as thought has not become conscious of self, it is a prey to perpetual confusions between objective and subjective, between the real and the ostensible; it values the entire content of consciousness on a single lane in which ostensible realities and the unconscious interventions of the self are inextricably mixed. It is thus not futile, but, on the contrary, indispensable to establish clearly and before all else the boundary the child draws between the self and the external world.

1. The result of a child's not learning that others think differently than he does is that
    A. the child will not be able to function as an adult
    B. when the child has matured, he will be innately egocentric
    C. when the child has matured, his reasoning will be poor
    D. upon maturity, the child will not be able to distinguish thought from objects
    E. upon maturity, the child will not be able to make non-ego-influenced value

2. Objectivity is the ability to
    A. distinguish ego from the external world
    B. dissociate oneself from others
    C. realize that others have a different point of view
    D. dissociate ego from thought

3. When thought is not conscious of self,
   A. one is able to draw the correct conclusions from his perceptions
   B. the apparent may not be distinguishable from the actual
   C. conscious thought may not be distinguishable from the unconscious
   D. the ego may influence the actual
   E. ontogeny recapitulates phylogony

4. The MAIN purpose of the passage is to
   A. argue that the child should be made to realize that others may not think like he does
   B. estimate the child's conception of the world
   C. explain the importance of distinguishing the mind from external objects
   D. emphasize the importance of non-ego-influenced perspective
   E. show how the child establishes the boundary between himself and the external world

5. The author *implies* that, if an adult is to think logically,
   A. his reasoning, as he matures, must be tempered by other viewpoints
   B. he must be able to distinguish one physical object from another
   C. he must be exclusively concerned with thought instead of things
   D. he must be able to perceive reality without the intrusions of the self
   E. he must not value the content of consciousness on a single plain

6. Realism, according to the passage, is
   A. the realization of the countless intrusions of the self
   B. final and complete objectivity
   C. a desire to be truly objective and absolute
   D. the ability to be perceptive and discerning
   E. none of the above

7. The child who is exclusively concerned with things
   A. thinks only objectivity
   B. is concerned with imitating the things he sees
   C. must learn to distinguish between realism and anthropomorphism
   D. has no innate ability
   E. will, through interaction with others, often prove his opinions

KEY (CORRECT ANSWERS)

1. C   5. A
2. E   6. E
3. B   7. B
4. D

TEST 8

DIRECTIONS: Each question or incomplete statement is followed by several suggested answers or completions. Select the one that BEST answers the question or completes the statement. *PRINT THE LETTER OF THE CORRECT ANSWER IN THE SPACE AT THE RIGHT.*

    Democracy is not logically antipathetic to most doctrines of natural rights, fundamental or higher law, individual rights, or any similar ideals—but merely asks citizens to take note of the fact that the preservation of these rights rests with the majority, in political processes, and does not depend upon a legal or constitutional Maginot line. Democracy may, then, be supported by believers in individual rights providing they believe that rights—or any transcendental ends—are likely to be better safeguarded under such a system. Support for democracy on such instrumental ground may, of course, lead to the dilemma of loyalty to the system vs. loyalty to a natural right—but the same kind of dilemma may arise for anyone, over any prized value, and in any political system, and is insoluble in advance.
    There is unanimous agreement that—as a matter of fact and law, not of conjecture—no single right can be realized, except at the expense of other rights and claims. For that reason their absolute status, in some philosophic sense, is of little political relevance. Political policies involve much more than very generable principles or rights. The main error of the older natural rights school was not that it had an absolute right, but that it had too many absolute rights. There must be compromise, and, as any compromise destroys the claim to absoluteness, the natural outcome of experience was the repudiation of all of them. And now the name of "natural right" can only creep into sight with the reassuring placard, "changing content guaranteed." Nor is it at all easy to see how many doctrine of inalienable, natural, individual rights can be reconciled with a political doctrine of common consent—except in an anarchist society, or one of saints. Every natural right ever put forward, and the lists are elusive and capricious, is every day invaded by governments, in the public interest and with widespread public approval.
    To talk of relatively attainable justice or rights in politics is not to plump for a moral relativism—in the sense that all values are equally good. But while values may be objective, the specific value judgments and policies are inevitably relative to a context, and is only when a judgment divorces context from general principle that it looks like moral relativism. Neither, of course, does the fact of moral diversity invalidate all moral rules.
    Any political system, then, deals only with relatively attainable rights, as with relative justice and freedoms. Hence, we may differ in given instances on specific policies, despite agreement on broad basic principles such as a right or a moral "ought"; and, per contra, we may agree on specific policies while differing on fundamental principles or long-range objectives or natural rights. Politics and through politics, law and policies, give these rights—and moral principles—their substance and limits. There is no getting away from the political nature of this or any other prescriptive ideal in a free society.

1. With which of the following would the author *agree*? 1.____
   A. Natural and individual rights can exist at all only under a democracy.
   B. While natural rights may exist, they are only relatively attainable.
   C. Civil disobedience has no place in a democracy where natural rights have no philosophic relevance.
   D. Utilitarianism, which draws its criteria from the happiness and welfare of individuals, cannot logically be a goal of a democratic state.
   E. Some natural rights should never be compromised for the sake of political policy.

2. It can be *inferred* that a democratic form of government
   A. can be supported by natural rightists as the best pragmatic method of achieving their aims
   B. is a form of government wherein fundamental or higher law is irrelevant
   C. will inn time repudiate all inalienable rights
   D. forces a rejection of moral absolutism
   E. will soon exist in undeveloped areas of the world

3. The MAIN purpose of the passage is to
   A. discuss natural rights doctrine
   B. compare and contrast democracy to individual rights
   C. discuss the reconciliation of a doctrine of inalienable natural rights with a political system
   D. discuss the safeguarding of natural rights in a democratic society
   E. indicate that moral relativism is antipathetic to democracy

4. The author indicates that natural rights
   I. are sometimes difficult to define
   II. are easily definable but at times unreconcilable with a system of government predicated upon majority rule
   III. form a basis for moral relativism
   The CORRECT answer is:
   A. I only   B. II only   C. I and II   D. III only   E. II and III

5. The fact that any political system deals with relatively attainable rights
   A. shows that all values are equally good or bad
   B. is cause for divorcing political reality from moral rules
   C. shows that the list of natural rights is elusive and capricious
   D. is inconsistent with the author's thesis
   E. does not necessarily mean that natural rights do not exist

6. The passage indicates that an important conflict which can exist in a democracy is the rights of competing groups, i.e., labor versus management
   A. adherence to the democratic process versus non-democratic actions by government
   B. difficulty in choosing between two effective compromises
   C. adherence to the democratic process versus the desire to support a specific right
   D. difficulty in reconciling conflict by natural rights

KEY (CORRECT ANSWERS)

1. B   4. A
2. A   5. E
3. C   6. D

READING COMPREHENSION
UNDERSTANDING AND INTERPRETING WRITTEN MATERIAL
EXAMINATION SECTION
TEST 1

DIRECTIONS: Each question or incomplete statement is followed by several suggested answers or completions. Select the one that BEST answers the question or completes the statement. *PRINT THE LETTER OF THE CORRECT ANSWER IN THE SPACE AT THE RIGHT.*

1. Most managers make the mistake of using absolutes as signals of trouble or its absence. A quality problem emerges—that means trouble; a test is passed—we have no problems. Outside of routine organizations, there are always going to be such signals of trouble or success, but they are not very meaningful. Many times everything looks good, but the roof is about to cave in because something no one thought about and for which there is no rule, procedure, or test has been neglected. The specifics of such problems cannot be predicted, but they are often signaled in advance by changes in the organizational system: Managers spend less time on the project; minor problems proliferate; friction in the relationships between adjacent work groups or departments increases; verbal progress reports become overly glib, or overly reticent; change occur in the rate at which certain events happen, not in whether or not they happen. And they are monitored by random probes into the organization—seeing how things are going.
According to the above paragraph,
    A. managers do not spend enough time managing
    B. managers have a tendency to become overly glib when writing reports
    C. managers should be aware that problems that exist in the organization may not exhibit predictable signals of trouble
    D. managers should attempt to alleviate friction in the relationship between adjacent work groups by monitoring random probes into the organization's problems

1.____

2. *Lack of challenge* and *excessive zeal* are opposite villains. You cannot do your best on a problem unless you are motivated. Professional problem solvers learn to be motivated somewhat by money and future work that may come their way if they succeed. However, challenge must be present for at least some of the time, or the process ceases to be rewarding. On the other hand, an excessive motivation to succeed, especially to succeed quickly, can inhibit the creative process. The tortoise-and-the-hare phenomenon is often apparent in problem solving. The person who thinks up the simple elegant solution, although he or she may take longer in doing so, often wins. As in the race, the tortoise depends upon an inconsistent performance from the rabbit. And if the rabbit spends so little time on conceptualization that the rabbit merely chooses the first answers that occur, such inconsistency is almost guaranteed.

2.____

According to the above paragraph,
- A. excessive motivation to succeed can be harmful in problem solving
- B. it is best to spend a long time on solving problems
- C. motivation is the most important component in problem solving
- D. choosing the first solution that occurs is a valid method of problem solving

3. Virginia Woolf's approach to the question of women and fiction, about which she wrote extensively, polemically, and in a profoundly feminist way, was grounded in a general theory of literature. She argued that the writer was the product of her or his historical circumstances and that material conditions were of crucial importance. Secondly, she claimed that these material circumstances had a profound effect on the psychological aspects of writing, and that they could be seen to influence the nature of the creative work itself.
According to this paragraph,
- A. the material conditions and historical circumstances in which male and female writers find themselves greatly influence their work
- B. a woman must have an independent income to succeed as a writer
- C. Virginia Woolf preferred the writings of female authors, as their experiences more clearly reflected hers
- D. male writers are less likely than women writers to be influenced by material circumstances

3.____

4. A young person's first manager is likely to be the most influential person in his or her career. If this manager is unable or unwilling to develop the skills the young employee needs to perform effectively, the latter will set lower personal standards than he or she is capable of achieving, that person's self-image will be impaired, and he or she will develop negative attitudes toward the job, the employer—in all probability—his or her career. Since the chances of building a successful career with the employer will decline rapidly, he or she will leave, if that person has high aspirations, in hope of finding a better opportunity. If, on the other hand, the manager helps the employee to achieve maximum potential, he or she will build a foundation for a successful career.
According to the above paragraph,
- A. If an employee has negative attitudes towards his or her job, the manager is to blame
- B. managers of young people often have a great influence upon their careers
- C. good employees will leave a job they like if they are not given a chance to develop their skills
- D. managers should develop the full potential of their young employees

4.____

5. The reason for these difference is not that the Greeks had a superior sense of form or an inferior imagination or joy in life, but that they thought differently. Perhaps an illustration will make this clear. With the historical plays of Shakespeare in mind, let the reader contemplate the only extant Greek play on a historical subject, the Persians of Aeschylus, a play written less than ten years after the event which it deals with, and performed before the Athenian people who had played so notable a part in the struggle—incidentally,

5.____

immediately below the Acropolis which the Persians had sacked and defiled. Any Elizabethan dramatist would have given us a panorama of the whole war, its moments of despair, hope, and triumph; we should see on the stage the leaders who planned and some of the soldiers who won the victory. In the Persians we see nothing of the sort. The scene is laid in the Persian capital, one action is seen only through Persian eyes, the course of the war is simplified so much that the naval battle of Artemisium is not mentioned, nor even the heroic defense of Thermopylae, and not a single Greek is mentioned by name. The contrast could hardly be more complete.
Which sentence is BEST supported by the above paragraph?
- A. Greek plays are more interesting than Elizabethan plays.
- B. Elizabethan dramatists were more talented than Greek dramatists.
- C. If early Greek dramatists had the same historical material as Shakespeare had, the final form the Greek work would take would be very different from the Elizabethan work.
- D. Greeks were historically more inaccurate than Elizabethans.

6. The problem with present planning systems, public or private, is that accountability is weak. Private planning systems in the global corporations operate on a set of narrow incentives that frustrate sensible public policies such as full employment, environmental protection, and price stability. Public planning is Olympian and confused because there is neither a clear consensus on social values nor political priorities. To accomplish anything, explicit choices must be made, but these choices can be made effectively only with the active participation of the people most directly involved. This, not nostalgia for small-town times gone forever, is the reason that devolution of political power to local communities is a political necessity. The power to plan locally is a precondition for sensible integration of cities, regions, and countries into the world economy.
According to the author,
- A. people most directly affected by issues should participate in deciding those issues
- B. private planning systems are preferable to public planning systems
- C. there is no good system of government
- D. county governments are more effective than state governments

6.____

Questions 7-11.

DIRECTIONS: Questions 7 through 11 are to be answered SOLELY on the basis of the following passage.

The ideal relationship for the interview is one of mutual confidence. To try to pretend, to put on a front of cordiality and friendship is extremely unwise for the interviewer because he will certainly convey, by subtle means, his real feelings. It is the interviewer's responsibility to take the lead in establishing a relationship of mutual confidence.

As the interviewer, you should help the interviewee to feel at ease and ready to talk. One of the best ways to do this is to be at ease yourself. If you are, it will probably be evident; if you are not, it will almost certainly be apparent to the interviewee. Begin the interview with topics for discussion which are easy to talk about and non-menacing. This interchange can be like the conversation of people when they are waiting for a bus, at the ballgame, or discussing the weather. However, do not prolong this warm-up too long since the interviewee knows as well as you do that these are not the things he came to discuss. Delaying too long in betting down too business may suggest to him that you are reluctant to deal with the topic.

Once you get onto the main topics, do all that you can to get the interviewee to talk freely with a little prodding from you as possible. This will probably require that you give him some idea of the area and of ways of looking at it. Avoid, however, prejudicing or coloring his remarks by what you say; especially, do not in any way indicate that there are certain things you want to hear, others which you do not want to hear. It is essential that he feel free to express his own ideas unhampered by your ideas, your values and preconceptions.

Do not appear to dominate the interview, nor have even the suggestion of a patronizing attitude. Ask some questions which will enable the interviewee to take pride in his knowledge. Take the attitude that the interviewee sincerely wants the interview to achieve its purpose. This creates a warm, permissive atmosphere that is most important in all interviews.

7. Of the following, the BEST title for the above passage is
   A. PERMISSIVENESS IN INTERVIEWING
   B. INTERVIEW TECHNIQUES
   C. THE FACTOR OF PRETENSE IN THE INTERVIEW
   D. THE CORDIAL INTERVIEW

8. Which of the following recommendations on the conduct of an interview is made by the above passage?
   A. Conduct the interview as if it were an interchange between people discussing the weather.
   B. The interview should be conducted in a highly impersonal manner.
   C. Allow enough time for the interview so that the interviewee does not feel rushed.
   D. Start the interview with topics which are not threatening to the interviewee.

9. The above passage indicates that the interviewer should
   A. feel free to express his opinions
   B. patronize the interviewee and display a permissive attitude
   C. permit the interviewee to give the needed information in his own fashion
   D. provide for privacy when conducting the interview

10. The meaning of the word *unhampered*, as it is used in the last sentence of the fourth paragraph of the above passage, is MOST NEARLY
    A. unheeded   B. unobstructed   C. hindered   D. aided

11. It can be INFERRED from the above passage that
    A. interviewers, while generally mature, lack confidence
    B. certain methods in interviewing are more successful than others in obtaining information
    C. there is usually a reluctance on the part of interviewers to deal with unpleasant topics
    D. it is best for the interviewer not to waiver from the use of hard and fast rules when dealing with clients

Questions 12-19.

DIRECTIONS: Questions 12 through 19 are to be answered SOLELY on the basis of the following passage.

Disabled cars pose a great danger to bridge traffic at any time, but during rush hours it is especially important that such vehicles be promptly detected and removed. The term *disable car* is an all-inclusive label referring to cars stalled due to a flat tire, mechanical failure, an accident, or locked bumpers. Flat tires are the most common reason why cars become disabled. The presence of disabled vehicles caused 68% of all traffic accidents last year. Of these, 75% were serious enough to require hospitalization of at least one of the vehicle's occupants.

The basic problem in the removal of disabled vehicles is detection of the car. Several methods have been proposed to aid detection. At a 1980 meeting of traffic experts and engineers, the idea of sinking electronic eyes into roadways was first suggested. Such *eyes* let officers know when traffic falls below normal speed and becomes congested. The basic argument against this approach is the high cost of installation of these eyes. One Midwestern state has, since 1978, employed closed circuit television to detect the existence and locations of stalled vehicles. When stalled vehicles are seen on the closed circuit television screen, the information is immediately communicated by radio to units stationed along the roadway, thus enabling the prompt removal of these obstructions to traffic. However, many cities lack the necessary manpower and equipment to use this approach. For the past five years, several east-coast cities have used the method known as *safety chains*, consisting of mobile units which represent the links at the *safety chain*. These mobile units are stationed as posts one or two miles apart along roadways to detect disabled cars. Standard procedure is for the units in the *safety chain* to have roof blinker lights turned on to full rotation. The officer, upon spotting a disabled car, at once assumes a post that gives him the most control in directing traffic around the obstruction. Only after gaining such control does he investigate and decide what action should be taken.

12. From the above passage, The PERCENTAGE of accidents caused by disabled cars in which hospitalization was required by at least one of the occupants of a vehicle last year was
    A. 17%   B. 51%   C. 68%   D. 75%

13. According to the above passage, vehicles are MOST frequently disabled because of
    A. flat tires   B. locked bumpers
    C. brake failure   D. overheated motors

14. According to the above passage, in the electronic eye method of detection, the *eyes* are placed
    A. on lights along the roadway
    B. on patrol cars stationed along the roadway
    C. in booths spaced two miles apart
    D. into the roadway

15. According to the above passage, the factor COMMON to both the *safety chain* method and the *closed circuit television* method of detecting disabled vehicles is that both
    A. require the use of *electronic eyes*
    B. may be used where there is a shortage of officers
    C. employ units that are stationed along the highway
    D. require the use of trucks to move the heavy equipment used

15.____

16. The one of the following which is NOT discussed in the above passage as a method that may be used to detect disabled vehicles is
    A. closed circuit television   B. radar
    C. electronic eyes   D. safety chains

16.____

17. One DRAWBACK mentioned by the above passage to the use of the closed circuit television method for detection of disabled cars is that this technique
    A. cannot be used during bad weather
    B. does not provide for actual removal of the cars
    C. must be operated by a highly skilled staff of traffic engineers
    D. requires a large amount of manpower and equipment

17.____

18. The NEWEST of the methods discussed in the above passage for detection of disabled vehicles is
    A. electronic eyes   B. the mobile unit
    C. the safety chain   D. closed circuit television

18.____

19. When the *safety chain* method is being used, an officer who spots a disabled vehicle should FIRST
    A. turn off his roof blinker lights
    B. direct traffic around the disabled vehicle
    C. send a ratio message to the nearest mobile unit
    D. conduct an investigation

19.____

20. The universe is 15 billion years old, and the geological underpinnings of the earth were formed long before the first sea creature slithered out of the slime. But it is only in the last 6,000 years or so that men have descended into mines to chop and scratch at the earth's crust. Human history is, as Carl Sagan has put it, the equivalent of a few seconds in the 15 billion year life of the earth. What alarms those who keep track of the earth's crust is that since 1950 human beings have managed to consume more minerals than were mined in all previous history, a splurge of a millisecond in geologic time that cannot be long repeated without using up the finite riches of the earth.
    Of the following, the MAIN idea of this paragraph is:
    A. There is true cause for concern at the escalating consumption of the earth's minerals in recent years.
    B. Human history is the equivalent of a few seconds in the 15 billion year life of the earth
    C. The earth will soon run out of vital mineral resources

20.____

21. The authors of the Economic Report of the President are collectively aware, despite their vision of the asset-rich household, of the real economy in which millions of Americans live. There are glimpses, throughout the Report, of the underworld in which about 23 million people do not have public or private health insurance; in which the number of people receiving unemployment compensation was 41 percent of the total unemployed, in which the average dole for the compensated unemployed is about one-half of take-home pay. The authors understand, for example, that a worker may become physically disabled and that individuals generally do not like the risk of losing their ability to earn income. But such realities justify no more than the most limited interference in the (imperfect) market for disability insurance. There is only, as far as I can tell, one moment of genuine emotion in the entire Report when the authors' passions are stirred beyond market principles. They are discussing the leasing provisions of the 1981 Tax Act (conditions which so reduce tax revenues that they are apparently opposed in their present form by the Business Roundtable, the American Business Conference, and the National Association of Manufacturers).

    In the dark days before the 1981 ACT, according to the Report, (*firms with temporary tax losses* (a condition especially characteristic of new enterprises) were often unable to take advantage of investment tax incentives. The reason was that temporarily unprofitable companies had no taxable income against which to apply the investment tax deduction. It was a piteous contingency for the truly needy entrepreneur. But all was made right with the Tax Act. Social Security for the disabled incompetent corporation: the compassionate soul of Reagan's new economy.

    According to the above passage,
    - A. the National Association of Manufacturers and those companies that are temporarily unprofitable oppose the leasing provisions of the 1981 Tax Act
    - B. the authors of the Report are willing to ignore market principles in order to assist corporations unable to take advantage of tax incentives
    - C. the authors of the Report feel the National Association of Manufacturers and the Business Roundtable are wrong in opposing the leasing provisions of the 1981 Tax Act
    - D. the authors of the Report have more compassion for incompetent corporations than for disabled workers

22. Much of the lore of management in the West regards ambiguity as a symptom of a variety of organizational ills whose cure is larger doses of rationality, specificity, and decisiveness. But is ambiguity sometimes desirable? Ambiguity may be thought of as a shroud of the unknown surrounding certain events. The Japanese have a word for it, *ma*, for which there is no English translation. The word is valuable because it gives an explicit place to the unknowable aspect of things. In English, we may refer to an empty space between the chair and the table; the Japanese don't say the space is empty but *full of nothing*. However amusing the illustration, it goes to the core of the issue. Westerners speak of what is unknown primarily in reference to what is known (like the space between the chair and the table, while most eastern languages give honor to the unknown in its own right.

Of course, there are many situations that a manager finds himself in where being explicit and decisive is not only helpful but necessary. There is considerable advantage, however, in having a dual frame of reference—recognizing the value of both the clear and the ambiguous. The point to bear in mind is that in certain situations, ambiguity may serve better than absolute clarity.
Which sentence is BEST supported by the above passage?
- A. We should cultivate the art of being ambiguous.
- B. Ambiguity may sometimes be an effective managerial tool,
- C. Westerners do not have a dual frame of reference.
- D. It is important to recognize the ambiguous aspects of all situations.

23. Everyone ought to accustom himself to grasp in his thought at the same time facts that are at once so few and so simple, that he shall never believe that he has knowledge of anything which he does not mentally behold with a distinctiveness equal to that of the objects which he knows most distinctly of all. It is true that some people are born with a much greater aptitude for such discernment than others, but the mind can be made much more expert at such work by art and exercise. But there is one fact which I should here emphasize above all others; and that is everyone should firmly persuade himself that none of the sciences, however abstruse, is to be deduced from lofty and obscure matters, but that they all proceed only from what is easy and more readily understood.
According to the author,
- A. people should concentrate primarily on simple facts
- B. intellectually gifted people have a great advantage over others
- C. even difficult material and theories proceed from what is readily understood
- D. if a scientist cannot grasp a simple theory, he or she is destined to fail

23.____

24. Goethe's casual observations about language contain a profound truth. Every word in every language is a part of a system of thinking unlike any other. Speakers of different languages live in different worlds; or rather, they live in the same world but can't help looking at it in different ways. Words stand for patterns of experience. As one generation hand its language down to the next, it also hands down a fixed pattern of thinking, seeing, and feeling. When we go from one language to another, nothing stays put; different peoples carry different nerve patterns in their brains, and there's no point where they fully match.
According to the above passage,
- A. language differences and their ramifications are a major cause of tensions between nations
- B. it is not a good use of one's time to read novels that have been translated from another language because of the tremendous differences in interpretation
- C. differences in languages reflect the different experiences of people the world over
- D. language students should be especially careful to retain awareness of the subtleties of their native language

24.____

9 (#1)

Questions 25-27.

DIRECTIONS: Questions 25 through 27 are to be answered SOLELY on the basis of the following passage.

The context of all education is twofold—individual and social. Its business is to make us more and more ourselves, too cultivate in each of us our own distinctive genius, however modest it may be, while showing us how this genius may be reconciled with the needs and claims of the society of which we are a part. Thought it is not education's aim to cultivate eccentrics, that society is richest, most flexible, and most humane that best uses and most tolerates eccentricity. Conformity beyond a point breeds sterile minds and, therefore, a sterile society.

The function of secondary—and still more of higher education is to affect the environment. Teachers are not, and should not be, social reformers. But they should be the catalytic agents by means of which young minds are influenced to desire and execute reform. To aspire to better things is a logical and desirable part of mental and spiritual growth.

25. Of the following, the MOST suitable title for the above passage is   25.____
    A. EDUCATION'S FUNCTION IN CREATING INDIVIDUAL DIFFERENCES
    B. THE NEED FOR EDUCATION TO ACQUAINT US WITH OUR SOCIAL ENVIRONMENT
    C. THE RESPONSIBILITY OF EDUCATION TOWARD THE INDIVIDUAL AND SOCIETY
    D. THE ROLE OF EDUCATION IN EXPLAINIING THE NEEDS OF SOCIETY

26. On the basis of the above passage, it may be inferred that   26.____
    A. conformity is one of the forerunners of totalitarianism
    B. education should be designed to create at least a modest amount of genius in everyone
    C. tolerance of individual differences tends to give society opportunities for improvement
    D. reforms are usually initiated by people who are somewhat eccentric

27. On the basis of the above passage, it may be inferred that   27.____
    A. genius is likely to be accompanied by a desire for social reform
    B. nonconformity is an indication of the inquiring mind
    C. people who are not high school or college graduates are not able to affect the environment
    D. teachers may or may not be social reformers

Questions 28-30.

DIRECTIONS: Questions 28 through 30 are to be answered SOLELY on the basis of the following passage.

Disregard for odds and complete confidence in one's self have produced many of our great successes. But every young man who wants to go into business for himself should appraise himself as a candidate for the one percent to survive. What has he to offer that is new or better? Has he special talents, special know-how, a new invention or service, or more capital than the average competitor? Has he the most important qualification of all, a willingness to work harder than anyone else? A man who is working for himself without limitation of hours or personal sacrifice can run circles around any operation that relies on paid help. But he must forget the eight-hour day, the forty-hour week, and the annual vacation. When he stops work, his income stops unless he hires a substitute. Most small operations have their busiest day on Saturday, and the owner uses Sunday to catch up on his correspondence, bookkeeping, inventorying, and maintenance chores. The successful self-employed man invariably works harder and worries more than the man on a salary. His wife and children make corresponding sacrifices of family unity and continuity; they never know whether their man will be home or in a mood to enjoy family activities.

28. The title that BEST expresses the ideas of the above passage is 28.____
    A. OVERCOMING OBSTACLES
    B. RUNNING ONE'S OWN BUSINESS
    C. HOW TO BECOME A SUCCESS
    D. WHY SMALL BUSINESSES FAIL

29. The above passage suggests that 29.____
    A. small businesses are the ones that last
    B. salaried workers are untrustworthy
    C. a willingness to work will overcome loss of income
    D. working for one's self may lead to success

30. The author of the above passage would MOST likely believe in 30.____
    A. individual initiative   B. socialism
    C. corporations   D. government aid to small business

KEY (CORRECT ANSWERS)

1.	C	11.	B	21.	D
2.	A	12.	B	22.	B
3.	A	13.	A	23.	C
4.	B	14.	D	24.	C
5.	C	15.	C	25.	C
6.	A	16.	B	26.	D
7.	B	17.	D	27.	D
8.	D	18.	A	28.	B
9.	C	19.	B	29.	D
10.	B	20.	A	30.	A

READING COMPREHENSION
UNDERSTANDING AND INTERPRETING WRITTEN MATERIAL
EXAMINATION SECTION
TEST 1

DIRECTIONS: Each question or incomplete statement is followed by several suggested answers or completions. Select the one that BEST answers the question or completes the statement. *PRINT THE LETTER OF THE CORRECT ANSWER IN THE SPACE AT THE RIGHT.*

1. The question *Who shall now teach Hegel?* is shorthand for the question *Who is going to teach this genre—all the so-called Continental philosophers?* The obvious answer to this question is *Whoever cares to study them.* This is also the right answer, but we can only accept it whole heartedly if we clear away a set of factitious questions. On such question is: *Are these Continental philosophers really philosophers?* Analytic philosophers, because they identify philosophical ability with argumentative skill and notice that there is nothing they would consider an argument in the bulk of Heidegger or Foucault, suggest that these must be people who tried to be philosophers and failed-incompetent philosophers. This is as silly as saying that Plato was an incompetent sophist, or that a hedgehog is an incompetent fox. Hegel knew what he thought about philosophers who imitated the method and style of mathematics. He thought they were incompetent. These reciprocal charges of incompetence do nobody any good. We should just drop the questions of what philosophy really is or who really counts as a philosopher.
Which sentence is BEST supported by the above paragraph?
    A. The study of Hegel's philosophy is less popular now than in the past.
    B. Philosophers must stop questioning the competence of other philosophers.
    C. Philosophers should try to be as tolerant as Foucault and Heidegger.
    D. Analytic philosophers tend to be more argumentative than other philosophers.

1.____

2. It is an interesting question: the ease with which organizations of different kinds at different stages in their history can continue to function with ineffectual leadership at the top, or even function without a clear system of authority. Certainly, the success of some experiments in worker self-management shows that bosses are not always necessary, as some contemporary Marxists argue. Indeed, sometimes the function of those at the top is merely to symbolize organizational accountability, especially in dealing with outside authorities, but not to guide the actions of those within the organization. A vice president of a large insurance company remarked to us that *Presidents are powerless; no one needs them. They should all be sent off to do public relations for the company.* While this is clearly a self-serving statement from someone next in line to command, it does give meaning to the expression being kicked upstairs. According to the author,

2.____

A. organizations function very smoothly without bosses
B. the function of those at the top is sometimes only to symbolize organizational accountability
C. company presidents are often inept at guiding the actions of those within the organization
D. presidents of companies have less power than one might assume they have

3. The goal of a problem is a terminal expression one wishes to cause to exist in the world of the problem. There are two types of goals: specified goal expressions in proof problems and incompletely specified goal expressions in find problems. For example, consider the problem of finding the value of X, given the expression 4X+5 = 17. In this problem, one can regard the goal expression as being of the form X = _____, the goal expression. The goal expression in a find problem of this type is incompletely specified. If the goal expression were specified completely—for example, X = 3—then the problem would be a proof problem, with only the sequence of operations to be determined in order to solve the problem. Of course, if one were not guaranteed that the goal expression X = 3 was true, then the terminal goal expression should really be considered to be incompletely specified—something like the statement X = 3 (true or false).
According to the preceding paragraph,
A. the goal of the equation 4X+5 = 17 is true, not false
B. if the goal expression was specified as being equal to 3, the problem 4X+5 = 17 would be a proof problem
C. if the sequence of operations of the problem given in the paragraph is predetermined, the goal of the problem becomes one of terminal expression, or the number 17
D. X cannot be found unless X is converted into a proof problem

4. We have human psychology and animal psychology, but no plant psychology. Why? Because we believe that plants have no perceptions or intentions. Some plants exhibit *behavior* and have been credited with *habits*. If you stroke the midrib of the compound leaf of a sensitive plant, the leaflets close. The sunflower changes with the diurnal changes in the source of light. The lowest animals have not much more complicated forms of behavior. The sea anemone traps and digests the small creatures that the water brings to it; the pitcher plant does the same thing and even more, for it presents a cup of liquid that attracts insects, instead of letting the surrounding medium drift them into its trap. Here as everywhere in nature where the great, general classes of living things diverge, the lines between them are not perfectly clear. A sponge is an animal; the pitcher plant is a flowering plant, but it comes nearer to *feeding itself* than the animal. Yet the fact is that we credit all animals, and only the animals, with some degree of feeling.
Of the following, the MAIN idea expressed in the above paragraph is:
A. The classification of plants has been based on beliefs about their capacity to perceive and feel
B. Many plants are more evolved than species considered animals

C. The lines that divide the classes of living things are never clear.
D. The abilities and qualities of plants are undervalued.

5. Quantitative indexes are not necessarily adequate measures of true economic significance or influence. But even the raw quantitative data speak loudly of the importance of the new transnationalized economy. The United Nations estimated value added in this new sector of the world economy at $500 billion in 2001, mounting to one-fifth of total GNP of the non-socialist world and exceeding the GNP of any one other country except the United States. Furthermore, all observers agree that the share of this sector in the world economy is growing rapidly. At least since 1980, its annual rate of growth has been high and remarkably steady at 10 percent compared to 4 percent for noninternationalized output in the Western developed countries.
One spokesman for the new system franklin envisages that within a generation some 400 to 500 multinational corporations will own close to two-thirds of the world's fixed assets.
According to the author, all of the following are true EXCEPT
A. Quantitative indexes are not necessarily adequate measures of actual economic influence.
B. The transnational sector of the world economy is growing rapidly.
C. Since 1980, the rate of growth of transnationals has been 10% compared to 4% for internationalized output in the Western developed countries.
D. Continued growth for multinational corporations is likely.

5.____

6. A bill may be sent to the Governor when it has passed both houses. During the session, he is given ten days to act on bills that reach his desk. Bills sent to him within ten days of the end of the session must be acted on within 30 days after the last day of the session. If the Governor takes no action on a ten day bill, it automatically becomes a law. If he disapproves or vetoes a ten day bill, it can become law only if it is re-passed by two-thirds vote in each house. If he fails to act on a 30 day bill, the bill is said to have received a *pocket veto*. It is customary for the Governor to act, however, on all bills submitted to him, and give his reason in writing for approving or disapproving important legislation.
According to the above paragraph, all of the following are true EXCEPT:
A. Bills sent to the Governor in the last ten days of the session must be acted on within thirty days after the last day of the session,
B. If the Governor takes no action on a 10 day bill, it is said to have received a *pocket veto*.
C. It is customary for the Governor to act on all bills submitted to him.
D. If the Governor vetoes a ten day bill, it can become law only if passed by a two-thirds vote of the Legislature.

6.____

7. It is particularly when I see a child going through the mechanical process of manipulating numbers without any intuitive sense of what it is all about that I recall the lines of Lewis Carroll: *Reeling and Writhing, of course, to begin with…and then the different branches of Arithmetic-Ambition, Distraction, Uglification, and Derision.* Or, as Max Beberman has put it, much more gently: *Somewhat related to the notion of discovery in teaching is our insistence that*

7.____

the student become aware of a concept before a name has been assigned to the concept. I am quite aware that the issue of intuitive understanding is a very live one among teachers of mathematics, and even a casual reading of the yearbook of the National Council of Teachers of Mathematics makes it clear that they are also very mindful of the gap that exists between proclaiming the importance of such understanding and actually producing it in the classroom.
The MAIN idea expressed in the above paragraph is:
- A. Math teachers are concerned about the difficulties inherent in producing an understanding of mathematics in their students.
- B. It is important that an intuitive sense in approaching math problems be developed, rather than relying on rote, mechanical learning.
- C. Mathematics, by its very nature, encourages rote, mechanical learning.
- D. Lewis Carroll was absolutely correct in his assessment of the true nature of mathematics.

8. Heisenberg's *Principle of Uncertainty*, which states that events at the atomic level cannot be observed with certainty, can be compared to this: In the world of everyday experience, we can observe any phenomenon and measure its properties without influencing the phenomenon in question to any significant extent. To be sure, if we try to measure the temperature of a demitasse with a bathtub thermometer, the instrument will absorb so much heat from the coffee that it will change the coffee's temperature substantially. But with a small chemical thermometer, we may get a sufficiently accurate reading. We can measure the temperature of a living cell with a miniature thermometer, which has almost negligible heat capacity. But in the atomic world, we can never overlook the disturbance caused by the introduction of the measuring apparatus.
Which sentence is BEST supported by the above paragraph?
- A. There is little we do not alter by the mere act of observation.
- B. It is always a good idea to use the smallest measuring device possible.
- C. Chemical thermometers are more accurate than bathtub thermometers.
- D. It is not possible to observe events at the atomic level and be sure that

the same events would occur if we were not observing them.

9. It is a myth that American workers are pricing themselves out of the market, relative to workers in other industrialized countries of the world. The wages of American manufacturing workers increased at a slower rate in the 1990s than those of workers in other major western countries. In terms of American dollars, between 1990 and 2000, hourly compensation increased 489 percent in Japan and 464 percent in Germany, compared to 128 percent in the United States. Even though these countries experienced faster productivity growth, their unit labor costs still rose faster than in the United States, according to the Bureau of Labor Statistics. During the 1990s, unit labor costs rose 192 percent in Japan, 252 percent in Germany, and only 78 percent in the United States.
According to the above passage,
- A. unit labor costs in the 1990s were higher in Japan than they were in Germany or the United States
- B. the wages of American workers need to be increased to be consistent with other countries

C. American worker are more productive than Japanese or German workers
D. the wages of American workers in manufacturing increased at a slower rate in the 1990s than the wages of workers in Japan or Germany

10. No people have invented more ways to enjoy life than the Chinese, perhaps to balance floods, famines, warlords, and other ills of fate. The clang of gongs, clashing cymbals, and beating of drums sound through their long history. No month is without fairs and theatricals when streets are hung with fantasies of painted lanterns and crowded with *carriages that flow like water, horses like roaming dragons*. Night skies are illumined by firecrackers—a Chinese invention—bursting in the form of flowerpots, peonies, fiery devils. The ways of pleasure are myriad. Music plays in the air through bamboo whistles of different pitch tied to the wings of circling pigeons. To skim a frozen lake in an ice sleigh with a group of friends on a day when the sun is warm is rapture, like *moving in a cup of jade*. What more delightful than the ancient festival called *Half an Immortal*, when everyone from palace officials to the common man took a ride on a swing? When high in the air, one felt like an Immortal, when back to earth once again human—no more than to be for an instant a god.
   According to the above passage,
   A. if the Chinese hadn't had so many misfortunes, they wouldn't have created so many pleasurable past times
   B. the Chinese invented flowerpots
   C. every month the Chinese have fairs and theatricals
   D. pigeons are required to play the game *Half an Immortal*

10.____

11. In our century, instead, poor Diphilus is lost in the crowd of his peers. We flood one another. No one recognizes him as he loads his basket in the supermarket. What grevious fits of melancholy have I not suffered in one of our larger urban bookstores, gazing at the hundreds, thousands, tens of thousands of books on shelve and tables? And what are they to the hundreds of thousands, the millions that stand in our research libraries? More books than Noah saw raindrops. How many readers will read a given one of them—mine, yours—in their lifetimes? And how will it be in the distant future? Incomprehensible masses of books, Pelion upon Ossa, hordes of books, each piteously calling for attention, respect, love, in competition with the vast disgorgements of the past and with one another in the present. Neither is it at all helpful that books can even now be reduced to the size of a postage stamp. Avanti! Place the Bible on a pinhead! Crowding more books into small spaces does not cram more books into our heads. Here I come to the sticking point that unnerves the modern Diphilus. The number of books a person can read in a given time is, roughly speaking, a historical constant. It does not change significantly even when the number of books available for reading does. Constants are pitted against variables to confound both writer and reader.
   Of the following, the MAIN idea in this passage is:
   A. It is difficult to attain immortality because so many books are being published.
   B. Too many books are being published, so fewer people are reading them.

11.____

C. Because so many books are being published, the quality of the writing is poorer.
D. Because so many books are available, but only a fixed amount of time to read them, frustration results for both the reader and the writer.

12. Until recently, consciousness of sexual harassment has been low. But workers have become aware of it as more women have arrived at levels of authority in the workplace, feminist groups have focused attention on rape and other violence against women, and students have felt freer to report perceived abuse by professors. In the last 5 years, studies have shown that sexual misconduct at the workplace is a big problem. For example, in a recently published survey of federal employees, 42% of 694,000 women and 15% of 1,168,000 men said they had experienced some form of harassment. According to the author, 12.____
   A. the awareness of sexual harassment at the workplace is increasing
   B. the incidence of harassment is higher in universities than workplaces
   C. sexual harassment is much more commonly experienced by women than men
   D. it is rare for men to experience sexual harassment

Questions 13-17.

DIRECTIONS: Questions 13 through 17 are to be answered SOLELY on the basis of the following paragraph.

Since discounts are in common use in the commercial world and apply to purchases made by government agencies as well as business firms, it is essential that individuals in both public and private employment who prepare bills, check invoices, prepare payment vouchers, or write checks to pay bills have an understanding of the terms used. These include cash or time discount, trade discount, and discount series. A cash or time discount offers a reduction in price to the buyer for the prompt payment of the bill and is usually expressed as a percentage with a time requirement, stated in days, within which the bill must be paid in order to earn the discount. An example would be 3/10, meaning a 3% discount may be applied to the bill if the payment is forwarded to the vendor within 10 days. On an invoice, the cash discount terms are usually followed by the net terms, which is the time in days allowed for ordinary payment of the bill. Thus, 3/10, Net 30 means that full payment is expected in thirty days if the cash discount of 3% is not taken for having paid the bill within ten days. When the expression Terms Net Cash is listed on a bill, it means that no deduction for early payment is allowed. A trade discount is normally applied to list prices by a manufacturer to show the actual price to retailers so that they may know their cost and determine markups that will allow them to operate competitively and at a profit. A trade discount is applied by the seller to the list price and is independent of a cash or time discount. Discounts may also be used by manufacturers to adjust prices charged to retailers without changing list prices. This is usually done by series discounting and is expressed as a series of percentages. To compute a series discount, such as 40%, 20%, 10%, first apply the 40% discount to the list price, then apply the 20% discount to the remainder, and finally apply the 10% discount to the second remainder.

13. According to the above paragraph, trade discounts are
    A. applied by the buyer
    B. independent of cash discounts
    C. restricted to cash sales
    D. used to secure rapid payment of bills

14. According to the above paragraph, if the sales terms 5/10, Net 60 appear on a bill in the amount of $100 dated December 5 and the buyer submits his payment on December 15, his PROPER payment should be
    A. $60   B. $90   C. $95   D. $100

15. According to the above paragraph, if a manufacturer gives a trade discount of 40% for an item with a list price of $250 and the terms are Net Cash, the price a retail merchant is required to pay for this item is
    A. $250   B. $210   C. $150   D. $100

16. According to the above paragraph, a series discount of 25%, 20%, 10% applied to a list price of $200 results in an ACTUAL price to the buyer of
    A. $88   B. $90   C. $108   D. $110

17. According to the above paragraph, if a manufacturer gives a trade discount of 50% and the terms are 6/10, Net 30, the cost to a retail merchant of an item with a list price of $500 and for which he takes the time discount, is
    A. $220   B. $235   C. $240   D. $250

Questions 18-22.

DIRECTIONS: Questions 18 through 22 are to be answered SOLELY on the basis of the following paragraph.

The city may issue its own bonds or it may purchase bonds as an investment. Bonds may be issued in various denominations, and the face value of the bond is its par value. Before purchasing a bond, the investor desires to know the rate of income that the investment will yield. In computing the yield on a bond, it is assumed that the investor will keep the bond until the date of maturity, except for callable bonds which are not considered in this paragraph. To compute exact yield is a complicated mathematical problem, and scientifically prepared tables are generally used to avoid such computation. However, the approximate yield can be computed much more easily. In computing approximate yield, the accrued interest on the date of purchase should be ignored, because the buyer who pays accrued interest to the seller receives it again at the next interest date. Bonds bought at a premium (which cost more) yield a lower rate of income than the same bonds bought at par (face value), and bonds bought at a discount (which cost less) yield a higher rate of income than the same bonds bought at par.

18. An investor bought a $10,000 city bond paying 6% interest. Which of the following purchase prices would indicate that the bond was bought at a PREMIUM?
    A. $9,000   B. $9,400   C. $10,000   D. $10,600

8 (#1)

19. During the year, a particular $10,000 bond paying 74% sold at fluctuating prices.
    Which of the following prices would indicate that the bond was bought at a DISCOUNT?
    A. $9,800   B. $10,000   C. $10,200   D. $10,750

    19._____

20. A certain group of bonds was sold in denominations of $5,000, $10,000, $20,000 and $50,000.
    In the following list of four purchase prices, which one is MOST likely to represent a bond sold at par value?
    A. $10,500   B. $20,000   C. $22,000   D. $49,000

    20._____

21. When computing the approximate yield on a bond, it is DESIRABLE to
    A. assume the bond was purchased at par
    B. consult scientifically prepared tables
    C. ignore accrued interest on the date of purchase
    D. wait until the bond reaches maturity

    21._____

22. Which of the following is MOST likely to be an exception to the information provided in the above paragraph? Bonds
    A. purchased at a premium   B. sold at par
    C. sold before maturity   D. which are callable

    22._____

Questions 23-25

DIRECTIONS: Questions 23 through 25 are to be answered SOLELY on the basis of the following paragraph.

There is one bad habit of drivers that often causes chain collisions at traffic lights. It is the habit of keeping one foot poised over the accelerator pedal, ready to step on the gas the instant the light turns green. A driver who is watching the light, instead of watching the cars in front of him, may *jump the gun* and bump the car in front of him, and this car in turn may bump the next car. If a driver is resting his foot on the accelerator, his foot will be slammed down when he bumps into the car ahead. This makes the collision worse and makes it very likely that cars further ahead in the line are going to get involved in a series of violent bumps.

23. Which of the following conclusions can MOST reasonably drawn from the information given in the above paragraph?
    A. American drivers have a great many bad driving habits.
    B. Drivers should step on the gas as soon as the light turns green.
    C. A driver with poor driving habits should be arrested and fined.
    D. A driver should not rest his foot on the accelerator when the car is stopped for a traffic light.

    23._____

24. From the information given in the above paragraph, a reader should be able to tell that a chain collision may be defined as a collision
    A. caused by bad driving habits at traffic lights
    B. in which one car hits another, this second car hits a third car, and so on

    24._____

9 (#1)

    C. caused by drivers who fail to use their accelerators
    D. that takes place at an intersection where there is a traffic light

25. The above passage states that a driver who watches the light instead of paying attention to traffic may   25.____
    A. be involved in an accident   B. end up in jail
    C. lose his license   D. develop bad driving habits

KEY (CORRECT ANSWERS)

1.	B		11.	D
2.	B		12.	A
3.	B		13.	B
4.	A		14.	C
5.	C		15.	C
6.	B		16.	C
7.	B		17.	B
8.	D		18.	D
9.	D		19.	A
10.	C		20.	B

21. C
22. D
23. D
24. B
25. A

TEST 2

DIRECTIONS: Each question or incomplete statement is followed by several suggested answers or completions. Select the one that BEST answers the question or completes the statement. *PRINT THE LETTER OF THE CORRECT ANSWER IN THE SPACE AT THE RIGHT.*

Questions 1-4.

DIRECTIONS: Each of the statements in this section is followed by several labeled choices. In the space at the right, write the letter of the sentence which means MOST NEARLY what is stated or implied in the passage.

1. It may be said that the problem in adult education seems to be not the piling up of facts but practice in thinking.
   This statement means MOST NEARLY that
   A. educational methods for adults and young people should differ
   B. adults seem to think more than young people
   C. a well-educated adult is one who thinks but does not have a store of information
   D. adult education should stress ability to think

   1._____

2. Last year approximately 19,000 fatal accidents were sustained in industry. There were approximately 130 non-fatal injuries to each fatal injury.
   According to the above statement, the number of non-fatal accidents was
   A. 146,000 B. 190,000 C. 1,150,000 D. 2,500,000

   2._____

3. No employer expects his stenographer to be a walking encyclopedia, but it is not unreasonable for him to expect her to know where to look for necessary information on a variety of topics.
   The above statement means MOST NEARLY that the stenographer should
   A. be a college graduate
   B. be familiar with standard office reference books
   C. keep a scrapbook of all interesting happenings
   D. go to the library regularly

   3._____

4. For the United States, Canada has become the most important country in the world, yet there are few countries about which Americans know less. Canada is the third largest country in the world; only Russia and China are larger. The area of Canada is more than a quarter of the whole British Empire.
   According to the above statement, the
   A. British Empire is smaller than Russia or China
   B. territory of China is greater than that of Canada
   C. Americans know more about Canada than they do about China or Russia
   D. Canadian population is more than one-quarter the population of the British Empire

   4._____

Questions 5-8.

DIRECTIONS: Questions 5 through 8 are to be answered SOLELY on the basis of the following paragraph.

A few people who live in old tenements have had the bad habit of throwing garbage out of their windows, especially if there is an empty lot near their building. Sometimes the garbage is food; sometimes the garbage is half-empty soda cans. Sometimes the garbage is a little bit of both mixed together. These people just don't care about keeping the lot clean.

5. The above paragraph states that throwing garbage out of windows is a 5.____
   A. bad habit
   B. dangerous thing to do
   C. good thing to do
   D. good way to feed rats

6. According to the above paragraph, an empty lot next to an old tenement is sometimes used as a place to 6.____
   A. hold local gang meetings
   B. play ball
   C. throw garbage
   D. walk dogs

7. According to the above paragraph, which of the following throw garbage out of their windows? 7.____
   A. Nobody
   B. Everybody
   C. Most people
   D. Some people

8. According to the above paragraph, the kinds of garbage thrown out of windows are 8.____
   A. candy and cigarette butts
   B. food and half-empty soda cans
   C. fruit and vegetables
   D. rice and bread

Questions 9-12.

DIRECTIONS: Questions 9 through 12 are to be answered SOLELY on the basis of the following paragraph.

The game that is recognized all over the world as an all-American game is the game of baseball. As a matter of fact, baseball heroes like Joe DiMaggio, Willie Mays, and Babe Ruth were as famous in their day as movie stars Robert Redford, Paul Newman, and Clint Eastwood are now. All these men have had the experience of being mobbed by fans whenever they put in an appearance anywhere in the world. Such unusual popularity makes it possible for stars like these to earn at least as much money off the job as on the job. It didn't take manufacturers and advertising men long to discover that their sales of shaving lotion, for instance, increased when they got famous stars to advertise their product for them on radio and television.

9. According to the above paragraph, baseball is known everywhere as a(n) _____ game. 9.____
   A. all-American   B. fast   C. unusual   D. tough

10. According to the above paragraph, being so well known means that it is possible   10.____
    for people like Willie Mays and Babe Ruth to
    A. ask for anything and get it
    B. make as much money off the job as on it
    C. travel anywhere free of charge
    D. watch any game free of charge

11. According to the above paragraph, which of the following are known all over   11.____
    the world?
    A. Baseball heroes   B. Advertising men
    C. Manufacturers   D. Basketball heroes

12. According to the above paragraph, it is possible to sell much more shaving lotion   12.____
    on television and radio if
    A. the commercials are in color instead of black and white
    B. you can get a prize with each bottle of shaving lotion
    C. the shaving lotion makes you smell nicer than usual
    D. the shaving lotion is advertised by famous stars

Questions 13-15.

DIRECTIONS: Questions 13 through 15 are to be answered SOLELY on the basis of the
              following passage.

That music gives pleasure is axiomatic. Because this is so, the pleasures of music may seem a rather elementary subject for discussion. Yet the source of that pleasure, our musical instinct, is not at all elementary. It is, in fact, one of the prime puzzles of consciousness. Why is it that we are able to make sense out of these nerve signals so that we emerge from engulfment in the orderly presentation of sound stimuli as if we had lived through an image of life?

If music has impact for the mere listener, it follows that it will have much greater impact for those who sing it or play it themselves with proficiency. Any educated person in Elizabethan times was expected to read musical notation and take part in a madrigalsing. Passive listeners, numbered in the millions, are a comparatively recent innovation.

Everyone is aware that so-called serious music has made great strikes in general public acceptance in recent years, but the term itself still connotes something forbidding and hermetic to the mass audience. They attribute to the professional musician a kind of initiation into secrets that are forever hidden from the outsider. Nothing could be more misleading. We all listen to music, professionals, and non-professionals alike in the same sort of way, in a dumb sort of way, really, because simple or sophisticated music attracts all of us in the first instance, on the primordial level of sheer rhythmic and sonic appeal. Musicians are flattered, no doubt, by the deferential attitude of the layman in regard to what he imagines to be our secret understanding of music. But in all honesty, we musicians know that in the main we listen basically as others do, because music hits us with an immediacy that we recognize in the reactions of the most simple minded of music listeners.

13. A suitable title for the above passage would be
    A. HOW TO LISTEN TO MUSIC
    B. LEARNING MUSIC APPRECIATION
    C. THE PLEASURES OF MUSIC
    D. THE WORLD OF THE MUSICIAN

13.____

14. The author implies that the passive listener is one who
    A. cannot read or play music
    B. does not appreciate serious music
    C. does not keep time to the music by hand or toe tapping
    D. will not attend a concert if he has to pay for the privilege

14.____

15. The author of the above passage is apparently inconsistent when he discusses
    A. the distinction between the listener who pays for the privilege and the one who does not
    B. the historical development of musical forms
    C. the pleasures derived from music by the musician
    D. why it is that we listen to music

15.____

Questions 16-18.

DIRECTIONS: Questions 16 through 18 are to be answered SOLELY on the basis of the following passage.

Who are the clerisy? They are people who like to read books. The use of a word so unusual, so out of fashion, can only be excused on the ground that it has no familiar synonym. The word is little known because what it describes has disappeared, though I do not believe is gone forever. The clerisy are those who read for pleasure, but not for idleness; who read for pastime, but not to kill time; who love books, but do not live by books.

Let us consider the actual business of reading—the interpretive act of getting the words off the age and into your head in the most effective way. The most effective way is not the quickest way of reading; and for those who think that speed is the greatest good, there are plenty of manuals on how to read a book which profess to tell how to strip off the husk and guzzle the milk, like a chimp attacking a coconut. Who among today's readers would whisk through a poem, eyes aflicker, and say that he had read it? The answer to that last question must unfortunately be: far too many. For reading is not respected for the art it is.

Doubtless there are philosophical terms for the attitude of mind of which nasty reading is one manifestation, but here let us call it end-gaining, for its victims put ends before means; they value not reading, but having read. In this, the end-gainers make mischief and spoil all they do; end-gaining is one of the curses of our nervously tense, intellectually flabby civilization. In reading, as in all arts, it is the means, and not the end, which gives delight and brings the true reward. Not straining forward toward the completion, but the pleasure of every page as it comes, is the secret of reading. We must desire to read a book, rather than to have read it. This change in attitude, so simple to describe, is by no means simple to achieve,, if one has lived the life of an end-gainer.

16. A suitable title for the above passage would be
    A. READING FOR ENLIGHTENMENT
    B. THE ART OF RAPID READING
    C. THE WELL-EDUCATED READER
    D. VALUES IN READING

    16.____

17. The author does NOT believe that most people read because they
    A. are bored
    B. have nothing better to do
    C. love books
    D. wish to say that they have read certain books

    17.____

18. The change in attitude to which the author refers in the last sentence of the above passage implies a change from
    A. dawdling while reading so that the reader can read a greater number of books
    B. reading light fiction to reading serious fiction and non-fiction
    C. reading works which do not amuse the reader
    D. skimming through a book to reading it with care

    18.____

Questions 19-22.

DIRECTIONS: Questions 19 through 22 are to be answered SOLELY on the basis of the following passage.

Violence is not new to literature. The writings of Shakespeare and Cervantes are full of it. But those classic writers did not condone violence. They viewed it as a just retribution for sins against the divine order or as a sacrifice sanctioned by heroism. What is peculiar to the modern literature is violence for the sake of violence. Perhaps our reverence for life has been dulled by mass slaughter, though mass slaughter has not been exceptional in the history of mankind. What is exceptional is the boredom that now alternates with war. The basic emotion in peacetime has become a horror of emptiness: a fear of being alone, of having nothing to do, a neurosis whose symptoms are restlessness, an unmotivated and undirected rage, sinking at times into vapid listlessness. This neurotic syndrome is intensified by the prevailing sense of insecurity. The threat of atomic war has corrupted our faith in life itself.

This universal neurosis has developed with the progress of technology. It is the neurosis of men whose chief expenditure of energy is to pull a lever or push a button, of men who have ceased to make things with their hands. Such inactivity applies not only to muscles and nerves but to the creative processes that once engaged the mind. If one could contrast visually, by time-and-motion studies, the daily actions of an eighteenth-century carpenter with a twentieth-century machinist, the latter would appear as a confined, repetitive clot, the former as a free and even fantastic pattern. But the most significant contrast could not be visualized—the contrast between a mind suspended aimlessly above an autonomous movement and a mind consciously bent on the shaping of a material substance according to the persistent evidence of the senses.

19. A suitable title for the above passage would be
    A. INCREASING PRODUCTION BY MEANS OF SYSTEMATIZATION
    B. LACK OF A SENSE OF CREATIVENESS AND ITS CONSEQUENCE
    C. TECHNOLOGICAL ACHIEVEMENT IN MODERN SOCIETY
    D. WHAT CAN BE DONE ABOUT SENSELESS VIOLENCE

19.____

20. According to the author, Shakespeare treated violence as a
    A. basically sinful act not in keeping with religious thinking
    B. just punishment of transgressors against moral law
    C. means of achieving dramatic excitement
    D. solution to a problem provided no other solution was available

20.____

21. According to the author, boredom may lead to
    A. a greater interest in leisure-time activities
    B. chronic fatigue
    C. senseless anger
    D. the acceptance of a job which does not provide a sense of creativity

21.____

22. The underlined phrase refers to the
    A. hand movements made by the carpenter
    B. hand movements made by the machinist
    C. relative ignorance of the carpenter
    D. relative ignorance of the machinist

22.____

23. The concentration of women and female-headed families in the city is both cause and consequence of the city's fiscal woes. Women live in cities because it is easier and cheaper for them to do so, but because fewer women are employed, and those that are receive lower pay than men, they do not make the same contribution to the tax base that an equivalent population of men would. Concomitantly, they are more dependent on public resources, such as transportation and housing. For these reasons alone, urban finances would be improved by increasing women's employment opportunities and pay. Yet nothing in our current urban policy is specifically geared to improving women's financial resources. There are some proposed incentives to create more jobs, but not necessarily ones that would utilize the skills women currently have. The most innovative proposal was a tax credit for new hires from certain groups with particularly high unemployment rates. None of the seven targeted groups were women.
    Which sentence is BEST supported by the above paragraph?
    A. Innovative programs are rapidly improving conditions for seven targeted groups with traditionally high unemployment rates.
    B. The contribution of women to a city's tax base reflects their superior economic position.
    C. Improving the economic position of women who live in cities would help the financial conditions of the cities themselves.
    D. Most women in this country live in large cities.

23.____

24. None of this would be worth saying if Descartes had been right in positing a one-to-one correspondence between stimuli and sensations. But we know that nothing of the sort exists. The perception of a given color can be evoked by an infinite number of differently combined wavelengths. Conversely, a given stimulus can evoke a variety of sensations, the image of a duck in one recipient, the image of a rabbit in another. Nor are responses like these entirely innate. One can learn to discriminate colors or patterns which were indistinguishable prior to training. To an extent still unknown, the production of data from stimuli is a learned procedure. After the learning process, the same stimulus evokes a different datum. I conclude that, though data are the minimal elements of our individual experience, they need be shared responses to a given stimulus only within the membership of a relatively homogeneous community: educational, scientific, or linguistic.
    Which sentence is BEST supported by the above paragraph?
    A. One stimulus can give rise to a number of different sensations.
    B. There is a one-to-one correspondence between stimuli and sensations.
    C. It is not possible to produce data from stimuli by using a learned procedure.
    D. It is not necessary for a group to be relatively homogeneous in order to share responses to stimuli.

24.____

25. Workers who want to move in the direction of participative structures will need to confront the issues of power and control. The process of change needs to be mutually shared by all involved, or the outcome will not be a really participative model. The demand for a structural redistribution of power is not sufficient to address the problem of change toward a humanistic, as against a technological, workplace. If we are to change our institutional arrangements from hierarchy to participation, particularly in our workplaces, we will need to look to transformations in ourselves as well. As long as we are imbued with the legitimacy of hierarchical authority, with the sovereignty of the status quo, we will never be able to generate the new and original forms that we seek. This means if we are to be equal to the task of reorganizing our workplaces, we need to think about how we can reeducate ourselves and become aware of our assumptions about the nature of our social life together. Unless the issue is approached in terms of these complexities, I fear that all the worker participation and quality of work life efforts will fail.
    According to the above paragraph, which of the following is NOT true?
    A. Self-education concerning social roles must go hand in hand with workplace reorganization.
    B. The structural changing of the workplace, alone, will not bring about the necessary changes in the quality of work life.
    C. Individuals can easily overcome their attitudes towards hierarchical authority.
    D. Changing the quality of work life will require the participation of all involved.

25.____

KEY (CORRECT ANSWERS)

1. D
2. D
3. B
4. B
5. A

6. C
7. D
8. B
9. A
10. B

11. A
12. D
13. C
14. A
15. C

16. D
17. C
18. D
19. B
20. B

21. C
22. B
23. C
24. A
25. C

SOCIAL STUDIES READING

EXAMINATION SECTION
TEST 1

DIRECTIONS: Each question or incomplete statement is followed by several suggested answers or completions. Select the one that BEST answers the question or completes the statement. PRINT THE LETTER OF THE CORRECT ANSWER IN THE SPACE AT THE RIGHT.

Questions 1-9.

DIRECTIONS: Questions 1 through 9 are to be answered SOLELY on the basis of the following passage.

When economists make projections for the future, they often focus on the gross national product (GNP) of the United States. GNP is the total dollar value of the final goods and services produced in a single year. Economists try to project the growth or decline of GNP in some future period. One way to do this is to analyze the four groups that buy goods and services: consumers, businesses, governments, and foreign interests.

Personal consumption expenditures make up the largest of these four components because consumers buy almost two-thirds of all goods and services. In making projections, economists must consider that consumers shift their purchases depending on circumstances. For example, when their incomes rise, consumers tend to buy relatively more durable goods, like cars, rather than nondurable goods, like food eaten at home. Compared to the spending of the other sectors, the overall level of consumer spending is more stable and thus more predictable.

Business investment is the most volatile component of GNP because, although consumers cannot wait until next year to buy food, businesses can often postpone the construction of a new factory. Typically, businesses will invest if they expect the economy to perform well. Economists often find business investment the most difficult sector to project accurately.

A third component of GNP is governmental purchases. In making projections, economists look closely at those categories of goods and services that federal, state, and local governments buy. For instance, state and local governments probably spend more on education than on any other single item in their budgets. A decline in the number of school-aged children might slow the growth of expenditures for education and result in a reduced impact of state and local governmental spending on GNP.

Finally, economists study foreign purchases of American goods and services. Foreigners are especially interested in buying highly technological items and basic foodstuffs. GNP is positively affected when the United States sells more to foreigners than it buys from them.

1. If businesses expected a recession, GNP *probably* would

    A. *increase* because businesses would want to take advantage of the situation
    B. *increase* because businesses would sell more abroad
    C. *decrease* because businesses would invest less
    D. *decrease* because businesses would buy more abroad

1.____

2. Although foreigners buy many goods and services from the United States, they are especially interested in items such as

   A. luxury automobiles
   B. standardized building materials
   C. computerized office equipment
   D. handmade furniture

3. Which event would *probably* have the GREATEST effect on United States sales to foreigners?

   A. An automobile workers' strike
   B. A decline in the housing industry
   C. A drought in wheat-growing regions
   D. Floods in New England rural areas

4. Which of these occurrences is LIKELY to result in a rise in GNP?

   A. The federal government announces a tax increase.
   B. Many state governments transfer money from education to road-building funds.
   C. Foreign automakers increase imports to the U.S.
   D. Consumers begin spending the part of their income they formerly saved.

5. Economists find the business sector's behavior hard to predict MAINLY because business investment *usually*

   A. constitutes only a small part of GNP
   B. is tied to governmental spending
   C. reflects future expectations
   D. follows no discernible pattern

6. If grain harvests abroad were bountiful, American GNP would *probably*

   A. decrease because America would sell less grain to foreigners
   B. increase because the total grain supply would be larger
   C. increase because the U.S. share of world grain supplies would fall
   D. not be affected

7. A 10 percent change in domestic consumer spending would affect GNP differently from a 10 percent change in foreign spending in the United States because

   A. domestic consumer spending is a much greater proportion of GNP than foreign spending
   B. foreigners pay no taxes to the U.S. government
   C. domestic consumer spending is more volatile than foreign spending
   D. foreigners spend more on business goods than on consumer goods

8. Business people *probably* would postpone investment if they

   A. foresaw a bright economic future
   B. were unsure of the future
   C. were waiting for governmental leadership
   D. believed the interest rates would rise in the future

9. Which of these factors would reflect a slowdown in the growth of GNP? 9._____
   - I. Rising unemployment
   - II. Reduced industrial output
   - III. Increased exports to foreign countries
   - IV. Lower interest rates on consumer loans

   The CORRECT answer is:

   A. I and II
   B. II and IV
   C. II, III, and IV
   D. All of the above

Questions 10-18.

DIRECTIONS: Questions 10 through 18 are to be answered SOLELY on the basis of the following passage.

The status of women in American society is still a topic for debate, as demonstrated in the following discussion.

Speaker 1

Although women in the United States are in the majority numerically, they still constitute a minority group. A minority group is defined as one whose members, *because of their physical or cultural characteristics, are singled out from the others in the society in which they live for differential and unequal treatment*.... As long as women are the objects of discriminatory practices, they must be viewed as a minority group.

Speaker 2

Of course women are treated differently from men: they are different, and those differences entitle them to the respect and care of every American male. What greater role could a woman play than that of mother and homemaker? To enable women to perform those duties well, women should be protected by law and custom and be given the privilege of shelter from the harsher life men must live.

Speaker 3

In governmental policymaking, women are nearly invisible. In the world of work, we are confined to subordinate positions—how many women head great corporations? Even in institutions of higher education, faculties and administrators are predominantly male. How can we be full and equal members of our society as long as these inequalities are permitted to exist?

Speaker 4

The separate status of women reflects their own conception of themselves. Women wish to be considered and treated differently; they wish to identify themselves as a group apart from the males in society. Why else do women support so many women's clubs, magazines, study programs—all focusing on their problems and interests as distinguished from those of men?

Speaker 5

The statuses of blacks and women display some remarkable similarities. To be sure, blacks have faced harsher discrimination than women, but both have had to overcome social and legal barriers erected to keep them *in their place*. The major difference is that the barriers erected by whites against blacks have been more successfully attacked than those erected by males against females. In both cases, however, more than the destruction of barriers is required. The full place of women and blacks in American society has yet to be realized.

10. Speaker 3 implies that American women are presently limited in their ability to

    A. travel freely
    B. join a voluntary organization of their choosing
    C. experience equal employment opportunities
    D. run for municipal office

11. Speakers _____ and _____ seem to believe that American women do NOT suffer from negative discrimination.

    A. 2; 3   B. 2; 4   C. 3; 5   D. 4; 5

12. Unlike blacks, American women have NEVER been denied the right to

    A. vote
    B. have an equal educational opportunity
    C. have American citizenship
    D. run for political office

13. Barbara Jordan, a former congresswoman from Texas and a supporter of equal rights for both blacks and women, would *probably* disagree MOST strongly with Speaker

    A. 1   B. 2   C. 3   D. 5

14. All the speakers seem to agree that

    A. women have moved more rapidly toward equality of status than blacks
    B. a minority status for women is generally approved in American society
    C. there is little difference in the status of women and blacks in American society
    D. women do in fact occupy a separate status in American society

15. Explicit in Speaker 4's argument is the belief that

    A. women see themselves as a distinct group in American society
    B. men see women as forming a separate group in American society
    C. women's organizations and clubs generally support the transformation of women's place in American society
    D. women's conception of themselves in society is undergoing rapid change

16. Some historians claim that many southern slave owners had a paternalistic attitude toward their slaves.
    Which speaker has a similar attitude toward women?

    A. 1   B. 2   C. 3   D. 5

17. Although the Fifteenth Amendment to the Constitution was a step forward for blacks, it was NOT one for women because it

    A. denied due process of law to women
    B. failed to remove gender as a barrier to voting
    C. allowed the states to establish voting requirements
    D. extended citizenship to black men but not black women

17.____

18. Which of these inferences can be drawn from Speaker 5's argument?

    I. The position of both women and blacks in American society requires improvement.
    II. Blacks are no longer fighting to change their status in American society.
    III. Discrimination against women has been more subtle than discrimination against blacks.

The CORRECT answer is:

    A. I only
    B. II only
    C. I and III
    D. II and III

18.____

Questions 19-27.

DIRECTIONS: Questions 19 through 27 are to be answered SOLELY on the basis of the following passage.

Psychologists generally agree that personality is the result of many interacting forces, but they disagree on which force is most important, as the following discussion indicates.

Speaker 1

I believe that the unconscious plays an important role in personality. Past experiences make an indelible impression on the mind, and even those that are seemingly forgotten can influence a person's behavior. I have also identified three components of personality: the *id*, the pleasure-seeking, unconscious aspect; the *ego*, the primarily conscious, reality-oriented aspect; and the *superego*, the moral aspect or conscience. If these three aspects are in balance, a healthy personality results. But if conflicts arise between one's conscious self and one's unconscious needs or desires, unhealthy behaviors result.

Speaker 2

I agree that personality is fashioned by a balance between the conscious and the unconscious, but I see the unconscious as having two parts. The personal part contains experiences one has forgotten or repressed, and the collective unconscious contains memory patterns inherited from our ancestors. The latter is universal and very influential in determining human behavior.

Speaker 3

I emphasize an individual's uniqueness and personal growth. Personality development is a continual effort to achieve self-actualization. For this to take place, people must first satisfy their basic needs, such as those for food, love, and security. Then they are free to fulfill their need for self-esteem and to attempt to develop their full potential.

Speaker 4

My theory relies heavily on people's self-concepts, what they believe to be true about themselves. Unless people behave in ways that support their self-concepts, conflict develops between their self-concepts and reality. To resolve the conflict, people have to rationalize their behavior or change their self-concepts to agree with the facts. Once self-concept is in line with behavior, individuals are able to function as complete human beings.

Speaker 5

I believe personality is determined by heredity and environment and base my theory on the principle of *operant conditioning*. People behave as they do either because they have been encouraged to do so through rewards – a practice I endorse – or because they've been discouraged by punishment. Thus personality is always subject to change depending on one's experiences.

19. By using the term *universal,* Speaker 2 indicates that the collective unconscious is

    A. common to all people
    B. influenced by daily situations
    C. different for each individual
    D. understood by people worldwide

20. Some parents wanted their young daughter to remember to pick up her toys, so each time she did, they gave her a dime. Soon she was picking up her toys WITHOUT any reminders.
    The parents had used the behavioral concept of

    A. matching self-concept with reality
    B. extroversion
    C. self-actualization
    D. reinforcement

21. A person on a lifeboat drinks his supply of water very quickly and later becomes thirsty. He considers stealing someone else's water.
    According to Speaker 1, what would keep him from stealing?

    A. Superego
    B. Id
    C. Personal unconscious
    D. Collective unconscious

22. According to Speaker 1, the id and the ego differ because the id

    A. is the ethical arm of personality, while the ego is the logical arm
    B. defines boundaries, while the ego helps a person stay within those boundaries
    C. controls the superego, while the ego works to maintain a balance among all three components
    D. is the center of needs and urges, while the ego determines how these needs are to be satisfied

23. When people *rationalize their behavior* (Speaker 4), they attempt to

    A. forget whatever behavior has occurred
    B. justify their behavior by making up acceptable, though untrue, reasons for it

C. interpret their behavior from a negative perspective
D. imitate the behavior of someone who seems better adjusted in life

24. Which speaker would be LEAST likely to be concerned with a person's inner drives, needs, or perceptions?

    A. 1   B. 3   C. 4   D. 5

25. Which speaker would be MOST likely to explain in part a person's fear of the dark by saying it is present because long ago humans experienced dangers in the dark?

    A. 1   B. 2   C. 4   D. 5

26. A belief that a person's behavior can be brought under the control of others and made predictable is MOST strongly implied by Speaker

    A. 1   B. 2   C. 4   D. 5

27. What means might Speaker 1 have used to learn what goes on in the unconscious?
    I. Hypnosis
    II. Dream analysis
    III. Free association

    The CORRECT answer is:

    A. II only   B. I and II
    C. I and III   D. All of the above

Questions 28-42.

DIRECTIONS: Questions 28 through 42 are NOT based on a reading passage. You are to answer these questions on the basis of your previous schoolwork in the social studies.

28. The United States Constitution allows state governments to

    A. coin their own currency
    B. levy taxes on their citizens
    C. repeal federal laws
    D. charge tariffs on goods imported from other states

29. President Jefferson's action in purchasing the Louisiana Territory from France led to

    A. his defeat in the 1804 election
    B. claims that he exceeded his constitutional authority
    C. stern objections from John Adams
    D. the Senate's refusal to ratify the purchase

30. Often pigeons that are to undergo operant conditioning experiments are reduced to a percentage of their normal weight.
    This is because

    A. subsequent feedings decrease the pigeons' fear of humans
    B. hungry birds are less active and thus easier to handle
    C. behavior extinction is impossible without this procedure
    D. food can be more effectively used as a reinforcer

31. _____ were concepts stressed by Englightenment thinkers.

    A. Natural law, reason, and progress
    B. Authority, obedience, and stability
    C. War, physical courage, and self-denial
    D. Change, social turmoil, and human depravity

31._____

32. Which of the following situations is an example of horizontal mobility? A(n)

    A. assembly line worker resigns to take a similar job at another factory
    B. foreman becomes assistant manager
    C. business student accepts a well-paying position upon graduation
    D. school teacher works as a house painter during the summer

32._____

33. One way in which a progressive income tax redistributes income is by allowing

    A. companies to reinvest more of their profit
    B. low-income families to retain a larger portion of their earnings than high-income families
    C. middle-income families to increase their savings
    D. all families to obtain necessities tax free

33._____

34. The state legislatures that elected delegates to the Constitutional Convention in Philadelphia in 1787 mandated these delegates to

    A. revise the Articles of Confederation
    B. write the Declaration of Independence
    C. propose a Bill of Rights
    D. devise a national court system

34._____

35. Peter the Great helped change Russia with his

    A. support for the Roman Catholic church
    B. determination to *westernize* his country
    C. attempts to institute democratic programs
    D. establishment of a lasting peace in Europe

35._____

36. Human slavery is PRIMARILY associated with culture systems that

    A. have essentially agricultural economies
    B. have easy access to seaports
    C. are European or direct descendants of European cultures
    D. have a monotheistic belief system

36._____

37. Medieval society and culture can be described as being all of the following EXCEPT

    A. communally or cooperatively oriented
    B. highly religious
    C. hierarchically structured
    D. socially and geographically mobile

37._____

38. In a pure laissez-faire economic system, governmental regulations of business activity would

    A. apply to only monopolistic practices
    B. be enforced on the state level
    C. affect only international trade
    D. not exist

39. The Constitution grants all of the following powers to the President EXCEPT the power to

    A. recommend legislation
    B. grant pardons
    C. formally declare war
    D. recognize countries and governments

40. One outstanding characteristic of fascism is its

    A. emphasis on international cooperation to attain peace
    B. belief that all members of a society should have a voice in determining policies
    C. total subordination of the individual to the state
    D. tendency to avoid government interference in the lives and decisions of individuals

41. Which of these factors did Karl Marx believe would cause a society to evolve from capitalism to socialism?
    I. Class conflict
    II. Natural selection
    III. Cultural lag

    The CORRECT answer is:

    A. I only
    B. II only
    C. I and II
    D. All of the above

42. In nineteenth century America, the *Social Darwinist* misapplication of Charles Darwin's theory regarding the *survival of the fittest* had its STRONGEST support among

    A. farmers
    B. ethnic minorities
    C. businessmen
    D. laborers

Questions 43-50.

DIRECTIONS: Questions 43 through 50 are to be answered SOLELY on the basis of the following passage.

In the 1950's, many public leaders who debated the source of America's problems with the Soviet Union focused on the Yalta Conference, held in February 1945. It was the last wartime conference that Franklin D. Roosevelt, Joseph Stalin, and Winston Churchill attended together. The following speakers express the varying attitudes toward the decisions reached at Yalta.

Speaker 1

Roosevelt was sick and was victimized at Yalta. His health was failing, and he was outmaneuvered by Stalin. FDR made concessions in Poland and the rest of Eastern Europe that allowed a Soviet takeover after the war. This was a shameful surrender of the principles of the Atlantic Charter.

Speaker 2

Churchill was right! The United States should have gone into Europe by way of *its soft underbelly.* He urged FDR to do this as early as 1943 to prevent communist domination of Eastern Europe, but since we didn't get there first to limit the communists militarily, we could only limit them diplomatically. And look at Yalta! The only concession gained from Stalin was a promise to hold free elections in Eastern Europe.

Speaker 3

Roosevelt should never have allowed Stalin to have the Kurile Islands and the southern half of Sakhalin Island in return for vague promises to aid the U.S. in the war against Japan. We didn't need the Russians. This was just an example of Soviet imperialism.

Speaker 4

FDR was correct in his concessions. He exchanged some islands in the Pacific for Stalin's promise to help defeat Japan after Germany surrendered. He also exacted promises of democratic elections in Eastern Europe and support for Chiang Kai-shek's government in China after the war. FDR cannot be blamed because Stalin did not live up to his word.

Speaker 5

FDR. did make concessions to Stalin in Europe, in the Far East, and in the United Nations. However, he made them on the basis of projected war losses and without knowing whether the atomic bomb could bring the Pacific war to a rapid end. He believed that Soviet aid in the Pacific war could save thousands of lives. The Yalta agreements must be seen in historical perspective. In 1945, there was a need for unity among the Allies.

43. Speaker 1 argues that the Soviets were able to dominate Eastern Europe because of

    A. Soviet military superiority
    B. the devastated condition of Eastern Europe
    C. Soviet geographic proximity to the region
    D. a lack of U.S. diplomatic skills at Yalta

44. Speaker 2 argues that the CHIEF factor in determining United States policy at Yalta should have been

    A. concern for the cost of the war effort
    B. concern for closer relations with the Soviet Union after the war
    C. the anticipation of communist imperialism in the postwar period
    D. the establishment of a postwar peacekeeping organization

45. The passage indicates that, at the Yalta Conference, Stalin specifically promised to

    A. liberalize communist doctrine in the Soviet Union
    B. ease demands for reparations from Germany
    C. roll back Soviet troops to Poland
    D. enter the war against Japan

46. In return for territorial and other concessions, Stalin agreed at the Yalta Conference to

    A. evacuate Soviet troops from Eastern Europe
    B. become a member of the U.N.
    C. allow free elections in Eastern Europe
    D. reunite North and South Korea after Japan's surrender

47. Speaker 5's assessment of the significance of the atomic bomb in World War II assumes that WITHOUT its use, the

    A. war would have lasted longer
    B. U.S. would probably have lost the war
    C. U.S. and the Soviet Union would have remained friends
    D. Soviet Union would have become dominant in the Far East

48. Which speaker MOST clearly disagrees with the argument that FDR's concessions resulted in the postwar *loss* of China to the communists?

    A. 2   B. 3   C. 4   D. 5

49. Speaker 4 suggests that the basis for FDR's actions at Yalta was

    A. his belief that Stalin would honor the agreements
    B. British advice that a balance of power be created in Europe
    C. a revision of earlier military strategy
    D. an interest in Eastern European nations as potential allies

50. Which speaker argues MOST directly that the need to maintain Allied unity led Roosevelt to postpone controversial territorial and political decisions until a final victory over the Axis powers was assured?

    A. 2   B. 3   C. 4   D. 5

KEY (CORRECT ANSWERS)

1. C	11. B	21. A	31. A	41. A
2. C	12. C	22. D	32. A	42. C
3. C	13. B	23. B	33. B	43. D
4. D	14. D	24. D	34. A	44. C
5. C	15. A	25. B	35. B	45. D
6. A	16. B	26. D	36. A	46. C
7. A	17. B	27. D	37. D	47. A
8. B	18. C	28. B	38. D	48. C
9. A	19. A	29. B	39. C	49. A
10. C	20. D	30. D	40. C	50. D

EXAMINATION SECTION
TEST 1

PASSAGE

By far, the best-known industry in Steuben County is the manufacture of glass. Just after the Civil War, the Flint Glass Company moved from Brooklyn to Coming, One reason why the company chose to settle in Coming was that the railroad from Pennsylvania to Corning brought coal for fuel at a low cost. In the early days, the company made lantern chimneys, bottles, and such familiar products. Later, it began making electric light bulbs. Now it manufactures all kinds of glass products. It makes Pyrex, a kind of glass that resists heat so well that it is used for cooking and baking. The company also makes glass wool, which is used for insulation and other purposes, and glass bricks, out of which the walls of some modern buildings are built.

1. The Flint Glass Company moved to Corning because it   1.____
   A. would be exempt from local taxes
   B. had been promised free land for its buildings
   C. could obtain coal cheaply
   D. could make glass bricks there

2. Glass wool, made in Corning, is used for   2.____
   A. insulation
   B. low cost fuel
   C. manufacturing lantern chimneys
   D. making electric blankets

3. Since its early days in Corning, the number and variety of the products of the glass industry have   3.____
   A. decreased   B. remained about the same
   C. increased slightly   D. increased greatly

4. The county in which Corning is located is   4.____
   A. Chautauqua   B. Cortland   C. Seneca   D. Steuben

5. Pyrex is used for   5.____
   A. antifreeze   B. cooking utensils
   C. curtain material   D. refrigeration

KEY (CORRECT ANSWERS)

1. C
2. A
3. D
4. D
5. B

TEST 2

PASSAGE

While Admiral Dewey was waiting in Manila Bay, exciting events were happening in the Atlantic. Soon after the start of the war, a Spanish fleet under Admiral Pascual Cervera set sail from the coast of Spain. An American fleet under Admiral William T. Sampson set out to give battle to Cervera's fleet. On May 19, Cervera's fleet came to anchor in the Cuban harbor of Santiago. Sampson's fleet quickly took up its position just outside the channel in order to blockade the harbor, which was too well defended by forts for the Americans to sail in. An American army was landed on the coast a few miles south of Santiago. On July 1-2, this force captured the outer defenses of the city at San Juan Hill and began a siege of Santiago. One of the regiments of volunteers that took part in the charge at San Juan Hill had been recruited by Theodore Roosevelt, who was second in command. The victory of the American army caused the Spaniards to give up hope. The Spanish commander in Cuba ordered Admiral Cervera to put to sea and save his fleet if he could. On July 3, Cervera, with his ships under full steam, started out of Santiago Harbor.

1. The paragraph describes a campaign in the

    A. War of 1812 B. Mexican War
    C. Civil War   D. Spanish-American War

2. At the time of the Cuban campaign, a new regiment was recruited by

    A. Cervera   B. Dewey   C. Roosevelt   D. Sampson

3. The American victory at San Juan Hill caused the enemy to

    A. lose confidence   B. surrender unconditionally
    C. retreat to San Juan Hill D. enter Santiago

4. The war was fought

    A. only in the Atlantic Ocean
    B. only in the Pacific Ocean
    C. on both land and sea
    D. off the coast of Tripoli

5. Sampson's fleet tried to

    A. keep Cervera's fleet from entering the harbor
    B. blockade Santiago Harbor
    C. attack San Juan Hill
    D. prevent the United States regiment from entering the battle

---

KEY (CORRECT ANSWERS)

1. D
2. C
3. A
4. C
5. B

TEST 3

PASSAGE

In the generation after Appomattox, the pattern of our present society and economy took shape. Growth - in area, numbers, wealth, power, social complexity, and economic maturity - was the one most arresting fact. The political divisions of the republic were drawn in their final form, a dozen new states were admitted to the Union, and an American empire was established. In a space of forty years, population increased from thirty-one to seventy-six million, fifteen million immigrants - an ever-increasing proportion of them from southern and eastern Europe - poured into the Promised Land, and great cities like New York, Chicago, Pittsburgh, Cleveland, and Detroit doubled and redoubled their size. In swift succession, the Indians were harried out of their ancient haunts on the high plains and in the mountains and valleys beyond and herded into reservations, the mining and cattle kingdoms rose and fell, the West was peopled and farmed, and by the end of the century, the frontier was no more. Vast new finds of iron ore, copper, and oil created scores of great industries; small business grew into big business.

1. Which one of the following terms BEST describes the period discussed?

   A. Expansion   B. Conservation   C. Regulation   D. Isolation

2. The policy of the Federal government toward the Indians was to

   A. break up the tribal governments
   B. disenfranchise the Indians
   C. educate all Indian children in public schools
   D. remove them to reservations

3. An IMPORTANT factor in the industrial development that followed the Civil War was the

   A. diversification of agriculture
   B. development of new mineral resources
   C. rapid transformation of farmers into industrial workers
   D. development of a colonial empire

4. The last stage in the development of the West was accomplished by

   A. Indians   B. farmers   C. ranchers   D. miners

5. Which one of the following statements is made concerning the United States during the period described in the paragraph? The United States

   A. established an empire
   B. secured special interests in the oil wells and copper mines of Mexico
   C. developed a policy of dollar diplomacy
   D. advocated the open-door policy

6. Which one of the following statements concerning the frontier is made in the paragraph?

   A. After the admission of twelve states, expansion ceased.
   B. An outstanding characteristic of the frontier people was their intense nationalism.
   C. At the end of the 19th century, the frontier came to an end.
   D. The frontier was most important in shaping our present society.

KEY (CORRECT ANSWERS)

1. A
2. D
3. B
4. B
5. A
6. C

TEST 4

PASSAGE

If George Washington could have visited the United States in the 1840's, his thoughts might have run somewhat like this:

"I find it hard to believe that over 20,000,000 people now live in the United States, and that towns have been built beyond the Mississippi River. In my day, there were only 4,000,000 people, and most of these lived along the Atlantic Coast. Can this great city be New York, where I took the oath of office as President? The city I knew had 60,000 inhabitants; today, they tell me, it is the largest city in the New World and has a population of 500,000. What is this engine belching smoke and sparks which carries people across the countryside? When I traveled from Mount Vernon to New York in 1789, I depended on horses. I see factories where machines spin thread to weave it into cloth. Who ever heard in my day of a machine that could spin eighty threads at one time? Here is a boat run by steam which travels against the current of a river! In my time, we depended on the wind to drive our boats. Who would have believed that this country could change so greatly in fifty years!"

1. How much GREATER was the population of the United States in 1840 than in 1789?

    A. Twice as great
    B. Five times as great
    C. Twelve times as great
    D. Twenty times as great

2. George Washington was inaugurated in

    A. Boston
    B. Mount Vernon
    C. New York
    D. Philadelphia

3. A method of transportation used in the 1840's but not in Washington's time was the

    A. airplane   B. automobile   C. sailboat   D. railroad

4. The changes described in the paragraph took place within a period of about _____ years.

    A. 10   B. 20   C. 50   D. 70

5. In Washington's time, MOST of the people in the United States lived

    A. beyond the Mississippi
    B. along the eastern seaboard
    C. in the deep South
    D. in the Northwest

KEY (CORRECT ANSWERS)

1. B
2. C
3. D
4. C
5. B

TEST 5

PASSAGE

In philosophy, the New Deal was democratic, in method evolutionary. Because for fifteen years legislative reforms had been dammed up, they now burst upon the country with what seemed like violence but when the waters subsided, it was clear that they ran in familiar channels. The conservation policy of the New Deal had been inaugurated by Theodore Roosevelt; railroad and trust regulation went back to the eighties; banking and currency reforms had been advocated by Bryan and partially achieved by Wilson; the farm-relief program borrowed much from the Populists, labor legislation from the practices of such states as Wisconsin and Oregon. Even judicial reform, which caused such a mighty stir, had been anticipated by Lincoln and Theodore Roosevelt. And in the realm of international relations, the policies of the New Deal were clearly continuations of the traditional policies of strengthening national security, maintaining freedom of the seas, supporting law and peace, and championing democracy in the Western world.

1. All of the following are suitable titles for the selection EXCEPT

   A. The New Deal - an Evolution
   B. The Radical Program of the New Deal
   C. Precedents for the New Deal
   D. Conservatism in the New Deal

2. Many students of history do not agree that legislative reforms had been *dammed up* during the fifteen-year period preceding the New Deal.
   All of the following legislative measures were passed during this fifteen-year period EXCEPT the _____ Act.

   A. Norris-LaGuardia
   B. Reconstruction Finance Corporation
   C. Sherman Antitrust
   D. Agricultural Marketing

3. This selection traces the origin of many of the policies of the New Deal to all of the following EXCEPT

   A. former Presidents
   B. legislation of the Western states
   C. minority parties
   D. the Supreme Court

4. All of the following were indications of isolationism in the New Deal period EXCEPT the

   A. *cash-and-carry* policy
   B. Johnson Debt-Default Act
   C. Lima Conference
   D. *America First* organization

5. Abraham Lincoln, Theodore Roosevelt, and Franklin Roosevelt had all of the following policies in common EXCEPT

   A. trust regulation
   B. expansion of executive powers
   C. land reforms
   D. economic betterment of the common man

6. According to the selection legislative reforms of the New Deal are characterized by all of the following adjectives EXCEPT

    A. democratic
    B. evolutionary
    C. reactionary
    D. traditional

7. All of the following Presidents were associated with banking reforms EXCEPT

    A. Warren Harding
    B. Andrew Jackson
    C. Abraham Lincoln
    D. Woodrow Wilson

8. According to the selection, some legislative precedents for the New Deal were furthered in the United States by all of the following Presidents EXCEPT

    A. Abraham Lincoln
    B. Theodore Roosevelt
    C. Calvin Coolidge
    D. Woodrow Wilson

9. The student seeking primary source material on the New Deal farm program should consult

    A. THE WORLD ALMANAC
    B. the CONGRESSIONAL RECORD
    C. an encyclopedia of the social studies
    D. WHO'S WHO IN AMERICA

KEY (CORRECT ANSWERS)

1. B
2. C
3. D
4. C
5. A
6. C
7. A
8. C
9. B

TEST 6

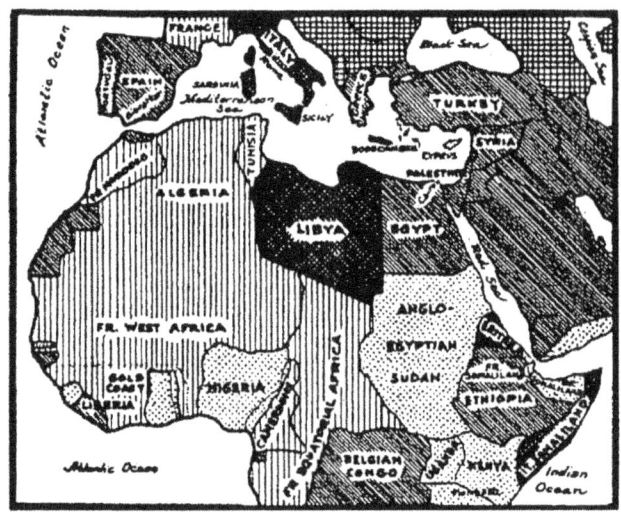

PASSAGE

London, August 14, 1948. A bankrupt empire was put for disposal in London this week. Although the empire, once the property of Italy, has few assets, bidding for the properties was spirited. Italy, despite her present domestic problems, was bidding strongly. Only Italy seemed to want the whole lot; others were angling for bits and pieces and odd parcels of the colonies. On the other hand, Great Britain, which wants the properties almost as badly as Italy, was bidding timidly as if she were afraid of running up the price too fast and too far.

The international auction sale was arranged last year when the winning powers in the recent war settled accounts with Italy. In the Italian peace treaty, Italy renounced all rights to her colonies. The Dodecanese promptly were ceded to Greece. In an annex to the treaty, the Big Four agreed that their Foreign Ministers should decide on the disposal of the other three colonies - Eritrea and Italian Somaliland on the east coast of Africa and Libya in North Africa. Failing a decision within one year, that is, by September 15, 1948, the Big Four agreed that they would hand over the problem to the United Nations General Assembly and abide by its verdict.

That year was nearly out when the deputies of the Big Four Foreign Ministers met, not to decide finally the future of the colonies, but merely to pass on recommendations to the Council of Foreign Minis- ters. When these deputies met last October, they sent out a four-power commission to investigate the situation in the colonies and the wishes of the inhabitants. Reports of that commission were in the hands of the deputies when they met this week.

1. The writer believes that the former Italian colonies   1._____

    A. have many fine resources
    B. are desired by some of the great powers
    C. are financially sound
    D. are strategically important to Russia

2 (#6)

2. The Italian colonies in Africa include 2.____

   A. Ethiopia, Eritrea, Libya
   B. Italian Somaliland, Eritrea, Libya
   C. Eritrea, Libya, and the Dodecanese
   D. Ethiopia, Tripoli, and the Dodecanese

3. Italy's African colonies bordered on the 3.____

   A. Mediterranean Sea
   B. Indian Ocean
   C. Atlantic Ocean and Red Sea
   D. Red Sea, Mediterranean Sea, and Indian Ocean

4. The MOST appropriate title for the article would be 4.____

   A. PROBLEMS OF WORLD EMPIRES
   B. FATE OF ITALY'S AFRICAN EMPIRE UNDECIDED
   C. FOUR POWERS INVESTIGATE ITALY'S COLONIES
   D. ITALY'S WEALTH IN AFRICA

5. Libya lies 5.____

   A. east of Algeria
   B. east of Egypt
   C. north of Egypt
   D. west of Tunisia

6. The author of the article 6.____

   A. thinks that the colonies will be restored to the natives
   B. says the colonies will be given to the Arabs
   C. predicts that the colonies will be returned to Italy
   D. makes no prediction as to the action of the United Nations Assembly

7. MOST of Libya's boundaries bordered on 7.____

   A. possessions of the French Empire
   B. possessions of the British Empire
   C. the sea
   D. independent countries

8. If the Big Four cannot agree upon the disposition of the Italian colonies, they will refer the problem to the 8.____

   A. International Court of Justice
   B. Trusteeship Council
   C. General Assembly of the United Nations
   D. Security Council of the United Nations

9. The author of the article states that 9.____

   A. the colonies were disposed of in the Italian peace treaty
   B. Greece received all the Italian colonies
   C. the Big Four were first assigned disposal of the colonies
   D. the United Nations Assembly would have to approve the disposal of the colonies

10. The author names the following countries as bidders in the disposal of the remaining colonies   10.____

    A. France and the Netherlands
    B. Great Britain and France
    C. Italy and Portugal
    D. Great Britain and Italy

11. By a study of this map, a student could determine the   11.____

    A. number of air miles from Rome to Cairo
    B. most densely populated areas
    C. notable topographic features of Ethiopia
    D. boundaries and comparative areas

12. Of the following statements selected from the article, the one that is CLEARLY a statement of opinion is that   12.____

    A. the Dodecanese were ceded to Greece
    B. the Big Four agreed to hand over the problem to the United Nations under certain conditions
    C. the deputies met in October, 1947
    D. Great Britain was afraid of running the price up too fast and too far

---

KEYS (CORRECT ANSWERS)

1. B
2. B
3. D
4. B
5. A

6. D
7. A
8. C
9. C
10. D

11. D
12. D

TEST 7

PASSAGE

"We hold these truths to be self-evident: that all men and women are created equal; that they are endowed by their Creator with certain inalienable rights; that among these are life, liberty, and the pursuit of happiness...

"The history of mankind is a history of repeated injuries and usurpations on the part of man toward woman, having in direct object the establishment of an absolute tyranny over her. To prove this, let facts be submitted to a candid world.

"He has never permitted her to exercise her inalienable right to the elective franchise.

"He has compelled her to submit to laws, in the formation of which she had no voice...

"He has so framed the laws of divorce, as to what shall be the proper causes, and in case of separation, to whom the guardianship of the children shall be given, as to be wholly regardless of the happiness of women - the law, in all cases, going upon a false supposition of the supremacy of man, and giving all power into his hands...

"He has monopolized nearly all the profitable employments, and from those she is permitted to follow, she receives but a scanty remuneration. He closes against her all the avenues to wealth and distinction which he considers most honorable to himself. As a teacher of theology, medicine, or law, she is not known.

"He has denied her the facilities for obtaining a thorough education, all colleges being closed against her..."

RESOLUTIONS ADOPTED AT THE SENECA FALLS CONVENTION, 1848

1. This selection appeals for support of the movement for

    A. temperance
    B. women's rights
    C. social security
    D. child labor legislation

2. Which served as a model for this selection?

    A. Federal Bill of Rights
    B. Emancipation Proclamation
    C. Mayflower Compact
    D. Declaration of Independence

3. An *inalienable right* is BEST defined as a right that

    A. cannot be taken away
    B. is granted to women only
    C. is granted to all except aliens
    D. is guaranteed by the preamble to the Federal Constitution

4. Which right did women enjoy at the time of the Seneca Falls Convention?

    A. The right to serve on juries
    B. The right of assembly
    C. Equal vocational opportunities
    D. Equal rights before the law

5. Which problem of the Seneca Falls Convention remains a legal issue in the United States today? 5.____

   A. A voice in making laws
   B. College admission
   C. Equal pay for equal work in industry
   D. Exclusion from the practice of medicine

6. About how long after the Seneca Falls Convention was the right to the elective franchise (referred to in the selection) achieved by a constitutional amendment? _____ years. 6.____

   A. 5 B. 50 C. 75 D. 100

KEY (CORRECT ANSWERS)

1. B
2. D
3. A
4. B
5. C
6. C

TEST 8

FROM THE FOUR CORNERS OF THE COUNTRY

1. The cartoon suggests that in the 82nd Congress

   A. harmony prevailed
   B. more agreement existed on domestic issues than on foreign policy
   C. only the reactionary Democrats opposed Truman's foreign policy
   D. there was disagreement within both the Democratic and the Republican parties

2. The cartoon specifically refers to division within the Republican party over

   A. foreign policy
   B. inflation
   C. civil rights
   D. taxation

3. Which of the following are leaders of the two Republican groups represented in the cartoon?

   A. Taft and Acheson
   B. Dewey and Hoover
   C. Austin and Dulles
   D. Stassen and Lehman

4. We can conclude from the cartoon that in the 82nd Congress, there was

   A. little prospect that either group in the Democratic party will take a world-minded view
   B. no possibility of any important legislation
   C. no possibility that the President's recommendations will receive favorable consideration
   D. little likelihood of settling significant foreign policy issues on strict party lines

5. Which of the following conclusions drawn from the cartoon can be readily proved?

   A. There was a reaction group in the Democratic party.
   B. All isolationists came from the same part of the country.
   C. The 82nd Congress was evenly divided between Republicans and Democrats.
   D. The Republicans were more interested in foreign policy than in domestic issues.

KEY (CORRECT ANSWERS)

1. D
2. A
3. B
4. D
5. A

TEST 9

FAMILY INCOME BEFORE TAXES
United States, 1946 and 1953

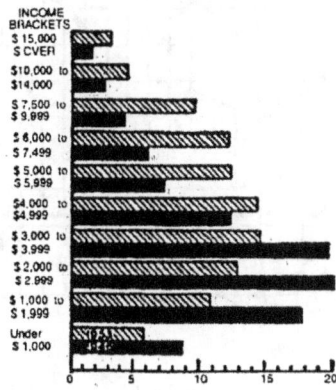

PERCENT OF FAMILIES

1. In 1953, the percent of families with incomes between $3000 and $3,999 was APPROXIMATELY

   A. 5%   B. 10%   C. 15%   D. 20%

2. In 1946, which income bracket included the largest percentage of families?

   A. $1,000 to $1,999   B. $2,000 to $2,999
   C. $3,000 to $3,999   D. $4,000 to $4,999

3. Which of these income brackets included a larger percentage of families in 1953 than in 1946?

   A. $1,000 to $1,999   B. $2,000 to $2,999
   C. $3,000 to $3,999   D. $4,000 to $4,999

4. In 1953, the percent of families with incomes less than $3,000 was about

   A. 30   B. 45   C. 60   D. 75

5. The average family income in 1953 was CLOSEST TO

   A. $1,500   B. $2,500   C. $4,500   D. $6,000

KEY (CORRECT ANSWERS)

1. C
2. B
3. D
4. A
5. C

TEST 10

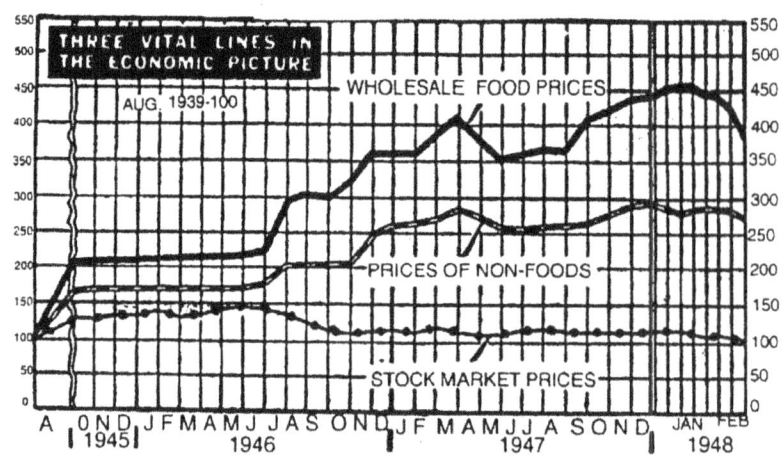

1. For the year 1948, the chart shows a _____ period.

   A. two-month   B. six-week   C. seven-week   D. eight-week

2. Throughout the period from October 1945 to February 1948, stock market prices

   A. rose sharply
   B. declined sharply
   C. remained comparatively steady
   D. fluctuated greatly

3. A comparison of wholesale food prices at the end of the second week in February 1948 with wholesale food prices in October 1945 shows an increase of APPROXIMATELY _____ points.

   A. 50   B. 100   C. 200   D. 300

4. In the period covered by the graph, wholesale food prices declined sharply

   A. once   B. twice   C. three times   D. four times

5. The prices of non-food items reached their highest peak in

   A. March 1946   B. December 1946
   C. March 1947   D. December 1947

6. For the period shown in 1948, all items

   A. rose   B. remained the same
   C. declined   D. fluctuated greatly

7. The month in which the GREATEST increase in wholesale food prices occurred was

   A. July 1946   B. October 1946
   C. September 1947   D. December 1947

8. The same wholesale order of groceries that cost $100 in August 1939 cost approximately $450 in

   A. November 1946   B. March 1947
   C. December 1947   D. January 1948

KEY (CORRECT ANSWERS)

1. C
2. C
3. C
4. B
5. D
6. C
7. A
8. D

INTERPRETATION OF LITERARY MATERIALS
EXAMINATION SECTION
TEST 1

DIRECTIONS: In the passages that follow, each question or incomplete statement that follows each passage is followed by several suggested answers or completions. Select the one that BEST answers the question or completes the statement. Base your choice in each case on the materials given and on your own understanding of the subject matter.

What things there are to write, if one could only write them! My mind is full of gleaming thoughts; gay moods and mysterious, mothlike meditations hover in my imagination, fanning their painted wings. They would make my fortune if I could catch them; but always the rarest, those freaked with azure and the deepest crimson, flutter away beyond my reach. The ever-baffled chase of these filmy nothings often seems, for one of sober years in a sad world, a trifling occupation. But have I not read of the great Kings of Persia who used to ride out to hawk for butterflies, nor deemed this pastime beneath their royal dignity?

1. The author believes that striving to write well is

    A. inappropriate for a mature person
    B. unappreciated
    C. unnecessary
    D. a trifling occupation
    E. a worthy occupation

2. The author finds that

    A. there are few subjects to write about
    B. he cannot capture the pictures of his imagination
    C. he is too old for writing gay trifles
    D. he cannot keep his mind on his writing
    E. it is easy to write

3. The theme of this paragraph is

    A. thoughts about butterflies
    B. the sport of kings
    C. the pursuit of ideas
    D. fortune out of reach
    E. the joy of writing

KEY (CORRECT ANSWERS)

1. E
2. B
3. C

TEST 2

DIRECTIONS: In the passages that follow, each question or incomplete statement that follows each passage is followed by several suggested answers or completions. Select the one that BEST answers the question or completes the statement. Base your choice in each case on the materials given and on your own understanding of the subject matter.

The single business of Henry Thoreau, during forty-odd years of eager activity, was to discover an economy calculated to provide a satisfying life. His one concern, that gave to his ramblings in Concord fields a value of high adventure, was to explore the true meaning of wealth. As he understood the problem of economics, there were three possible solutions open to him: to exploit himself, to exploit his fellows, or to reduce the problem to its lowest denominator. The first was quite impossible—to imprison oneself in a treadmill when the morning called to great adventure. To exploit one's fellows seemed to Thoreau's sensitive social conscience an even greater infidelity. Freedom with abstinence seemed to him better than serfdom with material well-being, and he was content to move to Walden Pond and to set about the high business of living, "to front only the essential facts of life and to see what it had to teach." He did not advocate that other men should build cabins and live isolated. He had no wish to dogmatize concerning the best mode of living—each must settle that for himself. But that a satisfying life should be lived, he was vitally concerned. The story of his emancipation from the lower economics is the one romance of his life, and WALDEN is his great book. It is a book in praise of life rather than of Nature, a record of calculating economies that studied saving in order to spend more largely. But it is a book of social criticism as well, in spite of its explicit denial of such a purpose. In considering the true nature of economy, he concluded, with Ruskin, that the cost of a thing is the amount of life which is required in exchange for it, immediately or in the long run. In WALDEN, Thoreau elaborated the text: "The only wealth is life."

1. In Thoreau's opinion, the price of a thing should always be measured in terms of

   A. time B. effort C. money
   D. romance E. life

2. According to Thoreau, the wealth of an individual is measured by

   A. the money he makes
   B. the experience he gains
   C. the amount he saves
   D. the books he writes
   E. his social standing

3. Thoreau's solution to the problem of living was to

   A. study Nature
   B. make other men work for him
   C. work in a mill
   D. live in a simple way
   E. write for a living

4. Thoreau was very

   A. active B. lazy C. dissatisfied
   D. unsociable E. stingy

5. Thoreau's CHIEF aim in life was to

   A. discover a satisfactory economy
   B. do as little work as possible
   C. convert others to his way of life
   D. write about Nature
   E. live in isolation

6. The theme of this paragraph is

   A. problems of economics
   B. Thoreau's philosophy of life
   C. WALDEN, Thoreau's greatest work
   D. how Thoreau saved money
   E. life at Walden Pond

KEY (CORRECT ANSWERS)

1.	E	4.	A
2.	B	5.	A
3.	D	6.	B

TEST 3

DIRECTIONS: In the passages that follow, each question or incomplete statement that follows each passage is followed by several suggested answers or completions. Select the one that BEST answers the question or completes the statement. Base your choice in each case on the materials given and on your own understanding of the subject matter.

A moment's reflection will make it clear that one can not live a full, free, influential life in America without argument. No doubt, people often argue on insufficient evidence and for insufficient reasons; no doubt, they often argue on points about which they should rather be thinking and studying; no doubt, they sometimes fancy they are arguing when they are merely wrangling and disputing. But this is only proof that argument is employed badly, that it is misused rather than used skillfully. Argument, at the right moment and for the right purpose and in the right way, is undoubtedly one of the most useful instruments in American life; it is an indispensable means of expressing oneself and impressing others.

1. The theme of this paragraph is

    A. the usefulness of argument
    B. principles of argument
    C. how to win arguments
    D. misuses of argument
    E. need for evidence in argument

2. Argument is an important factor in American life because it gives people a chance to

    A. talk about things of which they know little
    B. influence the ideas of others
    C. develop sufficient evidence
    D. have friendly conversations
    E. use argument at the right time and in the right way

3. Argumentation is being used unwisely when it results in

    A. understanding
    B. compromise
    C. deliberation
    D. bickering
    E. differences of opinion

KEY (CORRECT ANSWERS)

1. A
2. B
3. D

TEST 4

DIRECTIONS: In the passages that follow, each question or incomplete statement that follows each passage is followed by several suggested answers or completions. Select the one that BEST answers the question or completes the statement. Base your choice in each case on the materials given and on your own understanding of the subject matter.

The characteristic American believes, first, in justice as the foundation of civilized government and society, and, next, in freedom for the individual, so far as that freedom is possible without interference with the equal rights of others. He conceives that both justice and freedom are to be secured through popular respect for the laws enacted by the elected representatives of the people and through the faithful observance of those laws. It should be observed, however, that American justice in general keeps in view the present common good of the vast majority, and the restoration rather than the punishment of the exceptional malignant or defective individual. It is essentially democratic; and especially it finds sufferings inflicted on the innocent unintelligible and abhorrent.

Blind obedience and implicit submission to the will of another do not commend themselves to characteristic Americans. The discipline in which they believe is the voluntary cooperation of many persons in the orderly and effective pursuit of common ends. Thus, they submit willingly to any restrictions on individual liberty which can be shown to be necessary to the preservation of the public health, and they are capable of the most effective cooperation at need in business, sports, and war.

1. The American people believe in

    A. unquestioning obedience to their laws
    B. strict discipline
    C. liberty without restraint
    D. subservience to the President
    E. working together for a necessary purpose

2. American justice emphasizes

    A. the welfare of the minority
    B. retaliation for disobedience
    C. rehabilitation of wrongdoers
    D. the sufferings of the innocent
    E. punishment of criminals

3. The PRIMARY element in the American way of life is

    A. the right to vote
    B. freedom
    C. willingness to follow leaders
    D. justice
    E. popular respect for laws

4. The theme of this selection is
   A. American justice
   B. a plea for cooperation
   C. the basis of American democracy
   D. the American government
   E. liberty as the foundation of government

4. _____

KEY (CORRECT ANSWERS)

1. E
2. C
3. D
4. C

TEST 5

DIRECTIONS: In the passages that follow, each question or incomplete statement that follows each passage is followed by several suggested answers or completions. Select the one that BEST answers the question or completes the statement. Base your choice in each case on the materials given and on your own understanding of the subject matter.

The change in the treatment of his characters is a significant index to Shakespeare's growth as a dramatist. In the earlier plays, his men and women are more engaged with external forces than with internal struggles. In as excellent an early tragedy as ROMEO AND JULIET, the hero fights more with outside obstacles than with himself. In the great later tragedies, the internal conflict is more emphasized, as in the cases of HAMLET and MACBETH. He grew to care less for mere incident, for plots based on mistaken identity, as in the COMEDY OF ERRORS; he became more and more interested in the delineation of character, in showing the effect of evil on Macbeth and his wife, of jealousy on OTHELLO, of indecision on Hamlet, as well as in exploring the ineffectual attempts of many of his characters to escape the consequences of their acts.

1. The development of Shakespeare as a dramatist is MOST clearly revealed in his

    A. improved treatment of complications
    B. increased use of involved plots
    C. handling of emotional conflicts
    D. increased variety of plot
    E. decreased dependency on historical characters

2. In his later plays, Shakespeare became interested in

    A. plots based on mistaken identity
    B. great characters from history
    C. the history of his country
    D. the study of human nature
    E. the struggle of the hero with external forces

3. The theme of this paragraph is

    A. comedies and tragedies of Shakespeare
    B. Shakespeare's best plays
    C. Shakespeare's development as a dramatist
    D. the moral aspects of Shakespeare's later plays
    E. Shakespeare's interest in good and evil

KEY (CORRECT ANSWERS)

1. C
2. D
3. C

TEST 6

DIRECTIONS: In the passages that follow, each question or incomplete statement that follows each passage is followed by several suggested answers or completions. Select the one that BEST answers the question or completes the statement. Base your choice in each case on the materials given and on your own understanding of the subject matter.

Solitude is a great chastener when once you accept it. It quietly eliminates all sorts of traits that were a part of you - among others, the desire to pose, to keep your best foot forever in evidence, to impress people as being something you would like to have them think you are even when you aren't. Some men I know are able to pose even in solitude; had they valets they no doubt would be heroes to them. But I find it the hardest kind of work myself; and as I am lazy, I have stopped trying. To act without an audience is so tiresome and profitless that you gradually give it up and at last forget how to act at all. For you become more interested in making the acquaintance of yourself as you really are, which is a meeting that, in the haunts of men, rarely takes place. It is gratifying, for example, to discover that you prefer to be clean rather than dirty even when there is no one but God to care which you are; just as it is amusing to note, however, that for scrupulous cleanliness, you are not inclined to make superhuman sacrifices, although you used to believe you were. Clothes, you learn, with something of a shock, have for you no interest whatsoever....You learn to regard dress merely as covering, a precaution. For its color and its cut you care nothing.

1. The activities of everyday life seldom give us the chance to

    A. learn our own peculiarities
    B. keep our best foot forward
    C. impress people
    D. dress as we would like
    E. be immaculately clean

2. The desire to appear well-dressed USUALLY depends upon

    A. an audience
    C. personal pride
    E. a fondness for acting
    B. industriousness
    D. the need for cleanliness

3. In solitude, clothes

    A. constitute one item that pleases the valet
    B. make one careless
    C. are part of acting
    D. are valued for their utility only
    E. are tiresome

4. A desire to appear at your best is a trait that

    A. goes with laziness
    B. may disappear when you are alone
    C. depends primarily on clothes
    D. is inhuman
    E. is evil

5. The theme of this paragraph is
   A. carelessness in clothes
   B. acting without an audience
   C. discoveries through solitude
   D. showing off to best advantage
   E. being a hero to yourself

5.____

KEY (CORRECT ANSWERS)

1. A
2. A
3. D
4. B
5. C

TEST 7

DIRECTIONS: In the passages that follow, each question or incomplete statement that follows each passage is followed by several suggested answers or completions. Select the one that BEST answers the question or completes the statement. Base your choice in each case on the materials given and on your own understanding of the subject matter.

In width of scope, Yeats far exceeds any of his contemporaries. He is the only poet since the 18th century who has been a public man in his own country and the only poet since Milton who has been a public man at a time when his country was involved in a struggle for political liberty. This may not seem an important matter, but it is a question whether the kind of life lived by poets for the last two hundred years or so has not been one great reason for the drift of poetry away from the life of the community as a whole, and the loss of touch with tradition. Once the life of contemplation has been divorced from the life of action, or from real knowledge of men of action, something is lost which it is difficult to define, but which leaves poetry enfeebled and incomplete. Yeats responded with all his heart as a young man to the reality and the romance of Ireland's struggle, but he lived to be completely disillusioned about the value of the Irish rebellion. He saw his dreams of liberty blotted out in horror by "the innumerable clanging wings that have put out the moon." It brought him to the final conclusion of the futility of all discipline that is not of the whole being, and of "how base at moments of excitement are minds without culture"; but he remained a man to whom the life of action always meant something very real.

1. According to the writer of the paragraph, great poetry is MOST often produced by poets who

    A. are involved in the problems of life around them
    B. spend their time in contemplation
    C. drift away from the community
    D. break away from tradition
    E. take part in war

2. The writer implies that, as compared with older poetry, present-day poetry is more

    A. complete
    B. romantic
    C. alive
    D. ineffectual
    E. comprehensive

3. Yeats was PRIMARILY a

    A. soldier
    B. man of action
    C. dreamer
    D. rigid disciplinarian
    E. politician

4. The theme of this paragraph is

    A. basis of true poetry
    B. the necessity of culture
    C. action versus contemplation
    D. Yeats as a poet and patriot
    E. Yeats' part in the Irish rebellion

KEY (CORRECT ANSWERS)

1. A
2. D
3. B
4. D

TEST 8

DIRECTIONS: In the passages that follow, each question or incomplete statement that follows each passage is followed by several suggested answers or completions. Select the one that BEST answers the question or completes the statement. Base your choice in each case on the materials given and on your own understanding of the subject matter.

Only twice in literary history has there been a great period of tragedy, in the Athens of Pericles and in Elizabethan England. What these two periods had in common, two thousand years and more apart in time, that they expressed themselves in the same fashion, may give us some hint of the nature of tragedy, for far from being periods of darkness and defeat, each was a time when life was seen exalted, a time of thrilling and unfathomable possibilities. They held their heads high, those men who conquered at Marathon and Salamis and those who fought Spain and saw the Great Armada sink. The world was a place of wonder; manking was beauteous; life was lived on the crest of the wave. More than all, the poignant joy of heroism had stirred men's hearts. Not stuff for tragedy, would you say? But on the crest of the wave, one must feel either tragically or joyously; one cannot feel tamely. The temper of mind that sees tragedy in life has not for its opposite the temper that sees joy. The opposite pole to the tragic view of life is the sordid view. When humanity is seen as devoid of dignity and significance, trivial, mean, and sunk in dreary hopelessness, then the spirit of tragedy departs.

1. In an age of glory, one

   A. is not indifferent
   B. usually feels tragic
   C. feels happy
   D. is apathetic
   E. feels mean and hopeless

2. The two periods in which great tragedies were written were periods of

   A. gloom
   B. serenity
   C. defeat
   D. confusion
   E. valor

3. The mental attitude that finds tragedy in life is characterized by

   A. sordidness
   B. indifference
   C. exaltation
   D. triviality
   E. hopelessness

4. The theme of this paragraph is

   A. two thousand years of tragedy
   B. Periclean Athens
   C. the tragedy of war
   D. the psychology of happiness
   E. mainsprings of tragic drama

KEY (CORRECT ANSWERS)

1. A
2. E
3. C
4. E

TEST 9

DIRECTIONS: In the passages that follow, each question or incomplete statement that follows each passage is followed by several suggested answers or completions. Select the one that BEST answers the question or completes the statement. Base your choice in each case on the materials given and on your own understanding of the subject matter.

There are few books which go with midnight, solitude, and a candle. It is much easier to say what does not please us then than what is exactly right. The book must be, anyhow, something benedictory by a sinning fellow man. Cleverness would be repellent at such an hour. Cleverness, anyhow, is the level of mediocrity today, we are all too infernally clever. The first witty and perverse paradox blows out the candle. Only the sick mind craves cleverness, as a morbid body turns to drink. The late candle throws its beams a great distance, and its rays make transparent much that seemed massy and important. The mind at rest beside that light, when the house is asleep, and the consequential affairs of the urgent world have diminished to their right proportions because we seem them distantly from another and a more tranquil place in the heavens, where duty, honor, witty arguments, controversial logic on great questions, appear such as will leave hardly a trace of fossil in the indurated mud which will cover them — the mind then smiles at cleverness. For though at that hour the body may be dog-tired, the mind is white and lucid, like that of a man from whom a fever has abated. It is bare of illusions. It has a sharp focus, small and starlike, as a clear and lonely flame left burning by the altar of a shrine from which all have gone but one. A book which approaches that light in the privacy of that place must come, as it were, with open and honest pages.

1. At midnight in the solitude of one's room, the mind is

    A. tired   B. keen   C. sick
    D. troubled   E. clever

2. The author considers the average book of today

    A. inane   B. sinful   C. benedictory
    D. restful   E. open and honest

3. Naming the qualities of a book suitable for reading when one retires is

    A. logical   B. a clever job
    C. difficult   D. like lighting a candle
    E. tiresome

4. To make good reading at bedtime, a book must be

    A. light   B. witty   C. controversial
    D. historical   E. straightforward

5. The theme of this paragraph is

    A. reading by candlelight
    B. books for convalescents
    C. not a time to read
    D. books for tired minds
    E. books for midnight reading

KEY (CORRECT ANSWERS)

1. B
2. A
3. C
4. E
5. E

TEST 10

DIRECTIONS: In the passages that follow, each question or incomplete statement that follows each passage is followed by several suggested answers or completions. Select the one that BEST answers the question or completes the statement. Base your choice in each case on the materials given and on your own understanding of the subject matter.

Few things are move stimulating than the sight of the forceful wings of large birds cleaving the vagueness of air and making the piled clouds a mere background for their concentrated life. The peregrine falcon, becalmed in the blue depths, cruises across space without a tremor of his wide wings. Wild geese beat up in the sky in a compact wedge. Primeval force is in their strongly moving wings and their beautiful, outstretched necks, in their power of untiring effort, and the eager search of their wild hearts for the free spaces they love. The good fellowship of swift, united action, the joy of ten thousand that move as one, is in the flight of flocks of birds. When seagulls flash up from the water with every wing at full stretch, there is no deliberation; it is as if each bird saw a sweeping arc before it and followed its individual way faithfully. The unerring judgment of the grand curve when the wings are so near and yet never collide, the speed of the descent, are pure poetry.

1. He admires the ability of seagulls to

   A. coordinate their flight
   B. reach great heights
   C. stretch their wings
   D. rise from the water
   E. dive swiftly

2. The flight of the wild goose, as compared with that of the falcon, is MORE

   A. active
   B. beautiful
   C. poetic
   D. deliberate
   E. graceful

3. The author finds the sight of flying birds

   A. inspiring
   B. awesome
   C. joyful
   D. consoling
   E. primitive

4. The author admires the falcon's

   A. wild freedom
   B. effortless flight
   C. united action
   D. primitive force
   E. unerring judgment

5. The theme of this paragraph is

   A. our wild birds
   B. the superb falcon
   C. the beauty of flight
   D. citizens of the sky
   E. the lure of the wild

KEY (CORRECT ANSWERS)

1. A
2. A
3. A
4. B
5. C

TEST 11

DIRECTIONS: In the passages that follow, each question or incomplete statement that follows each passage is followed by several suggested answers or completions. Select the one that BEST answers the question or completes the statement. Base your choice in each case on the materials given and on your own understanding of the subject matter.

As we know the short story today, it is largely a product of the nineteenth and twentieth centuries and its development parallels the rapid development of industrialism in America. We have been a busy people, busy principally in evolving a production system supremely efficient. Railroads and factories have blossomed almost overnight; mines and oil fields have been discovered and exploited; mechanical inventions by the thousand have been made and perfected. Speed has been an essential element in our endeavors, and it has affected our lives, our very natures. Leisurely reading has been, for most Americans, impossible. As with our meals, we have grabbed bits of reading standing up, cafeteria style, and gulped down cups of sentiment on the run. We have had to read while hanging on to a strap in a swaying trolley car or in a rushing subway or while tending to a clamoring telephone switchboard. Our popular magazine has been our literary automat, and its stories have often been no more substantial than sandwiches.

1. From this selection, one would assume that the author's attitude toward short stories is one of

   A. approval   B. indifference   C. contempt
   D. impartiality   E. regret

2. The short story has developed because of Americans'

   A. reactions against the classics
   B. need for reassurance
   C. lack of culture
   D. lack of education
   E. taste for speed

3. The short story today owes its popularity to its

   A. settings   B. plots   C. style
   D. length   E. characters

4. The theme of this paragraph is

   A. *quick-lunch* literature
   B. life in the machine age
   C. culture in modern life
   D. reading while traveling
   E. the development of industrialism

KEY (CORRECT ANSWERS)

1. E
2. E
3. D
4. A

TEST 12

DIRECTIONS: In the passages that follow, each question or incomplete statement that follows each passage is followed by several suggested answers or completions. Select the one that BEST answers the question or completes the statement. Base your choice in each case on the materials given and on your own understanding of the subject matter.

If Shakespeare needs any excuse for the exuberance of his language (the high key in which he pitched most of his dramatic dialogue), it should be remembered that he was doing on the plastic stage of his own day what on the pictorial stage of our day is not so much required. Shakespeare's dramatic figures stood out on a platform-stage, without background, with the audience on three sides of it. And the whole of his atmosphere and environment had to come from the gestures and language of the actors. When they spoke, they provided their own scenery, which we now provide for them. They had to do a good deal more (when they spoke) than actors have to do today in order to give the setting. They carried the scenery on their backs, as it were, and spoke it in words.

1. The nature of the stage for which Shakespeare wrote made it necessary for him to

   A. employ only highly dramatic situations
   B. depend on scenery owned by the actors themselves
   C. have the actors shift the scenery
   D. create atmosphere through the dialogue
   E. restrict backgrounds to familiar types of scenes

   1.____

2. In comparison with actors of Shakespeare's time, actors of today

   A. carry the settings in their words
   B. pitch their voices in a lower key
   C. depend more on elaborate settings
   D. have to do more to make the setting clear
   E. use many gestures

   2.____

3. The theme of this paragraph is

   A. the scenery of the Elizabethan stage
   B. the importance of actors in the Shakespearean drama
   C. the influence of the Elizabethan stage on Shakespeare's style
   D. the importance of words
   E. suitable gestures for the Elizabethan stage

   3.____

KEY (CORRECT ANSWERS)

1. D
2. C
3. C

TEST 13

DIRECTIONS: In the passages that follow, each question or incomplete statement that follows each passage is followed by several suggested answers or completions. Select the one that BEST answers the question or completes the statement. Base your choice in each case on the materials given and on your own understanding of the subject matter.

It is no secret that I am not one of those naturalists who suffer from cities, or affect to do so, nor do I find a city unnatural or uninteresting, or a rubbish heap of follies. It has always seemed to me that there is something more than mechanically admirable about a train that arrives on time, a fire department that comes when you call it, a light that leaps into the room at a touch, and a clinic that will fight for the health of a penniless man and mass for him the agencies of mercy, the x-ray, the precious radium, the anesthetics and the surgical skill. For, beyond any pay these services receive, stands out the pride in perfect performance. And above all, I admire the noble impersonality of civilization that does not inquire where the recipient stands on religion or politics or race. I call this beauty, and I call it spirit—not some mystical soulfulness that nobody can define, but the spirit of man, that has been a million years a-growing.

1. The author implies that efficient operation of public utilities is

   A. expensive
   B. of no special interest
   C. admired by most naturalists
   D. mechanically commendable
   E. spiritual in quality

2. The aspect of city life MOST commendable to this author is its

   A. punctuality   B. free benefits
   C. impartial service   D. mechanical improvement
   E. health clinics

3. The author makes a defense of

   A. cities   B. prompt trains
   C. rural life   D. nature
   E. free clinics

4. The services rendered by city agencies are given

   A. only for pay
   B. on time
   C. only to people having a certain political allegiance
   D. to everybody
   E. to the spirit of man

5. The theme of this paragraph is

   A. the spirit of the city
   B. advantages of a city home
   C. disagreement among naturalists
   D. admirable characteristics of cities
   E. tolerance in the city

KEY (CORRECT ANSWERS)

1. E
2. C
3. A
4. D
5. D

TEST 14

DIRECTIONS: In the passages that follow, each question or incomplete statement that follows each passage is followed by several suggested answers or completions. Select the one that BEST answers the question or completes the statement. Base your choice in each case on the materials given and on your own understanding of the subject matter.

The annual survey of chemistry published by the American Chemical Society attributes the vast change in warfare to the airplane and, above all, to the motor fuels of today. We never think of gasoline as an explosive, yet it has to some extent taken the place of the artillery propellants of a quarter of a century ago. A bomber is hardly a gun, but it certainly performs the function of one, with a range of many hundred miles.

About fifteen years ago, we began to hear of iso-octane, a fuel used to measure antiknock qualities of high-compression gasoline. It was ideal for airplanes but quantity production was not practical Now we make lakes of it. Its performance is so remarkable that the planes propelled by it can carry loads that would have been inconceivable only ten years ago. As a result, octane numbers and indexes of antiknock properties have lost much of their former significance. It will probably be necessary to adopt some new standard. If we relate size and weight of engine to octane number, a truer picture of what aviation fuels really are is obtained. For each pound of weight, aviation engines of today produce, respectively, 100 percent and 50 percent more power than could those of 1918 and 1930.

1. The writer suggests that gasoline may be considered an explosive because

    A. it produces high compression
    B. modern bombing planes are essentially long-range guns
    C. guns now have greater range
    D. iso-octane is now manufactured in quantity
    E. it has replaced explosives in cannons

2. The proposed standard for measuring the quality of motor fuels is the

    A. ratio of power to weight
    B. antiknock index
    C. iso-octane number
    D. load-carrying ability
    E. relation of engine weight and size to octane number

3. Per pound of weight, the average engine now produces

    A. very much iso-octane
    B. high compression
    C. twice as much power as in 1930
    D. double the power of 1918
    E. 100 percent efficiency

4. The theme of this selection is 4._____
    A. the chemist speeds the airplane
    B. mass production of iso-octane
    C. improving the gasoline engine
    D. changing methods in warfare
    E. gasoline as an explosive

KEY (CORRECT ANSWERS)

1. B
2. E
3. D
4. A

TEST 15

DIRECTIONS: In the passages that follow, each question or incomplete statement that follows each passage is followed by several suggested answers or completions. Select the one that BEST answers the question or completes the statement. Base your choice in each case on the materials given and on your own understanding of the subject matter.

Once the rivers of America slid undisturbed between their banks, save when a birch canoe, manned by stolid Indians, sewed a narrow seam in the water. Then came a day when our rivers were broad highways filled with packets, lumber rafts, and houseboats. There were years when the rivers languished, deserted by the great commerce they had carried; years, too, of floods and devastation. Today, there is a difference. Efforts are being made to tame the untamed, to yoke the slow-sliding rivers to useful purpose. Dams are being built that will end the tragic flooding of the lowlands. Wasteful torrents are being taught economy, taught to irrigate the lands that lie fallow, needing only water to bring them to fruitfulness. The life-giving fluid to renewed utility is being fed into these rivers of ours, and they are again becoming a vital and integral part of our economy.

1. A MAJOR reason for flood control is

    A. provision of suitable streams for the Indians
    B. profits for the public utilities
    C. conservation of farming areas
    D. relief of unemployment
    E. restoring river commerce

2. America's rivers have

    A. been a steady commercial asset
    B. helped protect us against invasion
    C. brought serious destruction through floods
    D. alternated frequently between periods of usefulness and of destruction or neglect
    E. suffered complete neglect as railroads developed

3. Failing to utilize a country's rivers

    A. is economically wasteful
    B. makes the rivers sluggish
    C. restores their scenic beauty
    D. renews their picturesque traffic
    E. causes wasteful torrents

4. For the safety of property and people, rivers must be

    A. made into highways
    B. used for irrigation
    C. allowed to lie fallow
    D. utilized for commerce
    E. brought under control

5. The theme of this paragraph is
    A. from Indian canoe to modern boat
    B. conservation and our rivers
    C. the utility of water
    D. changing river traffic
    E. rivers, dams, and the public utilities

KEY (CORRECT ANSWERS)

1. C
2. C
3. A
4. E
5. B

INTERPRETATION OF READING MATERIALS IN THE NATURAL SCIENCES
EXAMINATION SECTION
TEST 1
PASSAGE

Less than 100 years ago, a fabulous *new era* of medicine—or so it was supposed to be—was ushered in by the *wonder drugs*, the germkillers extraordinary. Here, it seemed, were the ultimate weapons that could rout hordes of pestilential bugs. Once and for all, there was to be an end to the menace of dozens of infectious diseases. It was a heady dream—but it grossly underestimated the enemy.

The infections are still with us. The bugs have been fighting back. Their counter-attacks, indeed, have sometimes been so vicious that scientists have been forced to go to new lengths to try to repulse them. The battle today seesaws.

One of the latest examples of bug turnabout was noted a few weeks ago when tuberculosis experts met at an isoniazid *reunion* luncheon to take a look at that drug-ten years after it had been hailed as the conqueror of TB and after the first desperately ill patients to receive it got up out of their beds and danced exuberantly in hospital corridors. Currently, as many as 6 percent of TB patients are beyond help by isoniazid—infected with strains of tubercle bacilli impervious to the drug—and resistance to isoniazid is growing.

The trend, not yet calamitous, follows explosive epidemics produced by *hospital staph* bacteria that sneer at penicillin and many other antibiotics. There have been-and continue to be-troubles with numerous other disease organisms despite, and even because of, antibiotics.

As early as 1954, University of Michigan physicians, noting the ability, evident even then, of some germs to live with highly vaunted antibiotics, suggested that *man may be sitting on a time bomb, capable of *** shattering the illusion of medical miracles****.

1. What is meant by the statement in the passage that *man may be sitting on a time bomb*?

    A. The *bugs* may progressively develop resistances to the drugs.
    B. The idea of medical miracles is an illusion.
    C. There is a great chance that TB could develop into a more difficult disease to treat.
    D. As the *bugs* get stronger, the disease becomes more prevalent.
    E. One day the miracle drugs which have been discovered will cause more harm than good.

2. *The bugs have been fighting back,* states the passage. This means:

    A. Higher doses of a particular drug become required.
    B. Patients develop an immunity to the disease.
    C. The *bugs* increase in number as a result of the drug.
    D. Some people have no reaction to the antibiotics.
    E. As the drugs become stronger, so do the *bugs*.

3. *Wonder drugs* are not the ultimate weapon because

   A. it remains for a drug to be discovered which the *bugs* cannot fight
   B. they only treat one disease, not all
   C. they are limited to certain people, i.e., many are allergic
   D. they sometimes carry their own diseases, with which they replace the ones they cure
   E. scientists deny the existence of a foreseeable day when the *ultimate weapon* against disease can be evolved

3.___

4. Wonder drugs were discovered

   A. by Jonas Salk
   B. 20 years ago
   C. less than five decades ago
   D. over a century ago
   E. as a by-product of research done in nuclear physics

4.___

5. *Animalcules* is another word for

   A. antibiotics
   B. bacteria
   C. drugs
   D. penicillin
   E. oreomycin

5.___

6. Scientists realistically predict the day when

   A. there will be no more disease
   B. better drugs will be made
   C. the *bugs* may develop a resistance to all antibiotics
   D. antibiotics will not be needed to cure disease
   E. all bacteria will be conquered

6.___

KEY (CORRECT ANSWERS)

1. A   4. C
2. E   5. B
3. A   6. C

EXPLANATION OF ANSWERS

1. CORRECT ANSWER: A

   B is irrelevant; C is not stated; D is not stated or implied;
   E is pure conjecture and not inferred in the passage.

2. CORRECT ANSWER: E

   Items A and D are sometimes true but bear no relation to the question. C is false. Patients may develop an immunity to the antibiotics, but never to the disease. Therefore, B is false. The proper answer is E: *The battle today seesaws* (last sentence of the second paragraph).

3. CORRECT ANSWER: A

   While B and C are factually true, they do not satisfactorily complete the statement. D is scientifically unknown as yet. Item E is false. The correct answer is A (see the last sentence of the first paragraph).

4. CORRECT ANSWER: C

   The opening sentence is *Less than 50 years ago....a.... 'new era'....was ushered in by the 'wonder drugs'*. Therefore, C is the correct answer. The other answers are false.

5. CORRECT ANSWER: B

   Animalcules is a synonym for bacteria. Therefore, B is the proper answer. The other answers are completely incorrect as they are the substances which fight bacteria.

6. CORRECT ANSWER: C

   Though scientists are working constantly to perfect superior drugs, it has been their experience that the *bugs* are progressing in strength faster than the drugs can be improved. (See, particularly, the last paragraph.) Therefore, the correct answer is C.

TEST 2
PASSAGE

BILLINGS, Mont. — A 60-year-old Montanan traced on a map the other day the boundaries of the Bob Marshall Wilderness Area. As he lifted his finger, a smile creased his face. He said:

That's it. It has been pretty well explored for minerals, but you never can tell when somebody might want to try something again. Let's hope nobody can touch it now. It's something that should have been done long ago.

His reference was to the creation of the National Wilderness Preservation System, as set down in Public Law 88577, which went into effect September 3. The act is the compromise of a long and bitter fight to carve out of the national forests and other Federal lands a system that will, in the words of the legislation, *secure for the American people of present and future generations the benefits of an enduring resource of wilderness.*

The compromise was between conservationists and those who would put forest resources to commercial and other-than-wilderness uses.

It pins this down by its definition that a wilderness, *in contrast with those areas where man and his own works dominate the landscape, is hereby recognized as an area where the earth and the community of life are untrammeled by man, where man himself is a visitor who does not remain.*

1. The National Wilderness Preservation System was of great interest because it

    A. went into effect September 3
    B. was a compromise
    C. preserved an important resource
    D. worked hand-in-hand with commerce
    E. allowed for other-than-wilderness uses

2. What is meant by the statement ... *somebody might want to try something again*?

    A. It might be tapped for minerals
    B. Some party might damage the property.
    C. The property's resources might be tapped for commercial purposes.
    D. Building might take place.
    E. The general public might cause forest fires or sanitation problems.

3. *Untrammeled* means

    A. not trampled on
    B. not traveled
    C. something uninvestigated by man
    D. something abused by man
    E. something left in its original condition

4. After reading the passage, one gets the impression that the author

    A. appreciates the beauty of nature
    B. understands the needs of commerce in relation to natural resources
    C. is engaged in a bitter fight

D. will secure for the American people an enduring wilderness
E. is on the side of the conservationists

5. A good title for this passage would be

   A. THE BOUNDARIES OF THE WILDERNESS
   B. EXPLORING FOR MINERALS
   C. SAVING THE WILDS
   D. HOW COMMERCE MAKES USE OF NATURAL RESOURCES
   E. THE WILDERNESS

6. The TVA, a conservation act, was enacted during the Presidency of

   A. Theodore Roosevelt   B. Woodrow Wilson
   C. Dwight D. Eisenhower   D. Franklin D. Roosevelt
   E. Harry Truman

KEY (CORRECT ANSWERS)

1.	C	4.	E
2.	C	5.	C
3.	E	6.	D

EXPLANATION OF ANSWERS

1. CORRECT ANSWER: C

   Item C is the correct answer, and it is clearly delineated in the quotation contained in paragraph 3, viz., ... *secure for the American people ... an enduring resource of wilderness.*

2. CORRECT ANSWER: C

   When the speaker says, *It has been pretty well explored for minerals, but you never can tell when somebody might want to try something again,* he is referring to a similar possibility of an exploitation by industry. This would designate C as the proper answer. Though B, D, and E are possible occurrences, he is not, in this statement, referring to these.

3. CORRECT ANSWER: E

   The last clause of the passage indicates that A, B, and C are incorrect because man can visit a wilderness area and leave it *untrammeled*. D is incorrect because it infers the opposite of the word's correct meaning.

4. CORRECT ANSWER: E

   The passage is not about the author's love of nature or the needs of commerce, nor does his work match the events or aims suggested in C and D. E would be most suited to his position on natural resources, and is the correct answer.

5. CORRECT ANSWER: C

   The best answer presented here would be C. The theme of the passage is in no way related to items B and D. A and E could be considered, but C is much more directly related to the passage.

6. CORRECT ANSWER: D

   The correct answer is D, Franklin Roosevelt (1933).

TEST 3
PASSAGE

Where others saw unrelated, individually created flowers or birds or people, he saw a mass of altering, dissolving, and interrelated forms flowing onward through earth's history. Living creatures were like cloud shapes contorted by the winds of time. As it happens, the years have proved him right.

What made Darwin a scientist? Let us ask again in particular because by modern school standards and measurements he was not a very good pupil, let alone a candidate for genius. His career was undecided; he dawdled and misspelled words, enraged his father and, giving up a career in medicine, was packed off to Cambridge with the notion that he might at least learn enough to become a country parson.

We cannot analyze Darwin's entire life, but we can say that his quoted letter to Joseph Hooker is enormously important and revelatory. Charles Darwin was a millionaire of facts but they happened not to be the facts in which the schools of his day were interested. Indeed, he spoke of his Cambridge studies as *next thing to intolerable*. As a result, his formal educational career was no measure of his real capacities. Later, as he remembered his experience in South America, he was to speak of lonely desert travels in which *the whole of my pleasure was derived from what passed in my mind*.

Yet the influences at work upon him were not all of a solitary character. His grandfather Erasmus had entertained evolutionary ideas about which Charles had learned as a youth; a kindly botanist, John Henslow, had obtained for him his post as naturalist on the Beagle. On the outward voyage to South America, Darwin had read Sir Charles Lyell's PRINCIPLES OF GEOLOGY and been convinced by Lyell's then-heretical views that the earth was extremely ancient—a necessary prelude to grasping the slow pace of plant and animal evolution.

1. As opposed to the individually created flowers or birds, Darwin saw   1.____

    A. living creatures
    B. masses of altering and dissolving cloud shapes
    C. interrelated forms
    D. people
    E. winds of time

2. The reader can assume from the passage that the author feels a formal education is   2.____

    A. necessary even for a candidate for genius
    B. what made Darwin a scientist
    C. not always a measure of real capacities
    D. necessary for a scientist
    E. not able to help a pupil beyond his potential

3. His first ideas about evolution may well have come from   3.____

    A. his grandfather
    B. Joseph Hooker
    C. John Henslow
    D. PRINCIPLES OF GEOLOGY
    E. his voyage to South America

4. Sir Charles Lyell's ideas were

    A. about animal evolution
    B. about plant life
    C. unaccepted by his period
    D. Darwin's primary inspiration
    E. extremely ancient

5. A work of Darwin's is

    A. ZOOLOGY OF THE VOYAGE OF THE BEAGLE
    B. ON THE TENDENCY OF VARIETIES TO DEPART INDEFINITELY FROM THE ORIGINAL TYPE
    C. TRAVELS ON THE AMAZON AND THE RIO NEGRO
    D. THE BOTANIC GARDEN
    E. ZOONOMIA

6. The famous Scopes trial brought him into conflict with

    A. William Jennings Bryan
    B. Clarence Darrow
    C. the State of Tennessee
    D. J.T. Scopes
    E. the State of Kentucky

KEY (CORRECT ANSWERS)

1. C   4. C
2. C   5. A
3. A   6. C

EXPLANATION OF ANSWERS

1. CORRECT ANSWER: C

   He saw, states the passage (sentence 1), *altering, dissolving, and interrelated forms flowing onward through earth's history.* And as he saw these things, he was envisioning the relationships of all living things. He seemed to see, implies the author, no one thing independent of another. C, then, is the proper answer.

2. CORRECT ANSWER: C

   Judging from Darwin's various failures and indecisions discussed in paragraph 2, the reader can only accept C as the correct completion of the statement. While A, D, and E are probably acceptable statements in themselves, they have nothing to do with the man about whom the author is writing. B, apparently, is not the opinion of the author.

3. CORRECT ANSWER: A

   The evolutionary ideas about which he learned as a youth came from his grandfather long before, presumably, his many other influences. Therefore, A must be the correct answer.

4. CORRECT ANSWER: C

   The last paragraph mentions *Lyell's then-heretical views . . . .* Therefore, C is the only possible answer. Item D is not indicated in the passage, and A, B, and E are false.

5. CORRECT ANSWER: A

   Items D and E were works of Erasmus Darwin, grandfather of Charles. Items B and C are the works of Alfred Russell Wallace. Item A is the work of Charles Darwin-his work on the Beagle mentioned in the passage and is the correct answer.

6. CORRECT ANSWER: C

   Scopes was charged with teaching Darwinian evolution in violation of a state law forbidding such instruction. The state was Tennessee, and the correct answer is C. Clarence Darrow was attorney for the defense and William Jennings Bryan, attorney for the prosecution.

TEST 4
PASSAGE

The most fascinating thing about a greenhouse is the opportunity provided for growing unusual plants. A greenhouse gardener need not limit himself to the plants he once grew in his home. He can branch out to plants from all over the world–depending on the temperature maintained in the greenhouse.

In a greenhouse where the temperature is kept just above freezing, alpine plants can be grown. Edelweiss, bottle gentian, creeping phlox, and columbines like Aquilegia akitensis and A. flabellata are just a few of the candidates. A book on rock gardening or a catalogue from a specialist nursery will suggest many other plants. A practical advantage to growing these cold-greenhouse plants is the saving on wintertime fuel bills.

Under warmer conditions, many kinds of dwarf shrubs will be fun to grow. Do not overlook some of the berried kinds like pyracantha Victory, which is hardy outdoors only about as far north as Zone 7. Tender shrubs and trees such as kumquat, calamondin orange, and dwarf lemon are satisfying to grow, for they will often have flowers and fruit at the same time.

The charming wax plant, Hoya oarnosa, develops beautifully in a warm greenhouse. Others are hibiscus, lantana, oleander, and osmanthus or sweet olive.

1. According to the passage, kumquat is a

    A. sturdy shrub
    B. dwarfed plant
    C. tender shrub
    D. fruit
    E. form of berry

2. An oleander develops

    A. in a warm greenhouse
    B. in a cold greenhouse
    C. outdoors in a southern climate
    D. well in the home
    E. in a northern climate

3. The advantage to growing plants like edelweiss in the wintertime is

    A. they are far more attractive plants than most
    B. they are too fragile for summer cultivation
    C. temperature
    D. the saving on fuel bills
    E. that they are an alpine plant

4. A good title for the passage might be

    A. HOW TO GROW NORTHERN PLANTS
    B. HOW TO GROW TROPICAL PLANTS
    C. THE FLORIDIAN PLANTS: HIBISCUS, OLEANDER, LANTANA
    D. HOW TO GROW CITRUS IN A GREENHOUSE
    E. CANDIDATES FOR A GREENHOUSE

5. Broadly, the subject covered in the passage would come under the heading of

   A. botany
   B. nurseries
   C. gardens
   D. rock gardening
   E. pyracantha

6. A flowering plant, discovered by an American traveling in Mexico, and destined to become our most popular Christmas plant, thanks to the temperature control of the green house, is the

   A. mistletoe
   B. philodendron
   C. poinsettia
   D. rhododendron
   E. hibiscus

KEY (CORRECT ANSWERS)

1. C   4. E
2. A   5. A
3. D   6. C

EXPLANATION OF ANSWERS

1. CORRECT ANSWER: C

   Paragraph 3, sentence 3, contains the description of a kumquat as a *tender shrub,* indicating C as the correct answer.

2. CORRECT ANSWER: A

   Paragraph 4 contains the completion of the statement. It mentions Hoya carnosa as needing a warm greenhouse and goes on to state that, of other plants needing the same environment, one is oleander. Thus, the answer is A. Though an oleander will flourish outdoors in a southern climate, this is not indicated by the author in the passage.

3. CORRECT ANSWER: D

   The last sentence of paragraph 2 states that edelweiss is a cold-greenhouse plant and such plants are a *saving on wintertime fuel bills.* Therein lies its practical advantage. C and E could be considered adequate answers if the requirements only of the plant were the consideration, but D is the better answer because of the word *advantage* in the question (inferring that which is an advantage to the grower).

4. CORRECT ANSWER: E

   Though A, B, C, and D are all mentioned in the passage, the all inclusive title in item E presents the best possible choice and is the correct answer.

5. CORRECT ANSWER: A

   Botany being the science discussed in the passage is the most enveloping choice and, therefore, the best answer. Thus, the answer is A. B, C, D, and E, were they to be catagorized, would all come under the heading of A since they are all parts of the whole-botany.

6. CORRECT ANSWER: C

   Joel R. Poinsett, an American diplomat, discovered the flowering plant, poinsettia, in 1851, and it has since become our most popular Christmas plant. Thus, the answer is C.

TEST 5
PASSAGE

In a provocative series of experiments, a team of scientists at Western Reserve University in Cleveland has developed techniques to remove the brain of a monkey from its body and keep it alive for many hours. Bare except for two small bits of bone to help support it, the nerves and blood vessels that once connected it to the monkey's body severed, the brain is suspended above a laboratory table. Attached to it are the tubes of a mechanical heart to maintain its blood supply; from it run wires to recording instruments. Their measurements of its electrical activity not only show that it remains alive but even suggest that sometimes this isolated brain is conscious.

While the immediate goal of the team, headed by Dr. Robert J. White, is the development of methods for obtaining answers to basic questions related to the physiology of the brain, one cannot help being fascinated by less specifically scientific, but perhaps more profoundly philosophic, considerations. Can the truly *detached minds* of the Cleveland monkeys really be conscious? If so, conscious of what?

Sensation, for example, is an important ingredient of the conscious state. Does biological science give us any clues as to what sensations, if any, the conscious incorporeal brains of the Western Reserve monkeys could have felt? After all, the nerves that normally carry to the brain indications of touch, taste, odor, light, and sound were all cut, and the associated sensory organs were far removed. Does this mean that, during its conscious periods, the isolated monkey brain floated in a sensory void, with no flashes of touch, pain, sight, or sound to remind it of the kind of existence it once knew?

1. What is used by the scientists to support the brain?

    A. Nerves and blood vessels that once connected it to the monkey's body
    B. Two small bits of bone
    C. A mechanical heart
    D. A laboratory table
    E. The tubes of the mechanical heart

2. The suggestion that the brain is sometimes conscious comes from

    A. the measurements on the recording instruments
    B. associated sensory organs
    C. the memory of the kind of existence it once knew
    D. the maintenance of its blood supply
    E. the mechanical heart

3. By the term *incorporeal brains,* the author means

    A. brains without nerves
    B. brains with mechanical tubes
    C. brains in a sensory void
    D. that the brain, though isolated, has artificial support
    E. disembodied brains

4. The author states that the brain can be kept alive

   A. indefinitely
   B. until it normally expires corporeally
   C. until the mechanical heart fails
   D. a few minutes
   E. for many hours

5. Scientists, by such experiments as these, are PROBABLY trying to determine

   A. how certain parts of the brain can be mechanically replaced
   B. how the brain feels and thinks
   C. whether the brain of a monkey is superior to the human brain
   D. how they might duplicate this experiment with a human brain
   E. how long brains can be kept alive without their bodies

6. A part of the brain called the brainstem is

   A. the seat of mental activity
   B. the coordinator of muscular activity
   C. an extension of the spinal cord
   D. the mantle that fits the skull
   E. controller of voluntary action and the senses

7. The cerebral cortex is

   A. divided into two equal hemispheres
   B. that part of the brain through which all nerve impulses are channeled
   C. that part which controls breathing
   D. that part which controls heartbeat
   E. that part which generates feelings, i.e., hunger, anger, pleasure

KEY (CORRECT ANSWERS)

1. B   5. B
2. A   6. C
3. E   7. A
4. E

EXPLANATION OF ANSWERS

1. CORRECT ANSWER: B

   It is stated in paragraph 1 that the brain is *bare except for two small bits of bone to help support it*. The answer, then, is B. Items C and E refer to things connected to the brain but not supporting it.

2. CORRECT ANSWER: A

   Item C is stated as a question in the passage and goes unanswered. However, item A is stated in the last sentence of paragraph 1 and is the correct answer. Items D and E are artificial appendages on which the recording instruments depend, but cannot, themselves, estimate or measure consciousness.

3. CORRECT ANSWER: E

   Incorporeal means without a body, or a disembodied brain. Therefore, E is the correct answer. The other answers are characteristic of (or related to) the brain described in the passage but do not relate to the term *incorporeal*.

4. CORRECT ANSWER: E

   In sentence 1, paragraph 1, the author states there are techniques to *remove the brain. . . . and keep it alive for several hours*. Item E, then, is the correct answer. C is not correct because, should a mechanical heart fail, it would be replaced, and the brain would continue its *life course* for the prescribed length of time.

5. CORRECT ANSWER: B

   The correct answer is B (see paragraph two-*basic questions related to the physiology of the brain*). Item E, the scientists have obviously ascertained; items A, C, and D are neither mentioned nor implied in the passage.

6. CORRECT ANSWER: C

   Items A, D, and E relate to the cerebral cortex. Item B refers to the cerebellum.

7. CORRECT ANSWER: A

   Items B, C, D, and E refer to functions of the brainstem. Item A, which describes the make-up of the cerebral cortex, is the correct answer.

TEST 6
PASSAGE

The highest honors bestowed in the world of science were given last Thursday to an American, two Russians, and a British woman.

The Nobel Prize in physics was shared by Dr. Charles H. Townes, now provost of the Massachusetts Institute of Technology, and Drs. N.G. Basov and A.M. Prokhorov of the Soviet Union. The three men, during the early nineteen fifties, paved the way for a major invention: the maser. Dr. Townes also helped show how the maser principle could be applied to light, resulting in discovery of the laser.

The Nobel Prize in chemistry went to Mrs. Dorothy C. Hodgkin of Great Britain for her work in deciphering the structure of such complex molecules as those of penicillin and vitamin B-12. The latter is vital in treating a fatal form of pernicious anemia. Its structure was spelled out after eight years of work. *Never before,* the award announcement said, *has it been possible to determine the precise structure of so large a molecule.*

The analyses were performed by shining x-rays through crystals of the substance in question and recording the manner in which the rays were diffracted by the crystal structure.

Applied light was first achieved by Dr. Townes and his colleagues at Columbia University at a radar or *microwave* frequency. Hence, they called it *microwave amplification by stimulated emission of radiation,* or, more briefly, the maser, from the initials of these words.

When the same principle was applied to the production of intense light, it was called an optical maser or *laser*

One of the earliest applications of the maser was to increase many-fold the sensitivity of radar systems used to detect distant missiles.

1. The invention of the maser

   A. occurred in Great Britain
   B. made it possible to determine the precise structure of a molecule
   C. was related to the work of Drs. Basov, Townes, and Prokhorov
   D. was the work of Mrs. Dorothy C. Hodgkin
   E. was the work of Dr. Charles H. Townes

2. Vital in treating a form of pernicious anemia is

   A. deciphering the structure of complex molecules
   B. vitamin B-12
   C. the analysis performed by shining x-rays through crystals
   D. recording the manner in which the rays are defracted
   E. penicillin

3. The *laser* got its name from the

   A. microwave amplification by stimulated emission of radiation
   B. initials of its earliest application
   C. initials of the principle of the laser applied to light

D. application of the maser to increase the sensitivity of radar systems
E. optical laser

4. The Nobel Prize in physics was   4.____

   A. given for the work of deciphering the structure of molecules
   B. given for the invention of the laser
   C. given to Mrs. D.C. Hodgkin
   D. shared
   E. given to Drs. Basov and Prokhorov

5. The above passage might be found in a(n)   5.____

   A. scientific journal dealing with nuclear physics
   B. article on the detection of missiles
   C. brochure from the Massachusetts Institute of Technology
   D. article in a medical journal on the treatment of pernicious anemia
   E. article on Nobel Prize winners

6. A word MOST CLOSELY related to amplification is   6.____

   A. stimulation   B. enlargement
   C. emission   D. light
   E. radiation

KEY (CORRECT ANSWERS)

1. C   4. D
2. B   5. E
3. C   6. B

EXPLANATION OF ANSWERS

1. CORRECT ANSWER: C

   Paragraph 2 states, *The three men...paved the way for a major invention: the maser.* The correct answer, therefore, is item C. Item B relates to the work of Mrs. Hodgkin (item D), who lives in Great Britain (item A). Item E is incomplete and, therefore, false.

2. CORRECT ANSWER: B

   The answer is contained in paragraph 3, where it is stated, *...such complex molecules as those of penicillin and B-12. The latter is vital in treating...pernicious anemia.* The correct answer, then, is B. Item A relates to the work of Mrs. Hodgkin, as do items C and Item E is incorrect.

3. CORRECT ANSWER: C

   The laser is an optical maser (item E), but it got its precise name from the initials of the principle of the maser (item A) applied to light; that is, item C, which is the correct answer. The earliest application of the laser (item B) was item D and has nothing to do with the laser.

4. CORRECT ANSWER: D

   The prize was given to Drs. Basov, Prokhorov, and Townes. It was shared by these three men; therefore, the correct answer is D. E is incorrect because it is incomplete. The prize in Chemistry was given to Mrs. Hodgkin, item C. As for items A and B, if the reader were to check for the reason that the prize was given, he would find that it was the invention of the maser, discounting both A and B.

5. CORRECT ANSWER: E

   The correct answer, and the most inclusive one, regarding the source of the passage is item E. Item A is obviously false, as is C. B and D refer to things mentioned in the passage but not the substance or the main theme of it.

6. CORRECT ANSWER: B

   Item B is the correct meaning of amplification and, thus, the correct answer for the question. Items A, B, C, and E are incorrect.

TEST 7
PASSAGE

Thus for most of the earth's history, life, in the form of primitive algae, fungi, and bacteria, had little more than a toehold in these pools. The oldest fossil evidence of such algae dates back two or three billion years, yet diverse, large scale life forms did not appear in the fossil record until some 600 million years ago.

It is this sudden appearance of diverse life that has puzzled scientists. The assumption has been that the earlier record was destroyed or that previous life forms did not have shells or skeletons hard enough to leave a record. Yet soft plants and animals also leave their prints in the sands of time and they, too, were absent.

What really happened, according to the new hypothesis, was that when volcanic growth produced continents, and hence shallow pools of considerable extent, the pond-bottom plants slowly raised the oxygen content of the air until, at one percent of the present level, it was sufficient to filter out almost all the lethal ultraviolet. The latter, henceforth, could poison only the top few inches of the oceans and life, which had been hardly more than microscopic, erupted in all evolutionary directions.

The eruption of oceanic life increased photosynthesis and the oxygen level rose high enough to make the dry land habitable. This led to great forests and photosynthesis became so extensive that there was perhaps ten times as much oxygen in the air as today. The carbon dioxide of the air, that acts like the glass of a green-house in keeping the earth warm, was depleted, and the Permian ice ages of 250 million years ago resulted.

1. An example of algae is

    A. a form of mushroom plant
    B. fossiliferous
    C. seaweed
    D. a form of bacteria
    E. cryptogamous plants

2. The scientists were puzzled because

    A. of the production of shallow pools
    B. of the evidences of fossiliferous life prior to 600 million years ago
    C. they did not feel that the oldest forms of life did not have hard shells or skeletons
    D. they did not think volcanic growth produced continents
    E. they did not understand how plants could lower the oxygen content of the air

3. Continents were produced by

    A. fermentation
    B. a high level of oxygen
    C. photosynthesis
    D. volcanic growth
    E. the Permian ice ages

4. How could the ultraviolet poison only the top few inches of the oceans and life? Because

    A. salt water reflects the rays
    B. ultraviolet rays are poisonous to certain ocean plants
    C. the pond-bottom plants raised the oxygen content of the air
    D. the pond-bottom plants acted as a filter
    E. ultraviolet cannot penetrate below the ocean's surface

5. Ultraviolet rays are

    A. the strongest rays of the sun
    B. rays within the violet of the visible spectrum
    C. the rays of the sun which promote growth
    D. rays beyond the violet of the visible spectrum
    E. those rays which are attracted by salt or fresh water

6. Photosynthesis is the

    A. growth from within plant or animal life
    B. process by which plants manufacture food for their growth with the aid of light
    C. impulse of fluids to mix and become diffused through each other
    D. tendency of elements to pass through one another with unequal rapidity
    E. pressures produced by osmosis

KEY (CORRECT ANSWERS)

1. C 4. D
2. B 5. D
3. D 6. B

EXPLANATION OF ANSWERS

1. CORRECT ANSWER: C

   Algae is a subaqueous plant, that is a plant growing beneath the water. Therefore, the answer would be C. Items A and E are fungi. Item B, fossiliferous, means *containing or bearing fossils.* Item D is incorrect because algae is a form of plant life.

2. CORRECT ANSWER: B

   The answer to this question is to be found in paragraph 1, towards the end, and the beginning of paragraph 2. Items A and D are accepted concepts. Item E is a false statement, as is C. Item B is the correct answer.

3. CORRECT ANSWER: D

   At the beginning of paragraph 3, it is mentioned that *volcanic growth produced continents.* Therefore, item D is the correct answer, aside from being the only direct statement made about the production of continents. Items A, C, and E are not mentioned in relation to the production of continents.

4. CORRECT ANSWER: D

   The pond-bottom plants slowly raised the oxygen content of the air...until it was sufficient to filter out almost all the lethal ultraviolet states the passage in paragraph 3. Therefore, item D is the correct answer. A and E are false statements. Item C is true but not pertinent. Item B is misleading.

5. CORRECT ANSWER: D

   Ultraviolet rays are those short rays beyond the violet of the visible spectrum. A, B, C, and E are not applicable to ultra-violet rays.

6. CORRECT ANSWER: B

   Items C and D relate to the process of osmosis. Items A and E are incorrect.

TEST 8
PASSAGE

The discovery and use of metals was one of the crucial steps that put mankind on the long road to modern civilization.

New clues to the discovery were reported last week. They suggest that men were taking the first steps toward use of metal a millennium earlier than the dawn of real metallurgy. The clues are little bits of copper that appear to have been cold-hammered into shape as pins, a drill, and a sharply bent hook nearly 9,000 years ago by an artisan in one of man's earliest villages.

The copper specimens were discovered last summer by a team excavating an ancient village site at Cayonu, in southeastern Turkey.

Co-directors of the expedition that made the discoveries were Prof. Hale Cambel, from the University of Istanbul, and Prof. Robert J. Braidwood of the Oriental Institute and Department of Anthropology, University of Chicago.

In a telephone interview last week, Professor Braidwood said all the evidence indicates that the stone dwelling in which the tools were found was nearly 9,000 years old.

In the Shanidar Valley of northern Iraq, scientists from Columbia University independently have found a specimen that also seems to be cold-hammered copper and suggests the same conclusion as that reached by Professor Braidwood and his colleagues.

1. The discovery of the cold-hammered copper specimens was made

   A. in southwestern Turkey
   B. 9,000 years ago
   C. in Istanbul
   D. in the Shanidar Valley
   E. on the African continent

2. Why does the author suggest that metal was used before the dawn of real metallurgy? Because

   A. The scientists found evidences of copper
   B. The scientists found evidences of cold-hammers
   C. There was evidence of life in the site at Cayonu
   D. They assumed that people must have lived in Cayonu 9,000 years ago
   E. The scientists found copper worked into certain forms

3. Metallurgy is the

   A. discovery of metals
   B. discovery of minerals that could be worked into metals
   C. discovery of ore
   D. art of working metals
   E. application of metals to the body

4. A millennium is _____ years.

   A. thousands of
   B. a few thousand
   C. several thousand
   D. a thousand
   E. an incalculable number of

5. The dominant religion of Turkey today is

    A. Hinduism   B. Hebrew
    C. Islam   D. Buddhist
    E. Greek Orthodox

6. The capital of Turkey today is

    A. Istanbul   B. Ankara
    C. Constantinople   D. Smyrna
    E. Izmir

KEY (CORRECT ANSWERS)

1.	D	4.	D
2.	E	5.	C
3.	D	6.	B

EXPLANATION OF ANSWERS

1. CORRECT ANSWER: D

   A place, apart from Cayonu, where scientists found cold-hammered copper specimens is the Shanidar Valley, item D, which is the correct answer. Istanbul is the location of the university of one of the scientists (item C). And Cayonu is in southeastern Turkey, thus discounting item A. Item B refers to the age of the specimens. Item E is false.

2. CORRECT ANSWER: E

   The evidences that the scientists found were copper that had been cold-hammered into different shapes, indicating E as the correct answer. A and B are insufficient or incomplete answers. C does not represent enough evidence, nor does D.

3. CORRECT ANSWER: D

   Metallurgy is *the art of working metals*. It has nothing to do with the discovery of or the existence of metal substances, discounting items A, B, and C, but rather with such activities as smelting, refining, parting, etc. Thus, the correct answer is D. Item E is incorrect.

4. CORRECT ANSWER: D

   A millennium is a thousand years. Thus, the answer is D. Items A, B, C, and E are incorrect.

5. CORRECT ANSWER: C

   The dominant religion of Turkey is Islam. The other choices are practiced in Turkey, but have very small followings throughout the country.

6. CORRECT ANSWER: B

   Turkey's capital is Ankara, item B, which is the correct answer. Constantinople, item C, was the former name and the former capital; it was replaced by the name, Istanbul, in the 20's. Izmir is the present-day name for Smyrna, a change which was made coincidentally with that for Constantinople.

TEST 9
PASSAGE

A radically new concept of evolution is being discussed in scientific circles. As presented by two Texans, it would explain the chief puzzle in the record of life's history on earth: the sudden appearance, some 600 million years ago, of most basic divisions of the plant and animal kingdoms.

There is virtually no record of how these divisions came about. Thus, the entire first part of evolutionary history is missing.

The theory says that evolution of a large proportion of the diverse species that have inhabited the earth–plants, fish, trees, and so forth–took place in two gigantic *revolutions* of comparatively short duration.

There is now general agreement that the earth was born as barren of an atmosphere as is the moon today, but volcanoes poured out gases, including an abundance of water vapor - enough to fill the oceans and produce an envelope of *air*.

It is agreed that the early air was radically different from that of today. Volcanoes do not produce oxygen gas, and the early air was dominated by hydrogen compounds. Hence, it was transparent to ultraviolet sunlight that no longer reaches the earth. Recent observations in space have documented the nature of sunlight before filtering by the atmosphere. It is clearly rich in wavelengths of ultraviolet that are lethal to all known forms of life.

This light not only penetrated the original air, but even pierced the top 15 to 30 feet of the oceans.

Since oceanic water circulates, any drifting life would have been carried into the layer bathed in ultraviolet. Hence, it seems unlikely to Drs. Berkner and Marshall that life could have originated in the oceans. Instead, they believe it probably sprang forth independently on the bottoms of numerous deep pools, possibly warmed by the volcanic activity widespread at that time.

1. The earth, at its beginning,

    A. contained craters like the moon
    B. was barren
    C. was fertile
    D. had animal and plant life only in its oceans
    E. had only plants, fish, and trees

2. The doctors mentioned in the passage seem to believe that

    A. life could have originated in the oceans
    B. life came about as the volcanoes poured out gases
    C. a gigantic revolution took place before a large proportion of the diverse species could inhabit the earth
    D. life sprang forth from numerous deep pools
    E. oceanic water, at the beginning, did not circulate

3. How was the volcanic air different from that of today?

   A. It did not come from volcanoes.
   B. The gases did not contain water vapor.
   C. It was dominated by oxygen.
   D. Ultraviolet light could easily penetrate it.
   E. It was not dominated by hydrogen compounds.

4. The air of today can filter ultraviolet rays because

   A. there are no more volcanoes
   B. they are absorbed by the earth
   C. of its oxygen content
   D. of its hydrogen content
   E. the ocean absorbs them

5. The BEST definition of an hypothesis is a(n)

   A. theory or formula derived by inference
   B. tentative assumption made in order to draw out and test its logical or empirical consequences
   C. assumption made in the form of a concession
   D. interpretation of a practical situation or condition taken as the ground for action
   E. statement of order and relation in nature that has been found to be invariable under the same conditions

6. In relation to the content of the passage, the BEST definition of air is the(a)

   A. mixture of invisible gases which surround the earth
   B. surrounding or pervading influence
   C. medium of transmission
   D. compound of 2 parts hydrogen and 1 part oxygen
   E. volcanic gas

KEY (CORRECT ANSWERS)

1. B   4. C
2. D   5. B
3. D   6. A

EXPLANATION OF ANSWERS

1. CORRECT ANSWER: B

   The earth was born as barren of an atmosphere as is the moon today, states the passage in paragraph 4. The only difference was that it had volcanoes which poured out gases, which in turn produced oceans and air. But since the correct answer must refer to the earth at its beginning (refer back to the question stem), B is the only possible answer. Item A is not mentioned. Item C does not refer to the earth at its beginning. Item E took place much later, during the *revolutions* mentioned in paragraph 3. Item D is not stated in the passage.

2. CORRECT ANSWER: D

   At the end of the passage, the two doctors are mentioned as believing that life *probably sprang forth independently on the bottoms of numerous deep pools.* Therefore, D is the correct answer. E is a false statement. The doctors did not believe A or B. C is false because two *gigantic revolutions* took place, according to paragraph 3.

3. CORRECT ANSWER: D

   Volcanic air was transparent to ultraviolet sunlight because it did not produce oxygen gas and was dominated by hydrogen compounds (paragraph 5). Item E is false. It did contain hydrogen compounds. C is false because the reverse is true.
   Items A and B are incorrect because the opposites are true.

4. CORRECT ANSWER: C

   It is the oxygen content in the air which filters out the ultra-violet rays before they reach the earth or the oceans. Therefore, the correct answer is C, and can be found in paragraph 5. Items A, B, and E have nothing to do with the ability of the air to filter the rays. Hydrogen, mentioned in item D, is transparent to ultraviolet rays.

5. CORRECT ANSWER: B

   Item E refers to a law. A and C are insufficient as definitions. D is a broad definition but not so precise as item B, which is the most accurate definition presented, and the correct answer.

6. CORRECT ANSWER: A

   Since the passage is concerned with natural science, item A is far superior to items B and C. Items D and E are incorrect. The correct answer, then, is A.

TEST 10
PASSAGE

Some 25,000 infants suffocate each year in the United States alone. The infants, most of them premature, turn blue and choke and die.

They die from something that is not to this day in most current medical directories, dictionaries, or guides. It is a mysterious condition called hyaline membrane disease. Many years ago this disease killed Patrick Bouvier, the younger son of John F. Kennedy, and it usually kills about half of the infants it strikes.

About 2,000 of the nation's pathologists met in Miami this week for the joint annual session of the College of American Pathologists and the American Society of Clinical Pathologists. They heard a report suggesting that a cure for hyaline membrane has been found.

It was through a series of autopsies of 150 infants who died of hyaline membrane disease that the new treatment for this disease evolved.

The study was done by a Louisville pathologist, Dr. Daniel Stowens, Director of Laboratories at Children's Hospital.

From his autopsies, Dr. Stowens determined that babies who are victims of hyaline membrane disease had too much water in their bodies. The baby's major organ systems may be all right. But they attempt to get rid of the water through the lungs. This clogs these organs and prevents the normal absorption of oxygen into the blood. So the babies die.

There are many complicated theories about how hyaline membrane disease blocks the lungs. The new simple theory had led to a simple therapy.

It is the use of two epsom salts enemas. The first enema clears away the mucus; the second, which relies on epsom salts' affinity for water, draws fluid away from the lungs.

Dr. Stowens reported that gasping and choking babies have been dramatically relieved of their symptoms in a matter of a few minutes after the treatment. In the last eight months, 28 babies suffering from hyaline membrane disease have been treated by epsom salts enemas in five Louisville hospitals, and all are reported to be alive today.

1. The babies who are victims of hyaline membrane disease die because they   1.___

    A. are organically defective
    B. absorb oxygen into the blood
    C. lack sufficient water in their system
    D. get rid of excess water through their lungs
    E. do not attempt to get rid of the excess water in their system

2. Before the new method of treating the disease was discovered, it   2.___

    A. was always fatal
    B. killed half the infants it struck
    C. killed 25,000 infants a year all over the world
    D. killed 2,000 infants in the United States every year
    E. killed 150 infants a year

3. The success of the new method seems to

   A. be unpredictable
   B. be perfected
   C. involve some risk
   D. be disapproved of in some medical circles
   E. depend on the baby treated

4. The cause of death from hyaline membrane is

   A. the bloodstream
   B. the lungs
   C. the membrane
   D. suffocation
   E. the heart

5. Dr. Stowens might rightfully be compared to

   A. Dr. Spock
   B. the polio vaccine
   C. Dr. Teller
   D. Dr. Salk
   E. the hyaline membrane disease

6. Prior to the discovery of the therapy,

   A. there existed a simple theory about it
   B. hyaline membrane disease was not treated
   C. there was no theory on how to treat it
   D. the theories about causes were many and recondite
   E. there was a simple therapy

7. The new theory

   A. does not use epsom salts
   B. does not use water
   C. delivers fluid to the lungs
   D. relies on the affinity between epsom salts and water
   E. use various epsom salts enemas

8. With the new therapy, babies

   A. gasp and choke
   B. have been treated over the last 12 months
   C. are relieved of their symptoms in a matter of minutes
   D. are relieved of their symptoms in a few hours
   E. have now been treated in 28 hospitals

9. A pathologist is

   A. a doctor
   B. a specialist in children's diseases
   C. usually a pediatrician
   D. one versed in the nature of respiratory ailments
   E. one versed in the nature of diseases

KEY (CORRECT ANSWERS)

1. D   4. D   7. D
2. B   5. D   8. C
3. B   6. D   9. E

EXPLANATION OF ANSWERS

1. **CORRECT ANSWER: D**

   In the next to last sentence of paragraph 6, the reason is explained. The correct answer is D. Item B is incorrect because it is the prevention of the normal oxygen flow that leads to fatalities. C is incorrect because they have too much water in their system. Whether the baby is organically defective or not has nothing to do with the disease, discounting A. Item E is incorrect because the babies do make this attempt.

2. **CORRECT ANSWER: B**

   In the last sentence of paragraph 2, it is stated that the disease killed about half the infants it struck. Thus, the correct answer is B. 150 infants had autopsies performed (item E). 25,000 yearly in the United States died from it, discounting item C. Item A is false. The figure 2,000 in item D refers to the nation's pathologists.

3. **CORRECT ANSWER: B**

   It would seem, since all the babies treated are alive today, that Dr. Stowens' approach to the disease has been perfected and that the cure has been found. Therefore, the correct answer is B. Item D is not mentioned in the passage. And items A, C, and E are false.

4. **CORRECT ANSWER: D**

   The cause of death is suffocation. This is mentioned in the first sentence of the passage. The correct answer is D. Items A, B, C, and E are organs and parts of the body affected but not the cause of death. Item C refers to a part of the name of the disease.

5. **CORRECT ANSWER: D**

   Dr. Spock, a specialist in child growth and development, does not pioneer in the treatment of diseases, discounting A. Item C refers to a nuclear physicist. Item E refers to the disease Dr. Stowens sought to treat. But Dr. Salk, item D, found a way to treat polio successfully and, therefore, is the correct answer. Item B refers to the method he used.

6. **CORRECT ANSWER: D**

   The answer may be reached through paragraph 7, which ends in *The new simple therapy had led to a simple theory*. Before this, there were *many complicated theories about how ... disease blocks the lungs*. Therefore, item D is correct. (*Recondite* means complex, profound.) Item A is false; it occurred after the discovery of the therapy. Item B is false because it was treated. Item C is false; there were many theories. Item E is false although it contains a repetition of part of the statement appearing in the paragraph.

7. **CORRECT ANSWER: D**

   Item A is false because the opposite is stated in the passage. Item B is false for the same reason. Item C is false because fluid is drawn away from the lungs. Item D is correct because it is part of the second stage of the treatment (or therapy) indicated in paragraph 8. Item E is false because the two that are used do not justify the adjective *various*.

8. CORRECT ANSWER: C

   Item A is false because that is what occurs before they are treated. Item B is false because they have been treated over the last 8 months. Item C is correct, as indicated in para-graph 9. Item D is false because a different length of time *(a few minutes)* is mentioned in the passage. Item E is false because the passage actually states that 28 babies have been treated in 5 hospitals.

9. CORRECT ANSWER: E

   A pathologist is one versed in the nature of diseases. Therefore, E is the only possible answer and the correct one. Item A is insufficient. Items B, C, and D are false.

www.ingramcontent.com/pod-product-compliance
Lightning Source LLC
Chambersburg PA
CBHW082035300426
44117CB00015B/2493